NOT AS LEAN,
NOT AS MEAN,
STILL A MARINE!

MSgt A. A. Bufalo USMC (Ret)

ISBN 978-0-9745793-3-7

First Printing – November 2004
Printed in the United States of America

www.AllAmericanBooks.com

Not As Lean, Not As Mean, Still a Marine!

OTHER BOOKS BY ANDY BUFALO

SWIFT, SILENT & SURROUNDED
Sea Stories and Politically Incorrect Common Sense

THE OLDER WE GET, THE BETTER WE WERE
MORE Sea Stories and Politically Incorrect Common Sense

THE ONLY EASY DAY WAS YESTERDAY
Fighting the War on Terrorism

TO ERR IS HUMAN, TO FORGIVE DIVINE
However, Neither is Marine Corps Policy
A Book of Marine Corps Humor

HARD CORPS
The Legends of the Marine Corps

AMBASSADORS IN BLUE
In Every Clime and Place
Marine Security Guards Protecting Our Embassies Around the World

Not As Lean, Not As Mean, Still a Marine!

PREFACE

The title of this book, *Not As Lean, Not As Mean, Still A Marine*, is a nice way of saying that while each of us is truly "Once a Marine, always a Marine," we also have to pass the torch on to the "new breed" at some point. The stories which fill these pages are a combination of personal "sea stories," commentary, and articles which highlight the traits which make the Marine Corps the special brotherhood that it is. The volume ends with a poem by Robert A. Hall entitled *The Honor of Our Corps,* which talks about the old timers, (i.e. those of us who are no longer as lean and mean as we used to be) who have built the Corps' reputation and are still ready to answer our country's call if need be. It ends by asking the young Marines of today if they are ready to step up and accept the responsibility of carrying on our traditions. While the old-timers are certainly a tough act to follow, you will see how the young Marines of today are already building upon the legacy which has been passed to them. So all of you old salts can rest easy – our beloved Corps is in good hands!

Riverview, Florida
October 23, 2004

Not As Lean, Not As Mean, Still a Marine!

TABLE OF CONTENTS

Not As Lean, Not As Mean, Still a Marine!

Not As Lean, Not As Mean, Still a Marine!

THE WRATH OF GOD

"Sometimes it takes good people killing bad people to keep bad people from killing good people." - Phil Messina

This is an open letter I wrote in July of 2004 after terrorists in Iraq kidnapped a Marine corporal named Wassef Ali Hassoun and threatened to behead him if the U.S. did not release prisoners being held in Baghdad. I submitted the letter via the internet and asked that it be forwarded in the hope it would eventually reach the individuals holding the Marine hostage. It not only got forwarded - it circled the globe in less than two days, was added to dozens of websites, was reprinted in newspapers (including some in the Middle East), was read on the radio, and was even read by Oliver North on Fox News. Corporal Hassoun was eventually released, and although there were some questions about the circumstances of his capture and release I like to think my letter (and the efforts of all those who forwarded it) may have had something to do with the outcome. The only negative feedback I got was hate mail from representatives of some terrorist organizations, and a few complaints about me calling the terrorists "women." I responded to the latter, and explained that in the Muslim world calling a man a woman is a huge insult. My intent was not to denigrate women, but to call the terrorists cowards in terms they could easily understand. Most of those who complained wrote back and appreciated my explanation, but unfortunately a few did not understand:

Not As Lean, Not As Mean, Still a Marine!

To the terrorists currently operating in Iraq,

I see that you have captured a U. S. Marine, and that you plan to cut off his head if your demands are not met. Big mistake. Before you carry out your threat I suggest you read up on Marine Corps history. The Japanese tried the same thing on Makin Island and in a few other places during World War Two, and came to regret it. Go ahead and read about what then happened to the mighty Imperial Army on Tarawa, Iwo Jima and Okinawa. They paid full price for what they did, and you will too.

You look at America and you see a soft target, and to a large extent you are right. Our country is filled with a lot of spoiled people who drive BMWs, sip decaf lattes and watch ridiculous reality TV shows. They are for the most part decent, hard working citizens, but they are soft. When you cut off Nick Berg's head those people gasped, and you got the media coverage you sought, and then those people went back to their lives. This time it is different. We also have a warrior culture in this country, and they are called Marines. It is a brotherhood forged in the fire of many wars, and the bond between us is stronger than blood. While it is true that this country has produced nitwits like Michael Moore, Howard Dean and Jane Fonda who can be easily manipulated by your gruesome tactics, we have also produced men like Jason Dunham, Brian Chontosh and Joseph Perez. If you don't recognize those names you should. They are all Marines who distinguished themselves fighting to liberate Iraq, and there will be many more just like them coming for you.

Before the current politically correct climate enveloped our culture one of the recruiting slogans of our band of brothers was "The Marine Corps Builds Men." You will soon find out just how true that is. You, on the other hand, are nothing but a bunch of women. If you were men you would show your faces, and take us on in a fair fight. Instead, you are cowards who hide behind masks and decapitate helpless victims. If you truly represented the interests of the Iraqi people you would not be ambushing those who come to your country to repair your power plants, or sabotage the oil pipelines which fuel the Iraqi economy. Your agenda is hate, plain and simple.

When you raise that sword over your head I want you to remember one thing. Corporal Wassef Ali Hassoun is not alone as he kneels before you. Every Marine who has ever worn the uniform is there with him, and when you strike him you are striking all of us. If you think the Marines were tough on you when they were cleaning out Fallujah a few weeks ago you haven't seen anything yet. If you want to know what it feels like to have the Wrath of God called down upon you then go ahead and do it. We are not Turkish truck drivers, or Pakistani laborers, or independent contractors hoping to find work in your country. We are the United States Marines, and we will be coming for you.

Andy Bufalo
MSgt USMC (Ret)

THE PAINTING

"Every problem has a gift for you in its hands."
– Richard Bach

Years ago there was a very wealthy man who, along with his devoted young son, shared a passion for art collecting. Together they traveled around the world, adding only the finest art treasures to their collection. Priceless works by Picasso, Van Gogh, Monet and many others adorned the walls of the family estate. The widowed elder man looked on with satisfaction, as his only child became an experienced art collector. The son's trained eye and sharp business mind caused his father to beam with pride as they dealt with art collectors around the world.

As winter approached, war engulfed the nation and the young man left to serve his country in the Marine Corps. After only a few short weeks, his father received a telegram. His beloved son was missing in action. The art collector anxiously awaited more news, fearing he would never see his son again. Within days, his fears were confirmed. The young man had died while carrying a fellow Marine across a fireswept battlefield to a Corpsman. Distraught and lonely, the old man faced the upcoming Christmas holidays with anguish and sadness. The joy of the season - a season that he and his son had always looked forward to - would visit his house no longer.

On Christmas morning, a knock on the door awakened the depressed old man. As he walked through the large house to the door, the masterpieces of art on the walls only reminded him that his son was not coming home. He opened the door, and was greeted by a young Marine with a large package in his hand. He introduced himself to the man by saying, "I was a friend of your son. I was the one he was rescuing when he died. May I come in for a few moments? I have something to show you."

As the two began to talk, the Marine told of how the man's son had told him of his father's love of fine art. "I'm an artist myself," said the Marine, "and I want to give you this." As the old man unwrapped the package, the paper gave way to reveal a portrait of his son in his Dress Blues. Though the world would never consider it the work of a genius, the painting featured the young man's face in striking detail. Overcome with emotion, the man thanked the Marine, promising to hang the picture above the fireplace. A few hours later, after the Marine had departed, the old man set about his task. True to his word, the painting went above the fireplace, pushing aside many thousands of dollars worth of paintings. And then the man sat in his chair and spent Christmas gazing at the gift he had been given.

During the days and weeks that followed, the man realized that even though his son was no longer with him, the boy's life would live on because of those he had touched. He would soon learn that his son had rescued dozens of wounded Marines before a bullet stilled his caring heart. As the stories of his son's gallantry continued to reach him, fatherly pride and satisfaction began to ease the grief. The painting of his son soon became his most prized possession, far eclipsing any interest in the pieces for which museums around the world clamored. He told his neighbors it was the greatest gift he had ever received.

The following spring, the old man became ill and passed away. The art world was in anticipation. With the collector's passing, and his only son dead, those paintings would be sold at an auction. According to the will of the old man, all of the art works would be auctioned on Christmas day, the day he had received his greatest gift. The day soon arrived, and art collectors from around the world gathered to bid on some of the world's most spectacular paintings. Dreams would be fulfilled this day; greatness would be achieved as many would claim "I have the greatest collection." But the auction began with a painting that was not on any museum's list. It was the painting of the man's son. The auctioneer asked for an opening bid. The room was silent.

"Who will open the bidding with one hundred dollars?" he asked. Minutes passed. No one spoke.

From the back of the room came, "Who cares about that painting? It's just a picture of his son. Let's forget it and go on to the good stuff." More voices echoed in agreement.

"No, we have to sell this one first," replied the auctioneer. "Now, who will take the son?"

Finally, a friend of the old man spoke. "Will you take ten dollars for the painting? That's all I have. I knew the boy, so I'd like to have it."

"I have ten dollars. Will anyone go higher?" called the auctioneer. After more silence, the auctioneer said, "Going once, going twice. Gone." The gavel fell.

Cheers filled the room and someone exclaimed, "Now we can get on with it and bid on these treasures!"

After a few moments the auctioneer looked at the audience and announced the auction was over. Stunned disbelief quieted the room. Someone spoke up and asked, "What do you mean it's over? We didn't come here for a picture of some old guy's son. What about all of these paintings? There are millions of dollars of art here! I demand you explain!"

The auctioneer replied, "It's very simple. According to the will of the father, whoever takes the son... gets it all."

THE ANGELS OF DEATH

W. Thomas Smith Jr.

"In my entire life, I have never seen anything like you. You're taking care of the mission. You're taking care of each other. You're acting like Marines. I won't make a long speech here. I just want you to know that if I had a son, I'd want him to be a Marine." – General Tommy Franks, U.S. Army

Beginning this month, leathernecks from the 1st Marine Expeditionary Force will return to Iraq, replacing elements of the Army's 82nd Airborne Division. The return of the Marines is surely bad news for those desperate to undermine the liberation of Iraq.

Not to take anything away from the U.S. Army - its soldiers have performed magnificently, and will no doubt continue to do so - but America's enemies have a particular fear of U.S. Marines. During the first Gulf War in 1991, over 100,000 Iraqi soldiers were deployed along the Iraqi-Kuwaiti coastline in anticipation of a landing by some 17,000 U.S. Marines. Terrified by what they had been taught about the combat prowess of Marines, the Iraqi soldiers had nicknamed them "Angels of Death." The moniker - first published by Pulitzer-winner Rick Atkinson in his best-selling *Crusade* - carried over into the second Gulf war last year, as the 1st Marine Division swept across the Iraqi plains. Attacking American forces were unsettling enough, but reports of the seaborne "Angels of Death" being among the lead elements were paralyzing to many Iraqi combatants.

Despite less armor than other American ground forces, the

7

Not As Lean, Not As Mean, Still a Marine!

Marines were among the first to fight their way into Baghdad. And when intelligence indicated that foreign troops were coming to the aid of Iraqi diehards, Marine Brigadier General John Kelly stated, "We want all Jihad fighters to come here. That way we can kill them all before they get bus tickets to New York City." Typical Marine bravado, some say. But it works.

Best-selling author Tom Clancy once wrote, "Marines are mystical. They have magic." It is this same magic, Clancy added, that "may well frighten potential opponents more than the actual violence Marines can generate in combat."

Fear of Marines is not a new phenomenon, nor is it unique to Iraqi soldiers.

Established in 1775, the U.S. Marine Corps came of age in World War I during the 1918 Chateau Thierry campaign near the French village of Bouresches. There, Marines assaulted a line of German machine-gun nests on an old hunting preserve known as Belleau Wood. The fighting was terrible. Those Marines who weren't cut down by the enemy guns captured the nests in a grisly close-quarters slugfest. The shocked Germans nicknamed their foes "teufelhunden" (devil dogs).

"Marines are considered a sort of elite Corps designed to go into action outside the United States," read a German intelligence report following the battle. "They consider their membership in the Marine Corps to be something of an honor. They proudly resent any attempts to place their regiments on a par with other infantry regiments."

Twenty-four years later as the 1st Marine Division was steaming toward Guadalcanal, a Japanese radio propagandist taunted that which the Japanese soldiers feared most. "Where are the famous United States Marines hiding?" the announcer asked. "The Marines are supposed to be the finest soldiers in the world, but no one has seen them yet?"

Over the next three years, Marines would further their reputation at places with names like Tarawa, Saipan, and Iwo Jima. That reputation carried over into the Korean War. "Panic sweeps my men when they are facing the American Marines," confessed a captured North Korean major. It was a fear echoed by his Chinese allies.

In late 1950, Chinese premier Mao Tse Tung put out a contract on the 1st Marine Division. The Marine division, according to Mao in written orders to the commander of the Chinese 9th Army Group, "has the highest combat effectiveness in the American armed forces. It seems not enough for our four divisions to surround and annihilate its two regiments. You should have one or two more divisions as a reserve force." Though costly for both sides, the subsequent Chinese trap failed to destroy the 1st Marine Division. U.S. Army Major General Frank Lowe later admitted, "The safest place in Korea was right behind a platoon of Marines. Lord, how they could fight!"

Over a decade later, Marines were the first major ground combat force in Vietnam. Army General William C. Westmoreland, who commanded all American military forces in that country, conservatively stated he "admired the élan of Marines." But despite the admiration, some Army leaders found their equally proficient units wanting for similar respect.

In 1982, during the invasion of Grenada, Army General John Vessey, then chairman of the Joint Chiefs of Staff, telephoned one of his officers and demanded to know why there were "two companies of Marines running all over the island and thousands of Army troops doing nothing. What the hell is going on?"

The reputation of Marines stems from a variety of factors:

The Marine Corps is the smallest, most unique branch of the U.S. armed forces. Though it is organized as a separate armed service, it is officially a Naval infantry/combined-arms force overseen by the Secretary of the Navy. The Corps' philosophical approach to training and combat differs from other branches. Marine boot camp - more of a rite-of-passage than a training program - is the longest and toughest recruit indoctrination program of any of the military services. Men and women train separately. All Marines from private to Commandant are considered to be first-and-foremost riflemen. And special-operations units in the Marines are not accorded the same respect as they are in other branches. The Marines view special operations as simply another realm of warfighting. Marines are Marines, and no individual Marine or Marine unit is considered more elite than the other.

Consequently, newly minted Marines believe themselves to be superior to other soldiers, spawning understandable resentment from other branches. But do Marines actually fight better than other soldiers? Rivals argue it's not so much their ability to fight - though that's never been a question - but that Marines are simply masters in the art of public relations. President Harry Truman once stated that Marines "have a propaganda machine that is almost equal to Stalin's."

Fact is, while other armed services have lured recruits with promises of money for college, "a great way of life," or "being all you can be," the Marines have asked only "for a few good men (and today, women)" with the mettle to join their ranks.

Not surprisingly, there have been numerous unsuccessful efforts - primarily on the part of some Army and Navy officers - to have the Corps either disbanded or absorbed into the Army or Navy. Most of those efforts took place in the first half of the Twentieth Century. But even after the Marines' stellar performance in World War II, Army General Frank Armstrong proposed bringing them into the Army fold and condescendingly referred to the Corps as "a small bitched-up Army talking Navy lingo."

As late as 1997, Assistant Secretary of the Army Sara Lister took aim at the Marines. "I think the Army is much more connected to society than the Marines are," Lister said before an audience at Harvard University. "Marines are extremists. Wherever you have extremists, you've got some risks of total disconnection with society. And that's a little dangerous." Of course, the Commandant of the Marine Corps demanded an apology. Lister was fired. And Marines secretly said among themselves, "Yes we *are* extremists. We *are* dangerous. That's why we win wars and are feared throughout the world."

Despite its detractors, the Marines have become a wholly American institution - like baseball players, cowboys, and astronauts - in the eyes of most Americans. Marines indeed may be extreme, but America loves them, extremism and all. And fortunately for America, her enemies in the war against terror will continue to shudder upon hearing, "the Marines have landed."

A former U.S. Marine infantry leader and paratrooper, W. Thomas Smith Jr. is a freelance journalist whose work has appeared in a variety of national and international publications. His third book, *Alpha Bravo Delta Guide to American Airborne Forces,* has recently been published.

WHY I LIKE MARINES

Rear Admiral J. Stark, USN

"Marines are mystical. They have magic." – Tom Clancy

When someone mentions the often contentious relationship we have with our Navy brethren, I tend to think of the scene in "A Few Good Men" where the lieutenant played by Kiefer Sutherland says, "I like all you Navy boys. Every time we have to go somewhere to fight, you fellas always give us a ride." I know it doesn't come across as a compliment, but in a way it is. The Gator Navy brings us to the beach, naval gunfire supports out landings, and of course it is the Navy which provides our wonderful corpsmen and chaplains. And we have one other thing in common with sailors – they admire us... and so do we!

The first reason I like Marines: they set high standards - for themselves and those around them - and will accept nothing less.

I like the way Marines march.

I like the way Marines do their basic training whether it's Quantico, Parris Island, or San Diego.

I like the idea (that) Marines'cultivate an ethos conducive of producing hard people in a soft age.

I like the fact that Marines stay in shape.

I like the fact that the Marines only have one boss - the Commandant. And I like the directness of the Commandant.

I like the fact that Marines are stubborn.

I like the way Marines obey orders.

I like the way the Marines make the most of the press.

Not As Lean, Not As Mean, Still a Marine!

I like the wholehearted professionalism of the Marines.

It occurred to me that the services could be characterized by different breeds of dogs. The Air Force reminded me of a French Poodle. The poodle always looks perfect, sometimes seems a bit pampered, and always travels first class. But don't ever forget that the poodle was bred as a hunting dog and in a fight it's very dangerous. The Army is kind of like a St. Bernard. It's big and heavy and sometimes seems a bit clumsy. But it's very powerful and has lots of stamina. So you want it for the long haul. The Navy, God bless us, is a Golden Retriever. They're good natured and great around the house. The kids love 'em. Sometimes their hair is a bit long, they go wandering off for long periods of time, and they love water. Now, Marines I see as two breeds, Rottweilers or Dobermans, because Marines come in two varieties, big and mean, or skinny and mean. They're aggressive on the attack and tenacious on defense. They've got really short hair and they always go for the throat. That sounds like a Marine to me!

So what I really like about Marines is that 'first to fight' isn't just a motto, it's a way of life. From the day they were formed at Tun Tavern two hundred and twenty-one years ago, Marines have distinguished themselves on battlefields around the world. From the fighting tops of the *Bonhomme Richard,* to the sands of the Barbary coast, from the swamps of New Orleans to the halls of Montezuma, from Belleau Wood, to the Argonne Forest, to Guadalcanal, and Iwo Jima, and Okinawa and Inchon, and Chosin Reservoir and Hue City and Quang Tri and Dong Ha, and Beirut, and Grenada, and Panama, and Somalia and Bosnia and a thousand unnamed battlefields in godforsaken corners of the globe, Marines have distinguished themselves by their bravery, and stubbornness and aggressive spirit, and sacrifice, and love of country, and loyalty to one another.

They've done it for you and me, and this Country we all love so dearly. And they asked for nothing more than the honor of being a United States Marine. And *that's* why I like Marines!

From a speech by Rear Admiral J. Stark, USN, made in Newport, Rhode Island on 10 November 1995.

WELCOME TO COMMAND

"I was a PFC in the Marine Corps, so when I started playing officers (in the movies) I had a good opinion as to how they should be portrayed – from the bias of an enlisted man's viewpoint." – Lee Marvin

The Marine Security Guard program is the only place in the Marine Corps (other than the SNCO Academies) where an enlisted Marine officially fills the billet of "commander." It is a great opportunity for Staff NCOs to do a job normally reserved for officers, and allows them to mature as leaders. It is also a good opportunity for enlisted Marines to gain a better appreciation for the burdens their officers are required to shoulder.

Officers sometimes get a bad rap from the troops. Enlisted Marines give them a hard time, calling them "zeros" - in reference to the fact officer pay grades begin with the letter "O." It is sometimes forgotten by them that along with the perks of being an officer comes a great deal of responsibility.

One of the most important lessons of command, if not THE most important lesson, is that a commander can always delegate authority to someone else - but never responsibility. I'm sure you have seen those placards which say, "I have a very responsible position around here - every time something goes wrong, I'M RESPONSIBLE." That is very true, and it works both ways. That's because while leaders certainly do tend to get too much blame when things go awry, they also seem to get a lot more than their share of the credit when things go right.

One of the most difficult things about being in command

is enforcing rules and regulations with which you disagree. A perfect example is the one which says eighteen-year-olds are old enough to vote and die in combat, but not old enough to drink a beer - a subject I covered in detail in *Swift, Silent and Surrounded.* It just never made sense to me, but even so I enforced it - albeit grudgingly.

That's why the best leaders are the humble ones who are quick to accept blame, and even quicker to give credit where credit is due. Perhaps "humility" should be added as the fifteenth leadership trait, because in my experience people who don't take themselves too seriously tend to be the most successful leaders.

A good friend of mine named James Goethe is a perfect example of someone who fits into that category. Before being appointed a Warrant Officer, he served as a Force Recon Marine and later a Drill Instructor, and was awarded the Navy and Marine Corps Medal for saving the life of a recruit during a grenade throwing incident. With a résumé like that it would be easy for him to be a bit of an egomaniac. But he wasn't. Shortly after pinning on his bars James was preparing to go to Quantico to go through the Basic School, and just before leaving stated his biggest concern was the "frontal lobotomy" they would be performing on him there. A few years later I ran into him again. James was now an LDO Captain, and when I asked when he had gotten his commission, he replied, "They removed my spine about four years ago." What a guy.

Another officer who made an impression was my Company Commander during my tenure in the Congo, Lieutenant Colonel (later Colonel) Frank Duggan. Early in my tour the Colonel came to Brazzaville for a command visit, and one night over a couple of beers confided to me the reason he had become an officer (he was a Mustang) was he couldn't manage to get the cutting score for corporal. He was also the one who said to me, when I was having a difficult time dealing with a few issues, "Welcome to command, Gunny. It's not as easy as it looks, is it?" He was so right. Colonel Duggan is also the man who "read me the riot act" over the phone after I "invaded" the country of Zaire (see 'The NEO' in *Swift, Silent and Surrounded)* and who, after he had cooled down, called back to say he had probably blown his top "because he was a bit jealous." What a guy.

The officer in charge of my communications section at the end of my career was yet another Mustang named Captain Warren Dickey. He was easily the best communications officer I had ever worked with, and a hell of a Marine to boot, so we quickly developed an outstanding working relationship - and on our watch accomplished many great things. And we did so in spite of a less than ideal command structure. The company commander we had at the time was a pompous, self-promoting weasel, and his sergeant major was both self-important and dumb as a box of rocks. It pains me to say such things about fellow Marines, but that's just the way it was. In any case, my penchant for being "candid" got me in hot water with the sergeant major, who then convinced the colonel to transfer me (banish would be a better word) out of the company posthaste. I fought them tooth and nail over that, and it got pretty ugly, but Captain Dickey stood by my side every step of the way. He believed I was in the right, and put his career on the line to stand up for me. Ever since then I think of him whenever I hear someone use the word 'loyalty.' What a guy.

My last Commanding Officer before I retired was Lieutenant Colonel Bob Coates. He was a bit of a Neanderthal (I think he would consider that a compliment) and never one to stand on ceremony. His only concern was success in combat - period. I guess that's why he chose to have me accept the first piece of cake as the oldest Marine present at my last Birthday Ball, despite the fact he is a year older than me. Then a couple of years later - after I had retired - Coates (now a full Colonel) called to invite me to the ceremony at which he would assume command of Det 1, the Marine Corps' new special operations unit. During the conversation I repeatedly called the Colonel "sir" out of habit, until finally he stopped me and said, "Top, you're retired now. You don't have to call me 'sir' anymore." I replied that I wasn't calling him sir because of his rank. I was doing it because I had always been taught to respect my elders. His reply is not printable. What a guy.

These are the men who taught me more about leadership than any academy ever could. They brought the Leadership Traits to life, and through their actions set examples I will never forget. Because of them, I now feel qualified to look a young lieutenant or civilian executive in the eye when their burden has gotten a bit heavy and say... "Welcome to command. It's not as easy as it looks, is it?"

HERKY BIRD

"When you ain't got no money, you gotta get an attitude." – Richard Pryor

Ground pounding Marines like to give air-wingers a hard time about the (comparatively) cushy life they lead, but even so we never forget they are first and foremost Marines - just like us:

A Marine KC-130 Hercules landed here early this morning, winning an unprecedented cross-country race with an Air Force strategic airlift C-141. The Starlifter is expected in late tomorrow following crew rest entered into when the aircraft toilet could not be repaired within four hours of scheduled take-off time from Peterson Field, Colorado. The race, run between Travis AFB, California and McGuire AFB, New Jersey was dubbed the "Mission-Hacker's Marathon" because it was filled with planned command post obstacles throughout the ten-base route. The race required each aircraft to go through the different locations and upload/download cargo and personnel under challenging conditions.

The Starlifter's crew was contacted at Peterson Field just before entering crew rest with the toilet problems. The C-141's aircraft commander stated, "We knew it was a critical time for such a malfunction and it probably cost us the race, but what could we do? It just wouldn't flush." She then added, "Please congratulate the KC-130 crew for us."

The Hercules had been running approximately four bases ahead of the Starlifter throughout the race due to various turns of events. At the very first station, the C-141 crew took

Not As Lean, Not As Mean, Still a Marine!

off two hours late when fleet service failed to bring creamer for their coffee. Forced to remain overnight (RON) at their next stop due to a runway that was unfortunately closed following a C-5 landing, the Starlifter crew was thrown even further behind when they refused rooms they considered substandard. "The decor in that hotel was atrocious. I mean, there were green curtains with blue carpet," the aircraft commander fumed, adding, "pretty soon, they'll expect us to sleep in tents!" The nearest acceptable hotel rooms were seventy-five miles from the base, and that forced a late takeoff the following day.

At one point in the race it appeared the strategic airlift crew had turned the race around when a protest filed by the crew's parent wing commander, Colonel Norman Schaule, was accepted by Marine 2nd Lieutenant Jack W. Shelton, Jr. "I thought it unfair that the valid delays we took should penalize us when the Marine KC-130 crew was virtually invulnerable to them," explained Colonel Schaule regarding the protest. "I mean, Marine crews drink *yesterday's* coffee, and don't even care if they sleep in a bed. They just don't understand the philosophy of modern airlift. You can't compete with that type of mentality," he concluded.

Once the protest was accepted, the KC-130 was forced to fly the remainder of the race with its ramp down and cargo door open, pulling deployed A-22 chutes behind the aircraft in addition to the low speed refueling drogues being extended. The C-141 began making up ground rapidly, and actually tied the Hercules on the seventh stop despite another fleet service delay (no salad dressing in the box lunches!).

From the original story Marine Herk Nips Starlifter in '99 Face-off at McGuire AFB

CAMMIE UP!

Phillip Thompson

"The Marine Corps is slow and deliberate in making changes to the uniform. Then, when a change is made, mass confusion generally results." – Major H. G. "Dunk" Duncan

I don't know what it is about camouflage. When I was a young NCO, pretty much everything I owned was cammied-up in one way or another - and I don't think I was unusual in that regard. I also enjoyed applying cami-stick to my face - I guess because I thought it was reminiscent of Apaches on the warpath. I'm just glad I wasn't the <u>only</u> one who felt that way:

When I was on active duty, people would always ask, "Why did you join the Marine Corps?"

I usually gave a standard answer - "to be one of the few, the proud," et cetera - because I did not want to reveal the real reason, which was far too personal for most civilians to understand. Now, however, I'm prepared to reveal the reason I joined the military. Camouflage.

That's right, camouflage, the military's favorite fetish. Look around you. It's everywhere (though, ironically, you can see it). The services have camouflaged Humvees, uniforms, tanks, and trucks. There are even camouflage nets to cover the camouflaged vehicles. How's that for good old-fashioned military redundancy?

When I was a second lieutenant, our instructors at The Basic School would tell us solemnly that in the field, "camouflage is continuous."

21

It's also profitable. You can find camouflage notebooks, camouflage raincoats, even camouflage bikinis (not that there's anything wrong with that). Military kids go to school with camouflage pencils in their camouflage backpacks. A store at the Pentagon City mall near Washington, D.C. even carries - I'm not making this up - camouflage day-planner binders, I guess so officers can look professional and tactical at the same time.

You can even buy camouflage toilet paper!

The camouflage uniforms are the best, though. Of course Marines and soldiers wear camouflage. They need to. But sailors, too, are hard to see in cammies - SEALs wear them for the sneaky-Pete stuff they do.

The Marine Corps, though, has a particular passion for the stuff. The original, Vietnam-era jungle pattern has long since disappeared. It was replaced by the Cold War-chic "woodland" pattern in the early 1980s, a uniform all the services adopted. Unfortunately, the whiz kids with the slide rules designed the uniform to be too hot in the summer and too bulky to cut a dashing appearance.

Then came the speckled "desert" pattern in the 1980's, the one known by the silly, decidedly unwarlike name "chocolate chips." That was the uniform for the 1991 Persian Gulf War, until U.S. Central Command started issuing a newer version that looked even cooler than the chocolate chips.

Meanwhile, a new woodland pattern uniform came out. Same pattern, but a lighter material, with reinforced knees and elbows and a collar that didn't resemble a leisure suit. But most important, the blouse had two nifty tabs in the back so you could put a "military tuck" in the blouse and present a neat, military appearance while, say, putting down a civil disturbance in a Third World country.

Not As Lean, Not As Mean, Still a Marine!

But the Corps took things one step further. It designed its own special pattern in order to be unique among the other camo-clad services. True, Marines now look like a Croatian local militia (with better shaves), but at least they don't look like *soldiers*.

The Army, not to be outdone, devised four new patterns and polled soldiers as to which one they liked best. The soldier's favorite? The Marine Corps pattern. Guess they didn't learn from the beret debacle.

Now the Air Force has gotten into the game. Uniform gurus are testing - get this - a blue-and-gray tiger stripe pattern. Words fail me.

All of this hubbub over camouflage may sound frivolous to the average, noncammied-up civilian, but this is serious business for the military. Millions of dollars have gone into research, testing, manufacturing and procuring The Perfect Camouflage Uniform.

Sure, the Marine Corps could have stayed with the same pattern the other services had, rather than lay out the cash for its own special brand of camouflage. And the Army didn't have to spend all that money on research and development to come up with a decent pattern (plus three really nasty ones).

Who wants to look like the other guys, especially when there are hundreds of embedded reporters running all over the battlefield? They could easily mistake a Marine for a soldier or vice versa. Besides, looking good in combat is as important as having the best equipment money can buy. Right?

This article originally appeared in the Air Force Times in February of 2004.

23

MARINE'S MARINE

Brigadier General Edwin H. Simmons, USMC (Ret.)

"A battalion commander didn't need a staff, he got out in front of his battalion and he led it." - Chesty Puller

The average person on the street has never heard of Chesty Puller, and that is a shame. He simply never got the press his Army contemporaries got, and Hollywood never got around to making a movie about him the way they did with MacArthur, Patton and Eisenhower. Even so, Chesty is the ideal example of what a Marine should be, and this portrait by one who knew him personally clearly shows why:

Tomorrow is the U. S. Marine Corps' 203rd Birthday, and I suppose that is the reason I have been asked here today. I was given my topic. I am to talk about one of the Corps' best-known and most-loved characters: Chesty Puller. All those word's "best-known," "most-loved," and "character" - fit Chesty Puller particularly well. In our two hundred and three years of history, the Marine Corps has had at least its share and probably more than its share of colorful characters, but none more colorful than Chesty Puller. I remember when I first saw him - and heard him. It was late Fall or early Winter in 1942. I was a twenty-one-year-old lieutenant and a platoon leader in the Officers' Candidates Course. Captain Joseph Reynaud was my company commander. The battle for Guadalcanal was just ending, and a number of officers were being brought back to the Marine Corps Schools in Quantico to tell us about it. Chesty Puller was one of those who were brought back. He had commanded the 1st

Battalion, 7th Marines, and on the night of 24 October his battalion had held a mile-long front against the efforts of a Japanese regiment which was seeking to break through to Henderson Field. For this action Puller had been awarded his third Navy Cross, an award for valor second only to the Medal of Honor.

This was the man we were going to hear speak and I remember sitting in the auditorium of Breckinridge Hall and seeing him for the first time on the platform. Not very tall, he stood with a kind of stiffness with his chest thrown out, hence his nickname "Chesty." His face was yellow-brown from the sun and atabrine, the anti-malaria drug that was used then. His face looked, as someone has said, as though it were carved out of teak wood. There was a lantern jaw, a mouth like the proverbial steel trap, and small, piercing eyes that drilled right through you and never seemed to blink.

He was then forty-four years old. He had been born in the village of West Point, Virginia, where the waters of the Pamunkey and Mattaponi rivers come together to form the York River. That's Tidewater, and he had never lost his Tidewater, Virginia accent. His full name was Lewis (pronounced "Lewie") Burwell Puller and he was named for an ancestor, Lewis Burwell, who had settled in Virginia in the mid-17th Century. His father was a wholesale grocery salesman. His grandfather, Captain John W. Puller, had ridden with Jeb Stuart in the Civil War and had been killed at Kellys Ford in 1863. Young Lewis grew up on stories of the Confederacy. He finished high school in 1917 and went to Virginia Military Institute for a year, but when June 1918 came he told the Commandant of Cadets he was leaving because he didn't want the war to end without him. He enlisted in the Marine Corps, went through boot camp at Parris Island, and stayed on as a drill instructor. To his chagrin this kept him from going to France.

After the war ended he was sent to Officers' Training School, commissioned a second lieutenant in the Marine Corps Reserve, and placed on the inactive list. This was in June 1919. He then re-enlisted in the Marine Corps and was sent to Haiti where he served as a lieutenant in the gendarmerie. He remained there for five years, was in forty engagements against Haitian bandits, and began to build a reputation as a bush fighter.

He came back to the States in 1924 and received a commission as second lieutenant in the regular Marine Corps. He spent two years in the States, including an unsuccessful try at flight training at Pensacola, two years at Pearl Harbor, and then in 1928 he went to Nicaragua. Here he served as a captain in the Guardia Nacional. (The Gendarmerie d'Haiti and the Guardia Nacional of Nicaragua were both native constabularies officered for the most part by Marine Corps officers and NCOs serving at one or more levels above their Marine Corps ranks.)

He received his first Navy Cross for a series of five patrol actions fought against followers of one Augusto Cesar Sandino, a name that has reappeared recently in the news. In the current unrest in Nicaragua the opposition to the Somoza government has taken on to themselves the title "Sandinista." As a matter of interest, President Tachito Somoza, himself a West Point graduate, is the son of Tacho Somoza who was a Marine-trained member of the Guardia and who came to power after the Marines departed Nicaragua in 1933. But I am getting ahead of myself.

When Puller returned again to Nicaragua in 1931, one of the Managua newspapers welcomed him back with a front-page bulletin that read, "Los Marinos traen al 'Tigre de las Segovias' para combatir a Sandino." Translated it means,

Not As Lean, Not As Mean, Still a Marine!

"Marines bring back the Tiger of Segovia to fight Sandino."

Sandino is supposed to have welcomed Puller back by placing a price of five thousand pesos on his head. Puller, still a first lieutenant in the Marine Corps, went back into the Guardia as a captain and was soon back in his old haunts in northern Nicaragua - and he soon won his second Navy Cross for his patrol work.

The Marines never did catch Sandino but after they had left Somoza, who had become Jefe Director of the Guardia, caught him in 1934 and had him shot. By that time Puller had gone to North China for service with the Legation Guard in Peiping. Here, amongst other things, he commanded the famous Horse Marines - a detachment from the Legation Guard mounted on Mongolian ponies. A year later he went on board the cruiser *Augusta*, flagship of the Asiatic squadron, as commanding officer of the Marine Detachment. He came back to the States in 1936 and was assigned to The Basic School at the Philadelphia Navy Yard as a drill and tactics instructor. (The Basic School is the school attended by all new Marine Corps second lieutenants. It is now located at Quantico rather than in Philadelphia.) Puller saw three classes pass through The Basic School. He left a well-remembered mark on those young lieutenants who would be the captains, majors, and lieutenant colonels of the Marine Corps in World War II. On parade his leather and buttons seemed to shine more brightly than anyone else's, his khaki was more stiffly starched, and the creases in his trousers more sharply edged. Also, more fundamentally, he had not only his own experiences in Haiti and Nicaragua to recount, but also he was deeply read in military history.

In 1939 he left Philadelphia and went once again to China, to serve a year afloat aboard the *Augusta* and then to join the 4th Marine Regiment in Shanghai. He stayed with the spit-

and-polish 4th Marines until August of 1941, four months before Pearl Harbor. It was a good thing that he left when he did, because the 4th Marines left Shanghai at the end of November to go to the Philippines and were surrendered to the Japanese (by an Army General named Wainwright) when Corregidor fell.

Back in the States, Puller was given command of the 1st Battalion, 7th Marines in the newly formed 1st Marine Division, and this is the battalion he took to Guadalcanal. While he was there the Marines were visited by Eleanor Roosevelt, who was pretty tough herself in her own way. On meeting Puller, she asked him, "Tell me, Colonel, what are you fighting for?" thinking no doubt of some lofty set of ideals. Puller thought for a moment then answered, "Five hundred and forty-nine dollars a month, ma'am."

I can't vouch for that story because I wasn't there, but I do remember, quite clearly, some of the things Puller had to say when he came back to Quantico from Guadalcanal. Incidentally, his normal speaking voice was somewhere between a rasp and a growl and when he wanted to get your attention he could bark like a howitzer.

I remember in the question-and-answer period he was asked his opinion of Marine Corps staff action at the battalion level. He growled back that a battalion commander didn't need a staff - he got out in front of his battalion and he led it. And that was his tactical philosophy. Chesty led from out front and he expected his officers to do likewise, which perhaps accounted for the high rate of casualties amongst his officers.

Puller spoke not only at Quantico but also at many Army installations: Fort Benning, Fort Sill, Fort Riley, Fort Ord, and Leavenworth to name some of his stops. His message was that one American, properly trained, could handle two

Not As Lean, Not As Mean, Still a Marine!

Japanese. Marine Raiders were then very much in the news. Carlson's Raiders had landed at Makin Island. Edson's Raiders had fought well at Tulagi. I remember that one of the questions put to Puller at Quantico asked his opinion of the Raiders. "Marine Raiders," he rasped, "are just Marine riflemen with extra privileges."

He was happy when the lecture tour was finished and he was sent back to the 1st Marine Division. The tour had gotten him a personal letter of appreciation from General George C. Marshall, Chief of Staff of the Army, but when Puller got back to his old regiment in April of 1943 and was assigned as Executive Officer, he wrote the Commandant of the Marine Corps: "It is respectfully requested that my present assignment to a combat unit be extended until the downfall of the Japanese government."

The 1st Marine Division's next operation was Cape Gloucester, beginning in December of 1943. Puller landed with the 7th Marines and personally led two battalions, who had lost their commanding officers, in the successful assault of a heavily fortified Japanese position. For this he received his fourth Navy Cross. In February of 1944, still at Cape Gloucester, he was given command of the 1st Marine Regiment and, now a full colonel, would command the 1st Marines in the bitter fight for Peleliu in September and October of 1944. Following his philosophy of leading from the front, his regiment took terrible casualties - fifty-six per cent of the regiment dead or wounded in nine days of fighting. The 1st Marines, over Puller's protest, were pulled out of the line before the battle was finished and sent back to their base camp in the Russell Islands. Chesty received a Legion of Merit for Peleliu, but he did not again command combat troops in World War II.

When the Korean War began in June 1950, Puller was

commanding officer of Marine Barracks, Pearl Harbor - a very pleasant post. With him were his wife, Virginia, and his three young children. The oldest child, Virginia McCandlish, had been born in Shanghai in 1940. The twins, Martha and Lewis B. Puller, Jr., were born in 1945. But Puller was not one to sit out a war in comfort.

He went to the cable office and bombarded the Commandant, Assistant Commandant, and Commanding General, 1st Marine Division, asking for an assignment. He was given command of his old regiment, the 1st Marines. The regiment had gone inactive after World War II, and was being re-formed at Camp Pendleton.

I was then the Weapons Company commander in 1st Battalion, 6th Marines, based in Camp Lejeune, North Carolina. We were moved by troop train to Camp Pendleton and had our numbers changed to 3rd Battalion, 1st Marines. Thinking about those casualties at Peleliu, I have to admit that a kind of chill ran down my back when I heard that Chesty Puller was going to be our regimental commander.

Actually, I saw very little of him at Camp Pendleton and it wasn't until we were in Japan, getting ready for the Inchon landing, that I really made his acquaintance. All the field grade officers - that is, majors and above - in the regiment were gathered onboard the amphibious command ship, *Appalachian*, to be briefed on the forthcoming operation. The S-2 described the objective area, told us about the twenty-foot tides and the sea wall, and that we would be making an evening landing which would give us only about an hour to consolidate our position. The S-3 went into detail on the objectives. The 3rd Battalion, 1st Marines, was going to be on the extreme right flank of the beachhead. We were looking rather apprehensively at each other, when Chesty got up and planted himself in front of us:

"Forget what the S-2 told you," he growled. "We'll find out what's on the beach when we get there. You people are lucky. In my day we had to wait twenty years for a war. You get one every five years. You people have been living by the sword. You better, by God, be ready to die by the sword."

With those words of encouragement, we went back to our battalions. The next time I saw Chesty was on September 17th, D-plus-Two. We were firmly ashore at Inchon. The 3rd Battalion had passed into reserve and was bivouacked next to the 1st Marines' command post. We were told that General MacArthur had come ashore and wanted to give Chesty a medal. Chesty sent back a message, "If he wants to decorate me, he'll have to come up here."

And that's exactly what MacArthur did. He arrived by jeep, complete with crushed hat, sun-glasses, corncob pipe, and leather jacket, escorted by a body guard consisting of about a platoon of soldiers and two platoons of newspapermen and photographers. MacArthur presented Puller with a Silver Star, or actually, the promise of a Silver Star, because MacArthur had been rather liberal that morning and his aide had run out of medals. In due course, Puller would also get a second Legion of Merit from the Marine Corps for the landing at Inchon, the crossing of the Han River, and the capture of the city of Seoul.

Having taken the city, the Marines provided security for the triumphant entry of MacArthur and President Syngman Rhee into Korea's capital. That was my second and final glimpse of General MacArthur. After Seoul, the 1st Marine Division re-embarked, moved around to the east coast of Korea, landed at Wonsan, moved north to Hungnam, and then further north and inland, away from the sea, to the Chosin Reservoir. It was then that the Chinese hit us. The 5th and 7th Marines were out in front near a place called

Not As Lean, Not As Mean, Still a Marine!

Yudam-ni. The 1st Marines had its battalions strung out in three positions to the rear with ten to fifteen miles between them. The 3rd Battalion was at Hagaru-ri, the 2nd Battalion and regimental headquarters were at Koto-ri, and the 1st Battalion was at Chinhung-ni.

A Chinese division hit us at Hagaru-ri. We held them off until we were joined by the 5th and 7th Marines who had to fight their way through three Chinese divisions to get back to us. We got back to Koto-ri on 7 December by which time the Division had made contact with a total of eight Chinese divisions. I should say here that we were fighting not only the Chinese but also the weather. There was snow and temperatures as low as twenty-five degrees below zero. We were barely inside the Koto-ri perimeter when the senior officers of the 3rd Battalion were summoned to the regiment's operations tent. The scene was different, but in some ways the dialogue was the same as we'd had three months earlier aboard *Appalachian*. We were the told that the 3rd Battalion would be the rear guard from Koto-ri to Chinhung-ni - this was an honor that we would have been just as happy to have someone else have. The S-2 painted a gloomy picture of how many Chinese stood between us and Chinhung-ni. The S-3 outlined a complicated scheme of maneuver under which the battalion would occupy a succession of positions on the high ground on both sides of the road. Then, after all the Division's transport had passed, we were to come out of the hills and fall in on the rear of the column. Once again our faces must have shown our apprehension, because Colonel Puller, who as yet had not spoken, got up, braced himself with one foot up on a ration box, pulled his pipe from out between his teeth, and growled, "I don't give a blank-blank how many blank-blank Chinese laundrymen stand between us and the blank-blank sea, they

32

don't stand a blank-blank chance of stopping a U. S. Marine Corps regiment." You can fill in those blanks with words of your own choice. Having said this, Puller paused and said quietly, "And Christ, in His infinite mercy, will see you safely through."

We moved out on the 9th of December and had hard fighting for the next several days. Because our artillery was also moving to the rear we had very little artillery support, and had to depend on our own mortars to give us the high-angle fire we needed to get at the Chinese in defiladed positions. One of my 81mm mortar sections was firing in support of our Company H - we called it How Company in those days, it would be Hotel Company now - and was running out of ammunition. We had left Koto-ri with two truckloads of 81mm ammunition; one had broken through the ice crossing a stream and had to be blown up; the other had gotten lost in the Division column. I told the section sergeant to get down on the road and stop all trucks that seemed to have ammunition and to hi-jack any 81mm mortar ammunition they might have.

The sergeant did exactly what he was told. Chesty Puller came roaring up in his jeep to see who was holding up the column. The sergeant told him what he was doing. Chesty said, "I'll give you a hand." And there he was, in the middle of the road, stopping trucks, and when they found one with 81mm ammunition, helping to off-load the clover-leaves.

The next time I saw Chesty was a couple of days later. We were down off the plateau and through the Funchilin pass and were making a route march on the road. We came upon Chesty standing by the side of the road.

"Got any bullets left, Simmons?" he rasped. Cautiously, I allowed as how we had a few. He said, "Well, you're going to have to punch your way through a road block up ahead."

Luckily, the road block was gone by the time we got there. Maybe they heard us coming. Or maybe they heard Chesty. For the break-out from Koto-ri to Hungnam, Chesty received his fifth Navy Cross. No other Marine has ever won five Navy Crosses. For the same action he also received the Army's Distinguished Service Cross. In January, after we had evacuated Hungnam and were back in camp at Masan in the south of Korea, Puller was promoted to brigadier general and made the Assistant Division Commander.

General Puller returned to the States in May of 1951 and immediately attracted national attention, not all of it favorable. In San Francisco he told the press, "What the American people want to do is fight a war without getting hurt. You can't do that anymore than you can go into a barroom brawl without getting hurt." He also said, "Unless the American people are willing to send their sons out to fight an aggressor, there's just not going to be any United States. A bunch of foreign soldiers will take over."

He was also quoted, not quite accurately, that troops should be given beer and whiskey instead of ice cream and candy. This caused a furor in the press, and a blizzard of protesting letters descended on Headquarters Marine Corps. Puller was sent to his next duty station, Camp Pendleton, to take command of the new 3rd Marine Brigade - with the admonition to make fewer speeches.

He was promoted to major general in 1953, and the following year was given command of the 2nd Marine Division at Camp Lejeune, where he ended his legendary career.

General Simmons gave this address at a Fairfax Optimist Club Luncheon on Thursday, 9 November 1970.

LIKE FATHER, LIKE SON
A Tribute to Lewis B. Puller Jr.

"...The medals still represented the dignity and the caliber of my service and of those with whom I served... I could no more discard them than I could repudiate my country, my Marine Corps or my fellow veterans." - Lewis B. Puller Jr.

Chesty Puller, as you have just read, had a long and glorious career in the Marine Corps. In contrast, the career of his son Lewis Jr. was much shorter, and ended tragically when he stepped on a booby trap made from an artillery round while serving as a platoon commander in Vietnam. This letter was forwarded to me by a friend, and does much to show a side of the younger Puller most of the public never got a chance to see:

I don't know what he saw as he looked out into the room. Did he see the officers of the Second Marine Division, their attention already starting to blur from one too many drinks? Did he see what he was, or what he had been? We were waiting for him to speak. And what did *we* see?

I had been at HQMC the week the message regarding Puller's wounding came screaming in. I remember reading it later, hoping that he would die. The injuries were so bad you just wondered what was left to live with, and for. But he lived.

Puller pulled himself up to the lectern with a smooth practiced ease. You didn't notice the fingers. The lectern hid the missing lower body. And then he began to speak. That he

35

was there at all was a miracle itself. For a service that called itself a "band of brothers," only mostly unblemished ones were allowed to stay in the family. His father's heart was his ticket out.

All the General Officers within limo ride of HQMC, it seems, had gone to tell the old man that his son was wounded... badly. I didn't envy them. Mere mortals telling the God of War that one of his was not coming back wrapped in glory. Wrapped perhaps!

Did he scream? Did he cry? Did he turn away? Did he wonder that, had he been in charge, would it have happened? Did he think it was payback for all those other sons? I kept hoping he would die. But he lived.

In measured, even tones Puller began to talk. He didn't talk about his wounds - by now everyone knew about them. He didn't talk about a national healing or binding up the wounds of the fallen, and he didn't talk about the pain he must have endured that clung to him like an aura. He talked about what it meant to be an Officer of Marines.

He talked about the iron law of duty that Marine officers always took care of their men first. Always. You knew that he believed it, and you knew that he had paid the price and would have again. I never got the sense talking to him later that night that he begrudged any officer in that room. But you also noticed that not many made the trip across the room to talk with him. It was too bad, really. The trip was worthwhile.

His recent death was not an answer to an earlier prayer. He is with his father now. Both can spend endless centuries discovering why steel runs in some families, and how father and son were really more alike than they both ever knew.

Anyone who is unfamiliar with Puller's story should read his Pulitzer Prize-winning book *Fortunate Son*

A QUESTION OF LOYALTY

"You can tell (my mother) that when you found me, I was with the only brothers I had left. And that there was no way I was deserting them. I think she'd understand that." – Matt Damon in the movie *Saving Private Ryan* upon being told he was being sent home

This book is about honoring those who serve our country in these trying times, as well as those who went before. I don't want to turn it into a political statement; however I feel that I would be doing a disservice to those in uniform if I did not include this piece, which I wrote in early May of 2004. As all leaders of Marines know, the top priorities are "accomplish the mission" and "take care of your troops." They also know one of the most important Leadership Traits is LOYALTY – both up and down the chain of command.

Each day it is my custom to read the online news when I rise, and as I sat down with my cup of coffee this morning it looked like the usual collection of good news, bad news, and news of the weird - until I read two stories which really got my juices flowing.

The first, in and of itself, was rather innocuous. Just the usual bit of election year grandstanding with the obligatory photo op. It told of a pancake breakfast for six veterans in St. Louis, hosted by then-presumptive Democratic nominee John Kerry. My first thought was, "Hmm, he could only find *six* friendly veterans in *all* of St. Louis?" But I guess that's not so surprising, after all. So I just chuckled at that notion and continued to read. The article went on to mention (sadly) a former Marine in the group named Fields Black who suffers from emphysema. He said he may have contracted the disease in the oil fields of Kuwait during the Gulf War in 1991, and railed against President Bush for not providing the medical care he requires. My first thought was, the Gulf War was *thirteen* years ago. Did the disease wait a decade in order to appear during the Bush Administration? And if not, was Mr. Black saying the care provided by the VA during the eight years Bill Clinton occupied the White House was vastly superior to what he is getting now? I was a bit confused by this, but apparently Senator Kerry was not. He put his arm around the afflicted man's shoulder and quietly whispered, with all the compassion he could muster, that he would see what he could do to help. Gag.

When I tired of reading about such blatant political posturing I clicked on an article about, what else, Iraq. It told of a young Marine corporal named Jason Dunham who had thrown himself onto a live grenade in order to save the lives of the troops under his command. A truly selfless act. One that spoke volumes about the character of Corporal Dunham, and about his commitment to the welfare of those entrusted to his care. Although only twenty-two years old and "only" an enlisted man, that young American exhibited a greater degree of loyalty, courage and decisiveness in a *moment* than many of us do in a *lifetime*.

Reading those two stories back-to-back made me think of a question I would have liked to ask Senator Kerry if the opportunity had presented itself. Of course I fully realized the odds of that happening were rather remote, and I am also sure I would never have gotten a straight answer. But I would have felt better for having asked. I know that sounds awfully cynical, but consider the all questions which were asked, but remain unanswered.

Questions such as how Senator Kerry could possibly

criticize President Bush's service in the National Guard, after himself supporting the likes of *Bill Clinton.* During the 1992 presidential campaign he even went so far as to say this about the draft-dodging Clinton: "We do not need to divide America over who served and how. I have personally always believed that many served in many different ways." But I guess that only applies to members of *his* party.

Questions such as how Mr. Kerry could not manage to differentiate between a medal and a ribbon. He claimed there was no difference between the two, even though any recruit fresh from basic training knows that is ridiculous. I myself spent twenty-five years in the Marine Corps, and sat in open-mouthed disbelief during his televised "explanation." Please!

Questions such as how Kerry, who was born with a silver spoon in his mouth, lives in a half-dozen elaborate mansions, and has been married to not one but *two* heiresses worth hundreds of millions of dollars, could proclaim himself a champion of the common man? Come on, get real.

No, Senator Kerry, I will leave those (and many other) unanswered questions for others to pursue. My question was one which I felt was much more important for someone who aspired to be the Commander-In-Chief of the Armed Forces and leader of the Free World to answer. A question about loyalty and courage. A question which was answered in the blink of an eye by young Corporal Dunham at a checkpoint in Iraq, but which has yet to be answered by you.

My question was this: Why did you request to be transferred to Brooklyn after receiving that third "Purple Heart?" I am not even going to get into the questions surrounding your supposed "wounds" and whether or not they were real, or self-inflicted. The point is they were not much more than scratches, and you had only been in

Vietnam for three and a half months. You were a Naval officer in *command* of a boat and crew. Where was your loyalty to *them*?

I have read many accounts of our troops in Iraq which cite instances where Marines and soldiers have concealed their wounds because they didn't want to be evacuated and separated from their comrades. I'm not talking about scratches here. A Marine sergeant was shot in the shoulder and refused to leave the squad he commanded because they were *his men*, and in his mind he belonged wherever they were. Another Marine, a corporal, hitched a ride back to Iraq on an Air Force transport in order to get back to his men. He had been recovering from wounds in a hospital in Germany, and had a ticket home. Instead of using that ticket, he phoned his wife and told her a leader belongs with his men. Such conduct is not new. Throughout our history, many citations for heroism contain passages which read, "…while ignoring his own grievous wounds and refusing medical aid, he remained in command and led his troops to safety…"

I realize you may find it difficult to understand that sort of self-sacrifice, Mr. Kerry. Difficult to understand how a leader can, and should, put those under his command ahead of himself. Difficult to understand how your crew members must have felt when their "leader" used an obscure policy to get *himself* out of harm's way while leaving *them* to carry on with someone else at the helm.

I wonder what sort of loyalty you would have shown to the Armed Forces as a whole in the event you had become President? My guess is you would have backed down under political pressure and hang our valiant warriors out to dry whenever it suited your political agenda - much in the same way Bill Clinton pulled us out of Somalia after the 'Blackhawk Down' incident. Because of *that* action eighteen brave men died for nothing, and the word on the street is America will pack up and run away when given a bloody nose. That decision has emboldened the terrorists and shaped their strategy ever since.

Yes, Senator Kerry, loyalty must be a very difficult concept for someone like you to grasp. Too bad Corporal Dunham is no longer with us. He could have explained it to you.

Four months later a Vietnam Vet and former Army Ranger (and father of a Marine aviator) named Dexter Lehtinen placed a full page ad in the Army Times entitled "The Wounds That Never Heal" in order to draw attention to another disloyal act by then-Lieutenant (jg) Kerry - in this case his shameful and treasonous conduct after returning from Vietnam. The fact that he found it necessary to write and publish such a letter illustrates the importance of loyalty, integrity, and keeping faith with one other:

In 1971, I awakened after three days of unconsciousness aboard a hospital ship off the coast of Vietnam. I could not see, my jaws were wired shut, and my left cheekbone was missing, a gaping hole in its place.

Later, while still in that condition at St. Albans Naval Hospital, one of my earliest recollections was hearing of John Kerry's testimony before Congress. I remember lying there, in disbelief, as I learned how Kerry told the world that I served in an Army reminiscent of Genghis Khan; that officers like me routinely let their men plunder villages and rape villagers at will; that "war crimes" committed in Vietnam by my fellow soldiers "were not isolated incidents but crimes committed on a day-to-day basis with the full awareness of officers at all levels of command."

Then Kerry went to Paris and met with North Vietnamese

41

enemy officials, all while our soldiers still fought in the field. The pain and disbelief I felt listening to his words went deeper than the pain I felt from the enemy fire which seriously wounded my face.

Eighteen months later I was discharged from the hospital, the wounds inflicted by the enemy fully healed. But more than thirty years later, the wounds inflicted by John Kerry continue to bring pain to scores of Vietnam veterans. Those wounds - the bearing of false witness against me and a generation of courageous young Americans who fought and died in Vietnam - are much more serious than any wound warranting a Purple Heart. Those wounds go to the heart and soul. Those wounds never go away.

Today, my son is a Marine Corps weapons officer, flying the F/A-18 Hornet. He belongs to the same Marine Corps Kerry ridiculed with his 1971 book cover showing protestors simulating the Iwo Jima Memorial, raising an upside-down American flag. He flies the same F/A-18 fighter jet that Kerry voted against in the U.S. Senate. And today, Kerry's picture hangs in an honored place in Saigon's war museum, as a hero to the Vietnamese Communists. Yet, John Kerry shamelessly drapes himself in the imagery of Vietnam, military service and the support of veterans devoid of any media scrutiny. Meanwhile, the criticism and disapproval of Kerry by scores of veterans continues to fall on deaf ears. Worse yet, any legitimate criticism of Kerry's post-war record is discredited as a "personal" attack or an attack against his service.

John Kerry is quick to surround himself with a handful of veterans and claims overwhelming support from the veteran community. He ignores, however, the wounds he inflicted on millions of veterans.

CHARLIE BLACK

Marvin J. Wolf

"The U.S. Marine Corps has a propaganda machine to rival Stalin's." – President Harry S. Truman

Embedded reporters were not a new innovation of the Iraq War. During World War II a "regular guy" named Ernie Pyle was the best known correspondent, and during Vietnam, the first "TV war," there were a number of brave souls who went to the field with the grunts in order to tell their personal stories. Today, many of those men are members of the Combat Correspondents Association.

He wasn't what you'd call a writer, exactly. He was more a reporter, a man who just wrote what he saw and heard and felt, put it down in simple words. Who, what, when, where. Rarely *why*. Why didn't so much concern him. His readers, moms, dads, wives and kids back in Columbus, Georgia - they knew why. They knew why their husbands, sons and daddies were over in Vietnam: They were soldiers. Draftees, volunteers, privates, colonels, sergeants - soldiers all. In August of 1965 Lyndon Johnson had ordered them to go, and they went.

The families they left behind were from Illinois, Texas, California, New York, and everyplace in between. And most of them stayed in Columbus because that's where they were when their men left to spend a year in Vietnam. They had an insatiable thirst to know how their men were faring. Even many that had gone back home for the year took out a mail subscription to the *Columbus Enquirer*. And Charlie Black

43

Not As Lean, Not As Mean, Still a Marine!

told them what their men were doing in Vietnam.

Charlie told them in short sentences typed on a battered portable. Single-spaced, both sides of the page. Usually one of his friends in the Air Cav would put the copy in an envelope with a G.I.'s name for a return address and scrawl "Free" on the upper right-hand corner and mail it through the APO back to the *Enquirer*, back to the world, back to where nearly every word Charlie wrote was printed for the families of the men in Vietnam. Charlie had to do things that way, because Charlie didn't have an expense account, to speak of.

He drew his regular salary, something less than a couple of hundred a week - and all that, every dime after deductions, went to his wife. Old Maynard Ashworth, a WWI colonel and the publisher of the *Enquirer,* gave Charlie five hundred dollars for expenses and a roundtrip ticket to the war. "Come back when you've spent your expense money, Charlie," he said. "Come back in a couple of weeks and tell us how it was."

Charlie couldn't tell it in just a couple of weeks. He'd been a Marine Recon type during WWII and had lost a brother to the Communists in the Korean unpleasantness, killed in action, and Charlie couldn't tell the folks back in Columbus what this Air Cav war in Vietnam was like in a couple of weeks. So he lived in the field for weeks at a time. Longer than most of the grunts he went around with. In the field, Charlie could eat C-rations, sleep on the ground, and he didn't have to spend any of that five hundred. And when he did come back to our base camp at An Khe for a bath and some rest and the leisure to write about what he'd seen and heard and felt, the word got around pretty quickly among the troopers of the Cav: Charlie's money is no good. When he'd try to buy a beer for the guys he'd been sharing the mean end of a dirty war with, they wouldn't let him. Because when the money was gone, so was Charlie. And nobody wrote about the war like he did. Nobody.

Eventually the five hundred *was* gone. It took months. So Charlie cashed in his plane ticket and went out into the boonies to watch and learn and listen and write it all down and send it back to Columbus. When the plane fare money was gone, and he was totally and absolutely broke, he hitched a ride back on a Georgia Air National Guard plane. The pilot, a weekend warrior with a wife and a good civilian job, braved an Air Force court-martial for having an unauthorized civilian passenger on an intercontinental flight. But that's the way everybody felt about Charlie, who had to borrow a dime from the pilot to call his wife to come pick him up from someplace near Warner-Robins, Georgia.

In Vietnam, Charlie sometimes disappeared for weeks. More than once he was reported killed. And more than once, he was reported missing in action. One time he was out of touch for nearly a month, last seen with a squad that had been mauled in a firefight near one of those unpronounceable hamlets, someplace near Binh Dinh. But every time he'd show up again, gray under his grimy gaunt face, worn out, near collapse. And he'd say something like, "Hell no, I ain't dead yet." And he'd look for some place to lay his head for a few hours so he could think clearly while he filled in all those single-spaced lines on the old portable.

I first met Charlie at Camp Swampy, which was what everyone who'd ever been there called Ft. Stewart, Georgia. I was twenty-three and had bluffed my way into the photographer's slot with the Second Infantry Division PIO, and almost my first job was to drive a jeep and meet some guy named Black at a crossroads, grid coordinates such-and-such at first light. When I showed up on time, the only one more surprised than I was Charlie. He'd never met a PIO private who could read a map and sort-of drive a jeep.

We got rid of the jeep soon thereafter because what Charlie wanted to see that morning was a combat river crossing exercise. "Can't cover a war from the road," he told me. So we walked, this old man of forty-two and me, and I learned about the engineers and being quiet in the woods and how to make coffee by kicking a hole in the mushy earth and feeding a few dried pine needles to a tiny fire in it, then mixing C-ration instant coffee into iodined water in a blackened steel canteen cup until it was lukewarm.

And I learned how a reporter works. Charlie had an interviewing technique that's never been bettered. It was how he covered an exercise at Camp Swampy, and how he covered the Vietnam War. Mostly he didn't say much of anything. Mostly he listened, and nodded his head, and wrote stuff down on a pad. Once in awhile he would ask a few questions. First names and hometowns and such. And they were the names of privates and buck sergeants and a topkick now and then. The names that no one from the *Washington Post* or the *New York* or *Los Angeles Times* or the *Chicago Tribune* or even the *Charlotte Observer* ever wrote down. The names of the guys who were fighting the war.

My phone rang late one October night and an old, familiar voice from my Air Cav PIO days told me that Charlie Black was dead at fifty-nine. Dead of a massive heart attack at his home near Auburn, Alabama. I can still see him, caked with mud, an M-16 slung casual-like over his shoulder, pushing aside the mosquito net and easing into our tent at An Khe. Someone would holler, "Heard you'd been greased, Charlie, where the hell you been?" And he'd cackle, "Hell no, I ain't dead yet."

Myself, I'm not so sure he won't turn up again someday.

This story originally appeared in "Chicken Soup for the Writer's Soul"

THE RIGHT THING TO DO

Jess Levens

"Duty makes us do things well, but love makes us do them beautifully!"

When I reported in to my very first unit as a slick-sleeve private, the NCO in charge of my section was a corporal by the name of Bubba Lynch. He was tough, level-headed, and much respected. He was also perpetually pissed off. Bubba had joined the Marine Corps because he wanted to go to Vietnam and avenge his brother; but for some inexplicable reason he had to remain in the U.S. while draftees were sent in his place. I haven't thought about Bubba for almost thirty years, but this story reminded me of him:

They were inseparable. Born just one day apart, these small-town Minnesota boys were more than cousins; they were best friends. The Marine Corps brought them even closer, but war separated them forever.

Homemade punk music resounded through the small town of Kettle River, Minnesota as their band, *The Humbuckers*, regularly practiced. Martin Langhorst sang and played lead guitar, and his cousin, Moises Langhorst, sang and played rhythm guitar.

When they weren't practicing or making plans for the band, they were in the woods hunting for small game. They did almost everything together.

"When we were teenagers, it was all about the band," said Martin. "We got a little older, and it started to become more about the Marine Corps. Moises especially wanted to join.

47

Not As Lean, Not As Mean, Still a Marine!

He even painted his SUV camouflage."

As high-school graduation neared, Martin and Moises sought out their local Marine recruiter. They planned to enlist through a buddy program, but there was a problem.

"Moises was good to go, but there was a problem with my transcripts," said Martin. "I was home-schooled, so I didn't have the usual paperwork."

Moises joined as an infantryman while Martin stayed back to organize his paperwork. When Moises returned from recruit training, Martin was ready to go.

"Moises actually got recruiting points because I joined when he was home on leave," said Martin. "I'm a big reason he got promoted to PFC. We always helped each other out however we could."

Moises joined Infantry Training Battalion and Martin began recruit training nearly thirteen weeks later with Platoon 1065, Company B.

"Even though we were separated, I felt closer than I've ever felt to him," said Martin. "We were more than cousins or best friends. We were brothers in arms."

While Martin continued to pursue the title Marine, Moises deployed to Iraq to do his part in Operation Iraqi Freedom.

"We were up north at Edson Range when I was called in to see the company commander," recalled Martin. "My family passed a Red Cross message. Moises was killed in combat. I didn't get any details. I just know that on April 6th, my best friend died."

Actually, Moises died April 5th while serving with 2nd Battalion, 4th Marines, in the province of Al Anbar, Iraq during a firefight.

"He was devastated when he got the news," said Staff Sergeant John Maciel, Martin's senior drill instructor. "But his desire to become a Marine never wavered."

Not As Lean, Not As Mean, Still a Marine!

Company B leaders granted Martin emergency leave for Moises' funeral, and he returned to recruit training just in time for the Crucible, the most challenging training evolution in the cycle.

"When he came back from the funeral, the platoon gave him a welcome-back card," said Maciel. "He seemed more focused after that."

"I was really down before I went home for the funeral," said Martin. "I was so sad. But after I spent four days at home and went to Moises' funeral, I came back motivated. I don't take freedom for granted, and I want to ensure the next generations have the freedom I've had, the freedom I'm ready to fight for... the freedom Moises died for."

The pain of losing someone so close and dear is hard. The void in Martin's life is there, but it's been partially filled by his fellow platoon members and anyone else who wears the eagle, globe and anchor.

"To get through something like this while in recruit training shows that he has a lot of heart," said Maciel. "His potential is unlimited in or out of the Marine Corps."

Martin graduated with one goal in mind: go to Iraq and fight. "It's not even about revenge or anything like that," said Martin. "It's the right thing to do. I support this country, and I'm ready to die if I have to."

Now able to defend freedom, Martin spent ten days with his family and friends in Kettle River. With a population of one hundred and sixty-eight people and no gas station or grocery store, the town is relatively unknown. However, it is home to some good hunting, *The Humbuckers* - probably the only punk band in town history - and a family of patriots.

From the Marine Corps News, May 21, 2004

BARBER OF TOKTONG PASS

"I think when people begin to understand what happened in World War II they have a leg up on knowing who we are as a people, what we are, and how strong we can be if we need to be." – Bill Barber

This country needs more people like Bill Barber. As he correctly points out, we are doomed to repeat the mistakes of the past if we don't learn from them. He is one of the Marines who built the legacy of the Corps, and his wisdom is matched only by his bravery.

In 1950, Bill Barber saved the lives of eight thousand Marines. His five-day stand with two hundred and twenty men against a force of fourteen hundred is considered one of the greatest holding actions in Marine Corps history.

Barber was raised on a farm in Kentucky. After learning that Germany had invaded Poland, he joined the Marines at age nineteen. He received a Purple Heart at Iwo Jima, and the Legion of Merit in Vietnam. In between, he earned the country's highest military award, the Medal of Honor, for his heroism in Korea.

On November 28, 1950, the first of the five nights of the battle of Chosin Reservoir began. It was mercilessly cold - below zero - in the four thousand-foot-high Toktong Pass connecting eight thousand Marines on the North Korean front with their command center fourteen miles behind. Barber was captain of Fox Company, a group of Marines who left to patrol the narrow mountain pass.

No one expected that 120,000 troops from Communist China were lying in wait nearby, or that the sound of a bugle

Not As Lean, Not As Mean, Still a Marine!

would bring fourteen hundred of these soldiers out of the mountains to attack Barber's company. The battle continued all night. No one slept. Barber's lines broke once, but the enemy did not take advantage of this, and the lines reformed. Though Barber's men nearly ran out of ammunition, they held strong until daybreak, when fighting came to a halt.

The second night brought another wave of attack. Again the Chinese broke through, this time taking a machine-gun post and wounding Barber in the leg. He had not slept for two days, and the situation looked grim.

"There was a time I accepted the reality that I may not be able to hold," he remembers. "You don't ever want to think about that, but it would be foolish not to recognize the odds up against you."

Barber - wounded but still able to walk - rallied his men who regained the machine gun and drove out the Chinese. Soon, he received radio orders to fight his way to a safer position. Barber requested permission to stand fast. He did, and held the road for five nights, allowing Marines farther ahead to get out.

When their time to leave did come, only eighty-two of Barber's men were able to walk away. Over half were dead or wounded, and forty were too frostbitten to walk. They had killed one thousand enemy troops.

Today, Barber gives this advice to the younger generation: Know your history - especially World War II. "I think when people begin to understand what happened in World War II they have a leg up on knowing who we are as a people, what we are, and how strong we can be if we need to be."

THEY ARE NOT LIKE ME

Robert D. Kaplan

"In one flash, as we charged across (the street) amid whistling incoming shots, I realized that they were *not* like me. They were Marines." – Robert D. Kaplan

In April, after four Americans were fatally ambushed in Fallujah, writer Robert D. Kaplan went into that Iraqi city with the Marines. His report, "Five Days in Fallujah," appeared in the July and August 2004 issues of The Atlantic Monthly. An account of some of the heaviest close-quarter fighting of the Iraq war, the story vividly highlights the bravery of the troops, including Bravo Company, commanded by Captain Jason Smith. Herewith an excerpt:

Smith did not have to order his Marines to go straight into the direction of the fire. It was a collective impulse - a phenomenon I would see again and again over the coming days. The idea that Marines are trained to break down doors, to seize beachheads and other territory, was an abstraction until I was there to experience it. Running *into* fire rather than seeking cover from it goes counter to every human survival instinct - trust me. I was sweating as much from fear as from the layers of clothing I still had on from the night before, to the degree that it felt as if pure salt were running into my eyes from my forehead. As the weeks had rolled on, and as I had gotten to know the 1/5 Marines as the individuals they were, I had started deluding myself that they weren't much different from me. They had soft spots, they got sick, they complained. But in one flash, as we charged across (the street) amid whistling incoming shots, I realized that they were *not* like me. They were Marines.

Mr. Kaplan went on to write "The Real Story of Fallujah," and in doing so showed that while he may not BE a Marine, he certainly understands them better than most:

When Bravo Company of the First Battalion of the Fifth Marine Regiment led U.S. forces into the heart of Fallujah in the predawn hours of April 6, I was the only journalist present. It had been Bravo Company of the "First of the Fifth" that had been first inside the citadel of Hue in Vietnam in February 1968. Hue City, the sight of one of the most glorious chapters in Marine history - in which the Marines killed 5,113 enemy troops while suffering 147 dead and 857 wounded - was foremost in the minds of the Marine commanders at Fallujah.

The Marines never got proper credit for Hue, for it was ultimately overshadowed by My Lai, in which an Army platoon killed 347 civilians a month later. This was despite the fact that the Marines' liberation of Hue led to the uncovering of thousands of mass graves there - the victims of an indiscriminate communist slaughter. Thus, Hue became a metaphor for the military's frustration with the media - a frustration revisited in Fallujah.

Whenever the Marines with whom I was attached crossed the path of a mosque, we were fired upon. Mosques in Fallujah were used by snipers and other gunmen, and also to store weapons and explosives. Time and again the insurgents forfeited the protective status granted these religious structures as stipulated by Geneva Conventions. Snipers were a particular concern. In early April in nearby Ramadi, an enemy sniper wiped out a squad of Marines using a Soviet-designed Draganov rifle. "Twelve shots, twelve kills," a Marine officer told me. The marksmanship indicated either imported jihadist talent or a member of the old regime's military elite.

By the standards of most wars, some mosques in Fallujah deserved to be leveled. But only after repeated aggressions was any mosque targeted, and then sometimes for hits so small in scope that they often had little effect. The news photos of holes in mosque domes did not indicate the callousness of the American military - rather the reverse.

As for the close-quarters urban combat, I was in the city the first days of the battle. The overwhelming percentage of small arms fire - not to mention mortars, rockets and rocket-propelled grenades - represented indiscriminate automatic bursts of the insurgents. Marines responded with far fewer, more precise shots. It was inspiring to observe high-testosterone nineteen-year-old lance corporals turn into calm and calculating thirty-year-olds every time a firefight started.

There was nothing fancy about the Marine advance into Fallujah. Marines slugged it out three steps forward, two steps backward - the classic, immemorial labor of infantry. Little had changed since Hue, or since antiquity for that matter. As their own casualties mounted, the only time I saw angry or depressed Marines was when an Iraqi civilian was accidentally hit in the crossfire - usually perpetrated by the enemy. I was not surprised. I had seen Army Special Forces react similarly to civilian casualties the year before in Afghanistan. The humanity of the troops is something to behold. Contrary to the op-ed page of the New York Times, the word 'haji' in both Iraq and Afghanistan, at least among Marines and Special Forces, is more often used as an endearment than a slur. To wit, "let's drink tea and hang out with the hajis," "haji food is so much better than what they feed us," "a haji designed real nice vests for our rifle plates," and so on. Thus, it has been so appallingly depressing to read about Abu Ghraib prison day after day after day.

By April 7, two sleep-deprived Marine battalions had taken nearly twenty percent of Fallujah. The following day a third battalion arrived to join the fight, allowing the first two to rest and recover their battle rhythm. Just as the three well-rested battalions were about to start boxing in the insurgents against the Euphrates River at the western edge of the city, a cease-fire was announced.

As disappointing as the cease-fire was, the Marines managed to wrest positive consequences from it. It would free them up to resume mortar mitigation, a critical defense task today in Iraq. Mortars and rockets rain down continually on American bases. If left unchallenged, it may be only a matter of time before a crowded chow hall or MWR (morale, welfare, recreation) facility is hit. Just recall the 1983 attack on the Marine barracks in Beirut that killed 241 servicemen.

Furthermore, as soon as the First of the Fifth Marines departed Fallujah they headed for Al-Karmah, a town about half the size of Fallujah and strategically located between Fallujah and Baghdad. Al-Karmah was no less hostile than Fallujah. I went there several times in March with the Marines. The streets always emptied upon our arrival, and we were periodically fired upon. After the Fallujah operation, the Marines didn't just visit Al-Karmah. They moved inside, patrolling regularly, talking to people on the streets, collecting intelligence and going a long way toward reclaiming that city. As one company captain told me, "It's easily the most productive stuff we've done in Iraq."

If Al-Karmah is reclaimed, if Fallujah itself remains relatively calm, if the Marines can patrol there at some point, and if mortar attacks abate measurably - all distinct possibilities - the decision not to launch an all-out assault on

Fallujah could look like the right one.

But none of the above matters if it is not competently explained to the American public - for the home front is more critical in a counterinsurgency than in any other kind of war. Yet the meticulous planning process undertaken by the Marines at the tactical level for assaulting Fallujah was not augmented with a similarly meticulous process by the administration at the strategic level for counteracting the easily foreseen media fallout from fighting in civilian areas near Muslim religious sites. The public was never made to feel just how much of a military threat the mosques in Fallujah represented, just how far Marines went to avoid damage to them and to civilians, and how much those same Marine battalions accomplished after departing Fallujah.

We live in a world of burning visual images. As Marines assaulted Fallujah, the administration should have been holding dramatic slide shows for the public, the kind battalion and company commanders were giving their troops, explaining how a particular mosque was being militarily used, and how much was being done to avoid destroying them, at great risk to Marine lives. Complaining about the slanted coverage of Al-Jazeera - as administration officials did - was as pathetic as Jimmy Carter complaining that Soviet Communist Party boss Leonid Brezhnev had lied to him. Given its long-standing track record, how else could Al-Jazeera have been expected to report the story? You had the feeling the Pentagon was reacting, rather than anticipating.

And had the administration adequately explained to the public what the Marines were doing after Fallujah, there might have been less disappointment and mystification about quitting the fight there. But instead of a gripping storyline to compete with that of the global media's, spokesmen for the White House, Pentagon, Coalition Provisional Authority and the Baghdad-based military coalition, in their regular briefings about events in Iraq, continue to feed the public insipid summaries, with little visual context, that have all the pungency of watery gruel.

This is not to say that the Abu Ghraib prison scandal should be forgotten, that our government should deceive the public, or that the overall direction of events in Iraq is positive - far from it. I have been to towns and villages in the Sunni triangle where the CPA has no demonstrable presence, where the inhabitants have no functioning utilities, where crime is rampant, where the newly constituted police are powerless and only sheikhs have the power to haul in criminals, and where it is only the social glue of tribe and clan that keeps these places from descending into Middle Eastern versions of Liberia.

But I also found that there are many different Iraqs and different levels of reality to each of them. Presently, the administration lacks the public relations talent and the organizational structure for conveying even the positive elements of the Iraqi panorama in all their drama and texture.

Because the battles in a counterinsurgency are small scale and often clandestine, the story line is rarely obvious. It becomes a matter of perceptions, and victory is awarded to those who weave the most compelling narrative. Truly, in the world of postmodern, Twenty-first century conflict, civilian and military public affairs officers must become war fighters by another name. They must control and anticipate a whole new storm system represented by a global media, which too often exposes embarrassing facts out of historical or philosophical context.

Without a communications strategy that gives the public the same sense of mission that a company captain imparts to his noncommissioned officers, victory in warfare nowadays is impossible. Looking beyond Iraq, the American military needs battlefield doctrine for influencing the public in the same way that the Army and the Marines already have doctrine for individual infantry tasks and squad-level operations.

The centerpiece of that doctrine must be the flattening out of bureaucratic hierarchies within the Defense Department, so that spokesmen can tap directly into the experiences of company and battalion commanders and entwine their smell-of-the-ground experiences into daily briefings. Nothing is more destructive for the public-relations side of warfare than field reports that have to make their way up antiquated, Industrial Age layers of command, diluting riveting stories of useful content in the process. Journalists with little knowledge of military history or tactics and with various agendas to peddle can go directly to lieutenants and sergeants, yet the very spokesmen of these soldiers and Marines themselves - even through their aides - seem unable to do so.

The American public can accept fifty casualties per week if the path to some sort of success is convincingly laid out. If it isn't, the public won't accept even two casualties per week. It could not be helped that the shame of My Lai, as awful as it was, should have been allowed to blot out American heroism at places like Hue. The phenomenon of the media as we know it was new back then. But if the stain of Abu Ghraib, for example, is not placed in its rightful perspective against everything else that soldiers and Marines are doing in Iraq, Afghanistan, the Philippines, Colombia and many other places in the War on Terrorism, then it won't be the media's fault alone.

Mr. Kaplan is a correspondent for *The Atlantic Monthly*

DRILL INSTRUCTORS
Never Die

Brian L. Hipwell

"You will not *like* me, but the more you *hate* me, the more you will learn." – Drill Instructor Gunnery Sergeant Hartman in *Full Metal Jacket*

If you have read "Swift, Silent and Surrounded," you may recall the story in which I met R. Lee Ermy of "Full Metal Jacket" fame. What I didn't mention when I wrote that story was I nearly locked my body up at the position of attention when he first approached, despite the fact I held a higher rank than he had attained during his time in the Corps. Why? Because in my subconscious mind, he was a Drill Instructor - and I was eating a jelly donut!

I enlisted in the Marine Corps April 23, 1965 under the 120-day delay program while in my senior year at Stevens High School in Claremont, New Hampshire, and shortly after graduation I shipped out for PI. My father was a retired Marine Master Sergeant, and I had been a service "brat,' so I knew what I was in line for. There were no surprises at Boot Camp.

On day two at PI I joined Platoon 339 and met the one person who would have the most lasting impression upon my life, my Senior Drill Instructor, Staff Sergeant Ed Ricker, from Charlestown, New Hampshire - which happens to be the next town over from Claremont.

I needn't go into the details of Boot Camp at Parris Island during the summer of 1965. Vietnam was becoming a

59

household word, and everything was geared for eventually seeing service there. The first half of *Full Metal Jacket* brought it all back so clearly.

I graduated from PI as a PFC with orders for Marine Barracks, Kenitra, Morocco, 1st Guard Company at Sidi Yahia... the armpit of the world. Eventually I would see service in Vietnam and end up at Camp Lejeune twice, leaving the Marine Corps in 1969 with two Purple Hearts, five rows of ribbons and an Honorable Discharge. Every now and then I'd join in with other former Marines telling 'war stories' and everyone would always remember the name of their Senior Drill Instructor.

In 1983 I took advantage of my remaining GI Bill benefits and earned my degree in History (in 18th Century Studies). I subsequently had the occasion to be the Program Manager at "The Fort at #4," a re-creation of the 1740's fortified village and a living history museum simply known as Number Four - which would later be known as Charlestown.

One summer weekend the Fort sponsored a huge Eigtheenth Century event complete with hundreds of re-enactors, soldiers, camp followers, artillery, sutlers, white tents and officers marques. Authentically dressed soldiers and civilians representing French, Colonial, Prussian, and British forces were all crammed into the twenty-two acre site.

At ten o'clock the camps were given the order to 'TAP TO' and all was quiet. However, some of the 'townies' (local youths) decided to let off a few M-80's and various other forms of pyrotechnics and raise a little hell of their own. Being in charge of this affair, I didn't want the re-enactors being blamed for the afterhours 'fire-fight' - so I called the Charlestown Police.

Within a few minutes I received word from the gate

guards that a police cruiser was coming down, and I waited outside the office in my uniform of a British Sergeant Major of the 29th Regiment of Foot.

The cruiser slowly approached my position and stopped next to me. I could see the officer's arm resting on the door sill and noticed he had "USMC" and "Eagle, Globe, and Anchor" tattoos on his forearm. Not quite bending low enough to see his face, which was partially hidden by the brim of his 'Smokey' hat, I began telling him why he had been called. In the middle of my report the officer slowly moved his head out through the window and looked up into my eyes. I could now see his face, slightly lit by the office lights.

"HIPWELL, YOU @#%!%(#&@#$@#^&!....... GET DOWN AND GIVE ME FIFTY, NOW!"

I hadn't seen that face since outposting Parris Island for Camp Geiger in 1965... but there he was - Ed Ricker, my Senior Drill Instructor!

He slowly peeled himself out of the cruiser, slammed the door with meaningful irreverence, put his hands on his hips, feet slightly spread apart, and although we were about the same height he seemed seven feet tall. The brim of his Smokey cover was gently curved up, just like he had worn his campaign hat at PI. For a brief moment I WAS at Parris Island, and it was 1965. I was standing at attention, thumbs along the outboard seams of my 'breeches'... I was literally standing tall before THE MAN!

He smiled ever so slightly, stuck out his right hand, and firmly shook mine with a death grip. All while asking me, "WHAT'S YOUR ##$#$&%^&ing Fifth General Order?"

I actually answered "SIR, TO QUIT MY POST ONLY WHEN PROPERLY RELIEVED, SIR!"

He looked me squarely in the eye and said "Don't ever

forget that you %#^#^#%(**)(&%$!!.... You're a Marine. YOU take care of the problem, and don't call me for any more Mickey Mouse stuff the rest of the night. Now, get outta here!"

I did. I found the kids causing the problem, and relieved them of their firecrackers with a promise to call their parents. As I walked across the field with my 'booty,' relieved that the night would remain quiet, I could see the outline of a Charlestown police car parked just a couple of hundred feet away on the road shoulder. The lights were off and the engine was running. The car's spotlight shined on me and over the vehicle's loudspeaker came Ricker's voice, "You still owe me fifty!"

He turned his headlights on, flashed his blue roof lights and drove off. That was the last time I ever saw him.

A WISH COMES TRUE

"One of the most beautiful compensations of life is that no man can sincerely try to help another without helping himself." – Ralph Waldo Emerson

Marines will low-crawl through a thousand miles of barbed wire and broken glass to help a brother Marine or a member of his family - even when they have never met:

Larkann "Lynn" Stewart was only six months old when her father, Lance Corporal David Stewart, was killed in an ambush in Vietnam on January 13, 1968.

Nearly thirty years later, on her wedding day of August 30, 1997, she wanted someone who had served with her father to walk her down the aisle and give her away. The problem for the Memphis, Tennessee-born bride was that she didn't know anyone who could fill the bill.

Her plight reached retired Marine Fred Tucker, the Tennessee commissioner of Veterans Affairs. He took the problem as a personal challenge and issued press releases, made phone calls, conducted research and contacted several service-associated publications, including *Leatherneck* magazine.

Response was tremendous. Eventually he located Steven Meyer, who lived in Modesto, California near the site of the wedding, and verified that he had indeed served with Stewart.

Meyer said he was happy to be able to serve the daughter of a comrade in arms. At the request of the bride Tucker too took the walk down the aisle, and flew to the Sacramento, California, wedding at his own expense.

In spite of his death some twenty-nine years earlier Dave Stewart had, in spirit, been there to walk his daughter down the aisle, thanks to the Brotherhood of Marines to which he belonged.

Semper Fi, Dave.

BEIRUT TO BAGHDAD

Oliver North

"This is a time for all Americans to reflect on what it means to be an American. We have gone across the seas in years past to fight in the defense of the freedoms we hold so dear, but this time the battlefield is closer to home - too close." - Medal of Honor winner Colonel Harvey C. "Barney" Barnum USMC

Each September 11, Americans will commemorate one of the most tragic days in American history - a day when 2,998 of our friends and neighbors were murdered by fanatic terrorists. It is a day that will not be forgotten because, for so many Americans, September 11 marks the start of the war on terrorism.

But in fact, terrorists proclaimed war on Americans long before then, and every time American interests are targeted by these fanatics, there is one American family which suffers casualties, or is called upon to retaliate, or both. That American family is the United States Marine Corps.

Among their many other duties, Marines have the unique honor and responsibility of providing security at American embassies around the world, where the sentries are ordered to "take charge of this post and all government property in view." Unfortunately, embassies tend to be a favorite target of terrorists. The Corps' history of fighting terrorists dates to 1804, when Marine First Lieutenant Presley O'Bannon led his men to defeat the Barbary Pirates.

But the modern day war on terrorism is often traced to November 4, 1979, when Iranian militants seized the

Not As Lean, Not As Mean, Still a Marine!

American embassy in Tehran, Iran and took sisty-six Americans hostage – fifty-two of whom would be held in captivity for 444 days. Four years later, on April 18, 1983, the U.S. embassy in Beirut was attacked when a terrorist drove a pickup truck into the building, killing sixty-three people, seventeen of whom were Americans.

Six months later, U.S. Marines who were helping to keep the peace in Lebanon were the target of what was - prior to September 11, 2001 - the largest terrorist attack in American history. At 6:22 a.m. on Sunday, October 23, 1983, a homicide bomber crashed a large Mercedes truck loaded with over two thousand pounds of explosives through a barbed wire fence and other barriers into the four-story headquarters of the Marine compound located at Beirut's airport. The attack killed 241 Marines, sailors and one soldier, who were members of Battalion Landing Team 1/8 of the 24th Marine Amphibious Unit, and instantly turned the building into a pile of rubble.

At the time, the world was a dangerous place - as it is now. It was the height of the Cold War, and President Reagan had already branded the Soviet Union "the Evil Empire." One month before the Soviets had shot down a Korean airliner - Flight 007 - killing all 269 people on board, including sixty-one Americans, one of whom was U.S. Representative Larry McDonald.

Two days after the Beirut bombing Marines, along with other U.S. forces, landed on Grenada to rescue American medical students following a Marxist coup on the island. The threat of terrorism against Americans had become every bit as real as the dangers of the Cold War and Soviet expansion.

When the 24th Marine Amphibious Unit (MAU) was ordered to Lebanon from its home at Camp LeJeune, N.C., it was the fourth such Marine unit to serve in the country since

Not As Lean, Not As Mean, Still a Marine!

September 1982. They were invited there as part of a Multinational Peacekeeping Force along with France, Italy and, later, Great Britain to help enforce a tenuous peace arrangement between the various factions in Lebanon. The Marines' mission was to control the area around the Beirut International Airport – Lebanon's link to the outside world.

During better times, money from rich Arab states used to flow through the international banks in Beirut, and the city was known as the "Paris of the Middle East." But parts of the country were deteriorating, and outside the airport perimeter were slums that bred recruits for militant groups like Hezbollah, which was responsible for the October 23 bombing.

Since 1983, Marines and other U.S. military personnel have been targeted by terrorists in Kuwait, Bogota, Madrid, San Salvador, Frankfurt, West Berlin, Riyadh, Dhahran, Nairobi, Dar es Salaam and Aden, to name a few. Yet they continue the fight, and today in Afghanistan and Iraq they are not only defending Americans from terrorists, but their presence has allowed citizens in those countries to escape repressive and torturous regimes.

The war against terror, as the president repeatedly warned, will not be short in duration. Every October 23rd, Marines all over the world take a moment to salute their comrades who were murdered on that date, and then return to the fight until it is won.

Perhaps on that day, all Americans can take time to acknowledge the extraordinary contributions our fellow Marines have made to defend America's liberty throughout our history - particularly those who sacrificed their lives from Beirut to Baghdad to defend our nation and bring peace to a violent part of the world.

Semper Fidelis, Marines.

RAPID REQUEST

"Improvise, adapt and overcome." – Fictional Gunnery Sergeant Tom Highway

Early in my career I was assigned to 2nd Assault Amphibian Battalion as a communicator, and it wasn't long before I was on my first shipboard deployment to the Mediterranean. As a communicator it was my job to operate and maintain the radios in each of our fourteen "Amtrac" vehicles - and it was a tedious and thankless job to say the least. We did all of our work down on the "well deck" of our LST, and sometimes wouldn't see sunshine or fresh air for days at a time. Life was not good.

Then one day, as we were sailing around the Mediterranean in big lazy circles, I got an opportunity for a temporary reprieve - and I jumped on it. I was assigned to accompany our chief mechanic and a translator on a "contact team" to the Italian Marine base at San Marcos. Our mission was to survey the American-made AAVs the Italians were using, and assist them in performing maintenance on their equipment.

Before we boarded the helicopter to depart, my platoon commander gave me a PRC-77 man-packed radio and some "rapid request forms" for ordering parts. I was instructed to establish communication with the ship once we arrived at our destination, and radio back for any parts we needed by following the format on the forms. The only problem was the ship would end up being *way* out of radio range - which turned out to be quite fortunate for me.

In the Marine Corps toilet paper is known as "shit paper" - so much so that I'm surprised it doesn't actually *say* that on

68

the box it comes in. And since the products in our supply system are provided by the lowest bidder, it goes without saying the stuff we were getting wasn't what you would call "Charmin soft." In fact I liked to call it "John Wayne" shit paper, because it was rough, and it was tough, and it didn't take shit off of *anybody*.

As bad as our supply situation was in regard to sanitary products, the Italians had it worse. The first time I went to make a head call on their base I discovered they had no toilet paper of *any* kind. To make matters worse, I did not discover this problem until the moment I actually needed to use some. I think we have all been in this situation at one time or another, and it's not a good feeling. I looked around frantically for something which could serve as a substitute, but found nothing. Then it hit me. I had a pocket full of rapid request forms!

We never did make radio contact with the ship, so I ended up sharing the remainder of the forms with my buddies for the remainder of our stay. And of course, upon our return, the first thing the lieutenant asked me was if the rapid request forms had come in handy. I told him, in all honesty, that they had indeed…

GODDAMN MARINES!

"The U.S. Marine Corps is more than a crack military machine. It is a fraternity bonded in blood." – Clare Boothe Luce

I wonder how many times during Operation Iraqi Freedom the phrase "Goddamn Marines" was uttered? Even in the best of times, Army and Air Force officers have been heard muttering some epithet about Marines, invoking either heaven or hell. Interestingly enough, we Marines find it all rather reassuring and, at times, amusing.

Most of the time, Marines do not go out of their way to be obnoxious - we are just doing what Marines have done for over two hundred years. A good example is the fact that Marines always raise the American flag over mountains or cities they have conquered. From Mt. Suribachi to the City of Hue, to Kuwait City to Baghdad, U.S. Marines have raised the Stars and Stripes - in the latter examples, much to the chagrin of higher headquarters. You don't get these kinds of problems with the Army.

So what is it about U.S. Marines that causes them to stick U.S. flags on everything and do more with less - a "less" that is either old, or an Army hand-me-down? We call it Esprit de Corps, but it goes deeper than that. We learn and maintain myths of the past, which also means living up to those historical examples. Marine Corps boot camp is the longest of the services. It is where we mold young men and women into the mythical image called a Marine. You can be in the Army, you can join the Air Force, but you *become* a Marine. All of the other uniformed services have songs. U.S. Marines have a hymn. The basic pattern of Marine Corps uniforms comes from the late nineteenth century, and our emblem, "the Eagle, Globe and Anchor" has remained largely unchanged since 1868. The buttons on our dress blues, whites, and greens date back to the founding of our Corps. And the Marine Corps is the only service that requires its officers to carry a sword, whose pattern dates back to 1805.

I think the path of the Marines was established long ago. On the 10th of November 1775, the Marine Corps was first established... in a tavern. To this day, no matter where they are in the world, Marines celebrate the founding of their beloved Corps, much to the confusion of the other services.

A few years ago a congresswoman from Colorado felt that the Marine Corps was radical and extreme. She contended that the Marine Corps was not politically correct, nor did we seem to be part of the Department of Defense's transition to a "kinder and gentler" military. She was correct, and the Marine Corps took it as a compliment!

But the proof is in the doing, and during Iraqi Freedom the Marines demonstrated what Marines can do. I watched with some amusement as a reporter asked a young lance corporal about being in Iraq and under rifle fire. "Love it, sir!" was his response. The reporter was taken aback and asked, "No, really." The Marine then tried to explain that this is what he was *trained* to do, that he looked forward to doing it, and that he was now *happy* to be doing it. No doubt in boot camp he was told that he was "a minister of death praying for war." Contrast that with the poor U.S. Army Apache pilots who said that if they had to take life, they would do so reluctantly. You are either a warrior, or you are not.

Marines are mission oriented. Live or die, the most important thing to a Marine is accomplishing the mission. Whether taking the bridge, river or town, accomplishing the mission is the Holy Grail of being a Marine. How the mission is accomplished is not so important, as it is expected of all Marines to accomplish the mission with the tools available. This is probably why we heard that Marines in one engagement were fighting with knives and bayonets. This was hardly high tech, but it was effective. These Marines now have bragging rights, for they have proven they both talk-the-talk and walk-the-walk. I doubt there is a single Marine who is not envious.

Marines are practical, as well. I enjoyed hearing two reporters interviewing each other, one embedded with the Army, the other with the Marines. The reporter with the Army noted that the sandstorm had blown down many of the soldiers' cots. The other reporter countered that the Marines did not have this problem because they slept on the ground. The Marine learns to live with what he can carry on his back. He expects to be moved around on the battlefield via his two black Cadillacs (boots). If he is lucky and gets a ride on an amtrac, so much the better - but it is not expected. At the end of a mission, the priority for cleaning is weapon, then equipment, and finally, body. When the other services talk about "quality of life," they are referring to housing, clubs and food. Marines are talking about better weapons, equipment and training. Winning the battle and coming home alive is considered "quality of life."

All of this translates into combat power. In comparison to the U.S. Army's 3rd Infantry Division, the Marines of I Marine Expeditionary Force were lightly equipped. Yet, they battled through the heart of Iraq, fought to the center of Baghdad, and then moved off to Tikrit - taking that city as well.

The press was so enamored with the Marines that in the final days of the war they even credited the Marines with deeds actually accomplished by the Army. Little wonder we heard "Goddamn Marines!" so often. So we need to give the Marines some slack when they do something politically incorrect, such as raising the flag or appearing insensitive when killing the enemy. In the field, they look sloppy compared to the Army, but are aggressive in the attack and generally unhappy in the defense. Marines take pride in their work, even if that work is war. We are just Marines, and that is what we do.

MARINES DON'T DO THAT

"To see what is right, and not do it, is want of courage, or of principle." -Confucius

The following message, sent by then-Commandant Leonard Chapman to Marine Corps brass, was prompted by a letter he had received from a friend regarding the conduct of a Marine:

DEPARTMENT OF THE NAVY
HEADQUARTERS UNITED STATES MARINE CORPS
WASHINGTON, D.C. 20380

From: Commandant of the Marine Corps
To: All General Officers and All Commanding Officers – Active and Reserve

Subj: Marines Don't Do That

1. Early this month I received the following note from a distinguished friend:

"General Chapman:

Recently I was in an air terminal... (Most people there presented a pretty sloppy appearance) - coats unbuttoned, ties loosened, etc. There was a Marine Corporal (in uniform) who was just the opposite. I spoke to the Marine and pointed out the difference to him. I asked him why it was so? His answer was: 'The Marines don't do that.'

Best Regards,... "

Not As Lean, Not As Mean, Still a Marine!

2. "The Marines don't do that." A simple statement of fact which leaves no question in the mind of the listener.

3. Marines don't – wear a scruffy uniform.
   Marines don't – put their hands in their pockets.
   Marines don't – wear long hair.
   Marines don't – fail to respond with a "Yes, or No, Sir" when speaking with a senior.
   Marines don't – render a half-hearted or sloppy salute to the Stars and Stripes or to their seniors.
   Marines don't – gang up on each other.
   Marines don't – question lawful orders.
   Marines don't – lie, or cheat, or break their word.
   Marines don't – abandon a fellow Marine in time of need.
   Marines don't – let down their fellow Marines by succumbing to drug temptation.
   Marines don't – meet problems with "It can't be done" or questions or with the easy answer "No."
   Marines don't – knock the system without recommending appropriate change.
   Marines don't – (the list is all but endless!).

4. Marines don't do that. But why not? Because they are a breed apart. They are not the run of the mill; they are but a few good men. They are proud members of an elite Corps. They are as well trained as - if not better than - any military outfit, anywhere. They have led the way, in war and peace, for 196 years. And they know that today they are ready-combat ready - to move out, any time, with the Navy, go anywhere, take on anybody, fight and win. We must keep our balance, raise our quality, maintain our standards, and be ready to serve our Country. Marines do *that*!

L. F. Chapman, Jr. Commandant of the Marine Corps

TOAST YOURSELVES!

John Wintersteen

"Take courage then, seize the fortune that awaits you, repair to the Marine Rendezvous where, in a flowing bowl of punch, and three times three, you shall drink."
- Revolutionary War era recruiting poster

I'm sure Mr. Wintersteen speaks for all Marines, past and present. So pick up a glass, and toast yourself!

I'm sure most of you from "K" Company, 2nd Battalion, Marine Corps Recruit Depot, Parris Island, S.C. could look at your DD-214's and see that forty-four years ago today, you enlisted in the finest major fighting force in the world. That decision alone to take such a large step is impressive enough. To finish Boot Camp and become a Marine is even more so. We all know inside ourselves what it took to overcome whatever fears we might have had. For some, it was being away from home and family for the first time in our lives, for others it was self-doubt - could we cut the mustard? What if we didn't make it? Would we have to go back home and admit we failed? Maybe some worried about being sent to war. After all, the Korean War had ended just six short years before.

Now, after all this time, we know we had what it took. We know what a powerful influence the Corps has had on our lives. In our later years, we realize that many of our decisions, consciously or subconsciously, are and were guided by the principles of the Corps and that ever-present reminder to "do it right the first time." Or, "Adapt, improvise, overcome." Respect for God, Country and Corps were instilled in us, whether we knew it at the time or not. Our Drill Instructors did a number on us, and we all thought it was a bad thing at the time. How wrong we were! Now we see our DI's again and can thank them from the bottom of our green hearts for what they gave us.

Deep down, you now walk around confidently, knowing you did something, and are something, special - with no need to prove it to anyone else. When someone finds out you are a Marine, you can see the subtle change in the way they react or look at you. They don't even know why it happens themselves, because they haven't experienced the Brotherhood. They just know Marines have a long history of defending them and maybe they can't understand why someone would die for somebody else.

We had a very strong bond with our High School sports teammates, and some of those can last a lifetime. Most don't. But where else can you find the camaraderie we have with a million or more living Marines? Not to mention the bond we have with those who fought and died to bring us to where we are today. We carry on that proud tradition and try to live exemplary lives. How much is that worth to you? Would you not do it again? When our Series Officer, Colonel Alex Fazekas, met us for the first time since 1959 he stood up and said, "Y'all should be proud of yourselves for being such a big success." We won't ever forget that one.

So pick up your glass and toast yourselves. You have a right to do so with no immodesty. I will be toasting all Marines, and especially you, with whom I shared a frightening, then exhilarating, thirteen weeks forty-four years ago.

In order to PROPERLY toast yourself always use traditional Marine Corps "1775 Rum Punch." It is made by mixing four parts lime juice, one part dark Jamaican rum, maple syrup and Grenadine to taste. Ice liberally. Before drinking give the 'Corps and Country' toast: "Long live the United States, and success to the Marines!"

SEMPER FI TO SEMPER EYE

"You cannot depend on your eyes when your imagination is out of focus." - Mark Twain

Some years ago I heard the story of a Gunnery Sergeant who had returned from Vietnam blind in his left eye. He wanted to remain in the Corps more than anything, but knew he would probably be discharged due to his disability. Not one to give up easily (like most Marines), the Gunny reported to sick bay for the required physical, and when it was over he had passed with flying colors. How did he do it? When it came time for the eye test, the Gunny covered his left eye with his left hand and read the chart. When instructed to switch eyes, he simply lowered his left hand, raised the right, and placed it over his... left eye. Viola... 20/20!

Retired Gunnery Sergeant Donald A. Levesque comes from a small town in Massachusetts. In 1962, at the age of almost nineteen years old, Levesque joined the United States Marines. After graduating from Parris Island his assignments included "G" Company, 2nd Battalion, 4th Marines at Kanioi Bay, Philippines, "C" Company, 1st Battalion, 2nd Marines Camp Le Jeune, North Carolina; Drill Instructor at F Company, Second Recruit Training Battalion, Parris Island; and "L" Company, 3rd Battalion, 5th Marine Division, Viet Nam. After serving a little over seven years, at the age of twenty-five and having just completing his eighth combat operation, Gunny claims he received his "blessing of blindness." On April 10, 1969 at 3:33 PM Levesque, with the second-hand on the "3" on the waterproof Timex watch which he wore on his lapel, took a licking - and his watch stopped ticking. He proclaimed, "There must be something above me as to why I'm still kicking."

During the course of his treatment for injuries received in combat, one doctor commented, "We have no answer for the shrapnel passing clean through your head and missing your brain." And Don's reply was, "I don't have a brain." It is this spiritual connection and sick humor that still supports Levesque's ongoing career of helping others to help themselves.

In June of 1969, prior to Levesque's medical retirement, he was sent to the Veterans Administration's Northeast Blind Rehabilitation Center at West Haven, Connecticut on temporary assignment duty status. The core curriculum of the center had a four-pronged attack to the challenge of blindness: 1) mobility - use a long white cane to get from point A to point B; 2) manual skills - use of tools to enhance hand-mind-eye coordination; 3) living skills - use of household appliances, cleaning devices to enhance independent living; and 4) communication skills - use of tape recorder, Braille and other reading and writing devices. To Levesque's way of thinking, he'd be able to get back into the Marine Corps with a profile restricted to night maneuvers. Thus, the birth of his new attitude toward the disability came alive not as a challenge - it was simply an opportunity. An all-day night patrol! This conviction to be faithful to his Marine-hood was met with opposition by some rehabilitation specialists who tried to encourage him to drop the Marine idea and just become a veteran. Stoic at first, the Gunny's internal dialog was working overtime. "Who the *hell* are these civilians, telling me I'm not a Marine? You mean drop my principals of looking out for the welfare of the troops, knowing myself and seeking self-improvement, and completing the mission at hand?

Not As Lean, Not As Mean, Still a Marine!

From a rehabilitation standpoint, Levesque was at an all-time high in denying his blindness. It was at the peak, not even three months into his total blindness, that the following thoughts came to mind: "These poor government employees know not what they do. They not only have never walked in my shoes, they've never been a Marine. How can I get this message across?" It finally came to him one night in a sleepless sweat. It was a lesson he learned before his Marine Corps days from a former World War II Marine who worked back then as an ad man for his hometown newspaper. He told Levesque, who was about ten years old, to remember one thing: A picture is worth a thousand words. The very next day he was being sent to a restoration clinic in New York City to have artificial eyes made. He badgered the eye maker to make a Marine Corps emblem eye. He then wore it during the rest of his rehabilitation, and his message was loud and clear - Once a Marine, always a Marine!

In October of 1969, despite his unique and eccentric maverick approach to blind rehabilitation, Levesque also successfully completed his high school GED and used that to submit application to Providence College in Providence, Rhode Island. During his college years (he graduated in 1974 with honors), along with future employment with the Veteran's Administration, Levesque kept his Marine emblem eye in a water container, preserving it for annual cameo appearances at Marine Corps birthday celebrations and private parties with Marine friends to inspire them to "stay Marine no matter what." He never had a clue as to how to bridge his "die-hard Marine spirit" to mainstream society until December 1987, after Levesque had spent more that seventeen years helping blind veterans take their rightful place in the community no matter what their disability.

At that time the United States Department of Labor

Not As Lean, Not As Mean, Still a Marine!

Veterans program in New York was looking for a blind veteran to participate in a one hundred mile marathon preceded by a skydive event to be held in Death Valley. A colleague said that is was too dangerous for a blind person to jump out of an airplane. Levesque took this statement personally. He thought "It's time to set the record straight. It's up to the individual as to what he or she feels they can and cannot do. I have never sky-dived before, nor have I ran even a twenty-six mile marathon - however, I accept the challenge."

In February 1988 Levesque received national recognition when he successfully completed his second skydive with a standup landing, and completed his hundred mile marathon over the course of a week with thirteen other Vietnam veterans. Today he still serves as a volunteer. He has consistently demonstrated "ability over disability," participating in 10K races, jumping with the Royal Thai Marine Recon Battalion in Sadahip, Thailand, and helping veterans with their VA claims and benefits.

This means "ability over disability." Levesque says, "The more out-of-context experiences that we involve ourselves with, the more some sort of growth will occur. The determination, concentration, dedication, and patience I feel override the poisons of our mind, being worried, doubt, pessimism, and procrastination. One trick that I found is to go after something with a higher purpose than myself; for example, always the welfare of the troops via seeking self-improvement via the mission at hand. This is the kind of ticking that no longer makes me wonder why I outlived my Timex."

A few years ago Don joined forces with the USDOL VETS and the New York State Department of Labor to design and produce an "I Want You to Hire a Disabled

Veteran" poster. The poster reminds us of the sacrifices of our veterans and demonstrates to other severely disabled veterans that they don't have to spend their lives sitting in a rocker on the front porch. This poster is an absolute show-stopper and has put most viewers in a state of awe, reminding them of the sacrifice that we made for their freedom, as well as giving disabled people a message of the hope of "ability over disability."

GUNNY POPEYE

Jennie Haskamp

"A man's feet should be planted in his country, but his eyes should survey the world." - George Santayana

As Marine Gunnery Sergeant Nick Popaditch sat and watched his ten-year-old son play third base at Luckie Park in Twentynine Palms, California, he couldn't hide his enthusiasm. Popaditch hadn't planned on making it to these games.

"One month ago I was in Iraq, and I assumed I'd watch his first baseball season on videotape after I got home," he said from his red, white and blue canvas chair next to the dugout. "This is a real treat, being here for these games."

A real treat. Those three simple words provide a small preview of Popaditch's endlessly positive all-Marine attitude. The event that brought him home in time for little league was life-changing, but when he speaks of it he is humble and quick to change the focus of the conversation to the Marines he met recently, or to the support he has received from friends and strangers alike, rather than be hailed as a hero himself.

"These young Marines I met in the hospitals on my way home - they are the heroes," he said, telling story after story of the Marines he met in various stages of recovery while in hospitals in Landstuhl, Germany, Bethesda, Maryland, and San Diego on his way home to Twentynine Palms. "Marines like Corporal Ortiz."

Popaditch, still watching the game in front of him, retold Ortiz's story, a grin spreading across his chiseled, suntanned face.

"This kid was waiting for his buddy to be medevaced when a frag grenade came in. Ortiz could move, he could get out of the area, but his friend couldn't - so Ortiz covered his buddy with his own body, hoping their body armor would take up most of the blast. He used his arms to shield his friend's face, and at the last second this other Marine, shot and bleeding, wrenched his arm free to cover Ortiz's face, too."

Popaditch stopped, an amazed look on his face, and shook his head. "Man, they sure took a beating from the shrapnel, but they are both alive - they kept each other alive," he said. "They are heroes to me."

To fully understand why strangers across the country are sending well wishes to Nick Popaditch - a true American hero they've never met- one must rewind to Operation Iraqi Freedom and the liberation of Baghdad. In a famous event that truly symbolized the liberation, 1st Tank Battalion Marines pulled down a statue of Saddam Hussein. An Associated Press photographer captured then-Staff Sergeant Nick Popaditch grinning and smoking a stogie with the statue falling in the background.

This photo, which ended up on the front page of nearly every major paper in the United States, earned him the title of "the Cigar Marine."

Now fast forward to April 7th of this year. Popaditch, still a tank commander with 1st Tank Battalion, volunteered to redeploy to Iraq with another company when he found out his own company wasn't slated to go back yet.

For the thirty-six-year-old father of two, that fateful day in Fallujah was just another day at the office - or in the tank, if you ask him.

"We'd been in constant contact with the enemy for thirty-six hours," he started, absentmindedly tracing a scar above his right eyebrow. "We were on a street so narrow there wasn't even room to turn my turret."

With the enemy somewhere in front of them, Popaditch and his crew, which included a second tank, slowly traversed the narrow streets.

"We passed an alley no wider than those two poles, and I looked down the alley and saw anti-coalition forces fire (a rocket-propelled grenade) straight at us," he continued.

The poles he referred to were in the frame of the backstop, and as he made the analogy, he paused to watch the game being played in front of him, pointing out a kid in a pickle between first and second base.

"That RPG hit the side of my turret and it didn't penetrate, but I ordered my driver to stop and as I turned to engage them with my .50-caliber, another RPG was launched from a rooftop in front of us, and I guess that sucker had better aim," he laughed. "I'm not sure if he was aiming at my head, or at the hatch. The best I can figure is he split the difference."

Splitting the difference from a rooftop cost Popaditch his right eye - a fact he refuses to dwell on. Rather he speaks of the heroic actions of his twenty-six-year-old gunner, Corporal Ryan Chambers.

"When I got hit, I saw a flash of light and then everything went black. All I could hear was fuzz and static," he recalled, pausing to clap as his son's team brought in another runner, putting them ahead by five runs. "The force of the blast knocked me down into the tank, and I sat up and reached for my radio to start telling the driver we needed to get out of there. But my helmet was gone, so I had no radio."

Blinded, momentarily deaf and not yet feeling pain, Popaditch groped his way around the inside of his tank until he located Chambers.

"That guy, man, he was injured too, and he'd already climbed right up into the cupola - the same cupola I'd just been blown out of - and was assessing the situation," said Popaditch, stopping to laugh. "This is the funny part of the story. I grabbed him and screamed, 'Chambers, we have to get the tanks out of here,' and 'Chambers, you're going to have to call for a medevac.' He didn't answer me, so I shook him and screamed it three or four more times, until I realized he'd probably answered me but I couldn't hear him."

As the tank started moving he could faintly hear Chambers on the radio.

"I heard him hollering at both drivers, just doing what tank commanders do naturally," he said, admiration in his voice. "We were blocks and blocks deep into the city, and Chambers simply took control. That was comforting to me, to know that he had taken charge of the situation."

With Chambers in charge, Popaditch focused on himself for a moment and said he suddenly felt very tired.

"I wanted to lie down right there and go to sleep for a while, but I knew from first aid training that I had to stay awake," he laughed, shaking his head sheepishly. "I stood up, held on, and forced myself to stay awake. I don't remember anything about the trip back to the center of command, but there is a berm near the trestle we were based near, and when I felt the tank cross that berm, I knew we were home."

Popaditch said when his Marines and the medical crew pulled him out of the tank, he knew everything was going to be okay. He said he's still not sure if they were Army medics or Navy corpsmen, and laughingly apologizes for not knowing, saying, "Hey, I'd just been hit in the face with a grenade."

Not As Lean, Not As Mean, Still a Marine!

"When they started treating me I knew I was safe, and I knew my family would never see a picture of me hanging from a train trestle somewhere," he said. "It was such an emotionally charged feeling, such a sense of relief."

He remembers very little about being treated in Fallujah, or being medevaced to Germany, but what he does remember amazes him.

"I was on a cot, and they were working on me. I was very heavily medicated," he recalled, taking off the patch covering his right eye and rubbing his hand across his shaved head.

"All of a sudden, they said, 'Gunny, we're being mortared, so we're going to pile these flak jackets on you,' like it was no big deal."

Popaditch said they spread a flak vest on his legs, one on his torso and one over his head. He then lost consciousness until he was on the flight to Germany. In Germany, he spoke to his wife and parents on the telephone, and after surgery the doctors told him his right eye had been unsalvageable.

"I'm sure I left this guy on the floor of that tank," he smiled, gesturing to his swollen and closed right eyelid, surrounded with fresh pink scars and some small scabs peppered across his cheeks, mouth and forehead, "But it was nice of them to tell me I'd lost it. This other one is getting better every day though, and I expect to regain one hundred percent of my vision in this eye."

Now back at home in the Mojave Desert, Popaditch, who is still on convalescent leave, spends a few hours every day at the headquarters element of his battalion. The battalion surgeon asks him from time to time why he isn't convalescing at home.

"I told him, 'I want to wait until I feel good enough to enjoy the leave, Sir,' and I just like being around the battalion, seeing the guys, seeing what I can get into," laughs Popaditch, who, with the help of his wife of thirteen years, April, regularly drives three hours one-way to see a variety of doctors at Balboa Naval Medical Center, in San Diego.

"I can't believe these doctors. I really feel like I've got the greatest doctors in the world. There are so many of them, all specialists of some sort, and all interested in helping me make a full recovery."

When asked how he would sum up the whole experience, Popaditch thought for a minute and smiled. "This has been the most motivating experience of my life, and it has restored my faith in the youth of America," he said enthusiastically. "The people I've met along the way are amazing. Corporal Chambers saved my life that day, the doctors are working to give me the best quality of life possible, and people across America are coming forward to support not only me, but all of the guys fighting over there right now."

Along with his eye, Popaditch lost his sense of smell, suffered permanent hearing loss in his right ear, broke his nose and has undergone several surgeries to remove shrapnel from his head, eye and face. His sense of humor escaped unscathed however, as did his love of God, Corps and country.

"My friends and my Marines are still there, still fighting," he said softly. "Any Marine in their right mind would want to be right there with them. All I've really lost is about ten degrees of peripheral vision, and I'll be okay without that. I'm ready to be with my Marines again."

This article originally appeared on FreeRepublic.com

THE INTERPRETER

"Not only strike while the iron is hot, *make* it hot while striking." – Oliver Cromwell

If you have read my book *Swift, Silent and Surrounded,* you may recall a story called 'The Linguist.' It was about an "interpreter" who couldn't speak a word of Spanish, and whose inability to communicate was both funny and disconcerting. This story is much different. It is about an interpreter who *could* speak the language, but a little *too* well.

When I went on my first Med Cruise back in the 1970's my first liberty port was the Italian town of Reggio de Calabria. I was looking forward to my first exposure to a foreign culture, and my first glimpse of my Italian "roots." While I must admit there were some disappointments (authentic Italian pizza was nothing like I had imagined) all in all it was an interesting experience. The natives seemed friendly enough, and everywhere we went the locals would make it a point to smile, wave and say a few words in their native tongue. We of course couldn't understand a word they were saying, so we just smiled and waved back.

Everything was fine, until the day we went on liberty with PFC Tony Sciosiola. Tony had been born in Italy, and had emigrated to the United States with his family while still a teenager. Naturally, he spoke fluent Italian. Tony had not been on liberty with us the first couple of days because he had been assigned to translate for the ship's captain at a couple of official functions, so as we debarked *USS Barnstable County* on the morning of the third day we were looking forward to an especially exciting day. We got it.

As usual we passed several groups of Italians, and as usual they waved and shouted out their greetings. We all smiled and waved back as had become our custom - all except Tony. He had an uneasy look on his face, and finally stopped walking and asked us if we had any idea what those people had been saying. We admitted we didn't.

"They are telling you that they hate Americans, that we should leave their country, and that we are ugly, imperialistic swine," he told us. Our jaws dropped. Then it dawned on us that we had seen an awful lot of communist "hammer & sickle" logos spray painted on walls and fences. It was true. There was a heavy socialist influence in Italy, as well as in many other European countries.

Just then, as if on cue, an Italian man came walking by. He smiled, he waved, and he said something in Italian. Two seconds later he was lying flat on his back with blood gushing from his nose. One of our group (I'll call him Ron), who had clearly heard enough insults for one day had decked him.

Tony grabbed his head in his hands and said, "Ron, what did you do that for? *He* just said hello, and welcome to Italy!"

THE MEANING OF COURAGE

Chuck Tatum

"Only two kinds of people are gonna stay on this beach: those that are already dead, and those that are gonna die! Now get off your butts!" - Brigadier General Norman Cota at Normandy

The two bravest Marines I saw on Iwo Jima's black sandy beaches were Colonel Louis C. Plain and Gunnery Sergeant John Basilone. I don't know this for a true fact, but to the best of my knowledge the Colonel and the Gunny came in on the third wave. Basilone was the boat leader in Platoon Leader Second Lieutenant Roy Johnson's LVT (Landing Vehicle Tracked). In a private conversation with Lieutenant Johnson, while sailing from Saipan to Iwo Jima aboard LST-10, Basilone supposedly told Johnson he intended to win a Second Medal of Honor. This doesn't sound like John Basilone talking.

This short watery trip to the shores of Iwo Jima was through the courtesy of the 11th Amphibious Tractor Battalion. I *do* know for a true fact that when I looked back at the beach, the only Marines I saw standing upright and walking were the Colonel and the Gunny. Colonel Plain was the executive Officer of the 27th Marines. Manila John was the Gunnery Sergeant for C Company, 1st Battalion, 27th Marines.

I was surprised to see an officer of Colonel Plain's rank on an early wave. It was a good thing he was. The situation on the beach was becoming confused, and near pandemonium ruled the black sand of Iwo Jima. The invasion was stalled, and we hadn't made two hundred yards.

Not As Lean, Not As Mean, Still a Marine!

The wily Japanese General, Tudinichi Kuribayashi, had given the order to commence firing, and Japanese shells were hitting the beaches in ever increasing volleys and creating a firestorm of hell on earth. The main activity I was engaged in, along with nine thousand other Marines, was an attempt to dig my way to China as fast as my hands would let me. I had to use my hands, because my entrenching tool was strapped to the back of my pack and I couldn't get to it.

Now, what the Colonel and the Gunny did was get the invasion moving by leading the way. I don't know why I remember this so clearly fifty-four years plus after the battle for Iwo Jima. Colonel Plain's uniform was standard issue Marine green dungarees like all Marines were wearing, but with a difference. His dungarees had the look that only could come from a naval officer's laundry. The crease in the legs of his trousers was as sharp as a K-bar knife. His dungaree blouse had a crease that split the pockets perfectly in the center. His weapons included a map case and officer's field glasses, and a standard issue .45-caliber pistol was strapped to his cartridge belt, along with a canteen, gas mask and a first aid kit.

Gunny Basilone had a habit of not buckling his helmet strap, and sure enough he didn't have it buckled of the black sands of Iwo Jima. In fact he had it at the same jaunty angle he always wore it. Pushed to the back of his head, I could see his coal black hair and his famous ears. I wouldn't say he had really big ears, but they were the same size as the movie actor Clark Gable's. In his right hand he had a .30-caliber carbine, and he had a light pack and some hand grenades hooked to his shoulder straps. On his cartridge belt he had his canteen, gas mask, first aid kit, Ka-bar and a web magazine with extra ammo for his carbine.

The most important thing these two Marines brought to

the beach was their courage and leadership in combat. The fighting know-how and hands-on experience that only comes from having been in combat and having undergone the heat of battle. Almost single-handed, or double-handed, if you will, the Colonel and the Gunny got the invasion underway by extolling the men to get their asses moving, and then kicked a few to accomplish this. It was their example of courage under fire that inspired the Marines to quit digging in on the beach and start the attack. The black sand beaches were a death trap, and the Colonel and Gunny knew it. They knew they had to get the early waves moving inland to make room for the succeeding waves, which were timed to arrive in three-minute intervals.

As the area became more congested the better the target we became for the Japanese gunners now pouring a steady stream of lead and steel on the Marines stuck on the beaches of Iwo Jima. The black sands were turning red with the lifeblood of the Marines of the Fifth Amphibious Corps.

Gunny Basilone took charge of our group. Colonel Plain took charge of a second group. The attack to capture Motoyama Airfield #1 was underway - the first objective of the Iwo Jima invasion. On the way to take the airport, Gunnery Sergeant Manila John Basilone's heroic actions on the beach were recognized by his grateful country with the award of a Navy Cross to go with the Medal of Honor he had received for his actions at Guadalcanal in October of 1942. Basilone became the only enlisted Marine to receive the nation's two highest decorations, but his Navy Cross was awarded posthumously. The guns of Iwo Jima had claimed the life of one of America's heroes.

Colonel Louis C. Plain was awarded a Silver Star by our government. The Japanese Government's army gave him a wound in the arm. The Colonel wouldn't allow himself to be evacuated until he had written a battlefield report in the officer's message book that he carried in his starched dungaree pocket. Except for the blood on the sleeve of his dungarees, it was still parade-ground fresh. He was back aboard ship for the evening mess.

The battle on Iwo Jima was short lived for the Colonel and the Gunny - but full credit must go to these two valiant Marines for their courageous leadership on the Sands of Iwo Jima.

Colonel Plain's reputation had preceded him. Before coming on board the 27th Marines as Colonel Worham's Executive Officer, Colonel Plain had played a major role in the invasion of North Africa in November of 1942. On loan to the United States Army, he had acted as an advisor for the amphibious phase of the operation. Advisor or not, when the lead started flying Plain went into action.

According to a newspaper article written in August of 1942 (*Dateline Washington D.C.*) and a Letter of Commendation he received from Lieutenant General Thomas E. Holcomb, Commandant of the United States Marine Corps, Colonel Plain was a one-man task force. Second in Command of a naval assault party charged with the responsibility of assaulting the harbor at Arzew, Algiers on November 8th, 1942, the Colonel and the assault team he was attached to entered the harbor at Arzew aboard naval landing craft. This was in the wake of the main assault. Colonel Plain and his team endured heavy enemy fire from positions on the shore, and along the way the Colonel and his men captured three French merchant vessels and one enemy patrol boat. He then assisted in consolidating the port at Arzew, opening it for operations.

The letter of commendation went on to state that "Colonel Plain was quick to take independent action and was calm and effective under fire." General Holcomb's Letter of Commendation ends as follows:

"The efficiency, courage and initiative which you displayed as second in command were outstanding and in keeping with the highest traditions of the United States Marine Corps."

General Ike or someone in the United States Army must have liked the cut of Colonel Plain's jib. He was then asked to serve as a Marine Corps observer in England prior to the Invasion of France. He also took an active part in the channel crossing that eventually led to the defeat of Germany.

Colonel Plain ended thirty-two years in the Marines with his retirement in April of 1957 - a career that began in 1925, when he enlisted as a private in the Marine Corps. After serving three years as an enlisted man he was commissioned from the ranks. He was discharged on February 3rd, 1928 and the next day was commissioned a Second Lieutenant in the United States Marine Corps.

In his thirty-two year career of distinguished service, Plain saw and did it all. He served at numerous duty stations and posts, domestic and foreign. His last post was as Chief of Staff, Department of the Pacific, and upon his retirement in 1957 Colonel Louis C. Plain was promoted to the rank of Brigadier General. His career had spanned thirty-two years, from enlisted man to General.

Time did something his country's enemies couldn't do. He died on February 20th, 1983 - thirty-eight years and one day after the invasion of Iwo Jima, and more than fifty-five years after I learned the true meaning of courage on the black and bloody Sands of Iwo Jima from the Colonel and the Gunny.

Chuck Tatum served with B Company 1ˢᵗ Battalion 27th Marines 5th Marine Division on Iwo Jima in February, 1945

WHERE USS COLE
Got Her Name

"There is no time. War is upon us!" – Theoden, in the *Lord of the Rings* trilogy

Most Americans are familiar with the terrorist bombing of USS Cole while she was in Yemen for refueling in October of 2000, but very few know about the Marine for whom she was named:

On August 25, 1941 Darrell Samuel Cole enlisted in the Marine Corps for the duration of the National Emergency, and following boot camp at Parris Island, South Carolina was appointed to the Field Music School for training as a Marine Corps Field Music - the equivalent of a bugler. After completing instruction he was transferred to the First Marine Regiment, First Marine Division, and on August 7, 1942 reached the shores of Guadalcanal for the first American offensive of World War II.

Not too happy in his role of field music when he had joined a fighting outfit to *fight*, and after acquitting himself meritoriously as a machine gunner in the absence of the regular gunner, he applied for a change in rating, but was refused due to the shortage of buglers. Cole completed his first overseas tour of duty and returned to the United States in February of 1943, where he joined First Battalion, Twenty-Third Marines, then forming as a part of the Fourth Marine Division at Camp Lejeune. When the unit moved to California he again asked for relief as a Field Music and for permission to perform line duties, but was again refused due to the shortage of buglers in the Marine Corps.

Not As Lean, Not As Mean, Still a Marine!

During the first engagement of the Fourth Division at Roi-Namur in the Kwajalein Atoll Cole, again forsaking his bugle, went into action as a machine-gunner. Four months later, when the Division stormed ashore at Saipan, he had once again been assigned to a machine-gun unit, and because of his proven ability in combat he was designated as a machine gun section leader. During the battle his squad leader was killed and Cole, although wounded, assumed command of the entire squad and acquitted himself in such a manner he was awarded the Bronze Star Medal for "...his resolute leadership, indomitable fighting spirit and tenacious determination in the face of terrific opposition..." He was also awarded the Purple Heart Medal for wounds received in action.

A few days after the battle of Saipan Cole again led his squad ashore in the invasion of the neighboring island of Tinian, where he continued to live up to his growing reputation as "The Fighting Field Music."

After the Marianas campaigns he *again* requested a change of rating, and this time his request was approved and he was redesignated Corporal "line" and subsequently promoted to Sergeant. On February 19, 1945 Sergeant Cole led his machine gun section ashore in the D-Day assault of Iwo Jima. Moving forward with the initial assault wave, their advance was halted by a hail of fire from two Japanese emplacements which Sergeant Cole personally destroyed with hand grenades. His unit continued to advance until pinned down for a second time by enemy fire from three Japanese gun emplacements. One of these emplacements was silenced by Cole's machine gun, which then jammed. Armed only with a pistol and one hand grenade, Sergeant Cole made a one-man attack against the two remaining positions. Twice he returned to his own lines for additional grenades, and continued the attack under fierce enemy fire until he had succeeded in destroying the Japanese strong point. Returning to his own squad, he was instantly killed by an enemy grenade. By his one-man attack and heroic self-sacrifice, Sergeant Cole enabled his company to move forward against fortifications and attain their ultimate objective.

More than fifty years later, the Navy warship bearing his name was assaulted by terrorists. Although she was badly damaged, her crew responded to the attack with the same courage and determination that had been displayed by her namesake. He would have been proud.

THE REAL SURVIVORS

Lieutenant Colonel James G. Zumwalt USMCR (Ret)

"If you are able, save for them a place inside of you, and save one backward glance when you are leaving for the places they can no longer go. Be not ashamed to say you loved them, though you may or may not have always."
- Major Michael O'Donnell

As one reads through the list of combat medals - three Purple Hearts, three Silver stars, four Bronze Stars - one wonders how a single Marine could have seen so much action and managed to survive. But through two wars in Korea and Vietnam, Sergeant Major Louis Rountree has proven to be a survivor.

In Korea, Rountree found himself outnumbered at the Chosin Reservoir. Cut off from any escape route his regiment, commanded by Marine legend "Chesty" Puller, was surrounded by eight North Korean divisions. Breaking out of the encirclement, carrying their dead and wounded with them, the regiment fought its way back forty miles to friendly lines.

One would have thought his Korea experience would have been enough excitement for this gung-ho Marine, but Rountree wanted to serve again. In Vietnam, as an advisor to the South Vietnamese Army during the early days of the war, his unit was wiped out. Rountree escaped into the jungle where he evaded North Vietnamese forces before friendly reinforcements arrived to recover the dead. Initially listed as a KIA, when the body count came up one short his status was changed to MIA. Days later he emerged from the jungle, alive and well.

During a career that spanned four decades, Sergeant Major Rountree experienced both the highs and lows of military service. The "highs" included his service to country. The "lows" the loss of friends and comrades who served with him on Hell's battlefields. Through it all, Rountree was true to his country, true to his Corps, and true to himself.

Rountree continued to demonstrate was a survivor, but on a much different battlefield. Living in a VA hospital, he received medical attention for a profusion of life-threatening health problems. Considering his personal achievements, this tough, combat-hardened Marine seemed out of place confined to his bed and wheelchair. Time appeared to be accomplishing what no enemy soldier ever could.

To his credit though, time proved incapable of diminishing Rountree's fighting spirit and zest for life, and this became apparent to me during a personal visit with him. "Compassion in Action" Chairman Dannion Brinkley led a fire team of visitors to see the Sergeant Major at the Washington, D.C. VA Medical Center, and Rountree greeted us with a smile that lit up the room. When Dannion and I shared that we too were former Marines, an immediate bond formed among us.

Other visitors included my mother, who had been recently widowed by the passing of my father, Admiral Elmo R. Zumwalt, Jr. The visit brought back memories of time she spent in military hospitals during the Vietnam War thanking our young men for their sacrifices and encouraging them to get well. This visit was different though, for veterans such as Rountree would not be going home.

Despite the camaraderie that ensues whenever former Marines get together Rountree clearly wanted to spend time with the ladies in our group, so they escorted him to the recreation center. Dannion and I followed in trace.

As we reached the recreation room veterans Morris Moore, Joseph Thomas, Jr. and Benjamin Saunders sat aimlessly watching TV. Dannion immediately sprang into action. He began moving wheelchairs around and engaging the veterans in conversation. Everything happened so fast it must have reminded them of their first firefight. Appearing to quickly recover from the shell shock, they began sharing stories, telling jokes and recalling memories. Smiles replaced blank stares as laughter was heard throughout the center.

In his own dynamic way, Dannion clearly sent an important message to these four veterans. He told them, "We have not forgotten you. We still remember the sacrifices you made on our behalf. We love you."

In a serious moment, Dannion asked each man what message he would want to convey to Americans. Upon reflection, each spoke of patriotism, teamwork, and doing what was right for America. "What humility and selflessness," I thought to myself, "that men receiving so little attention and love in the twilight of their lives would respond only positively about their country and their military service."

As it came time to depart, we hugged each man. I felt a mixture of emotions. Jubilation over making four special new friends, yet immense sadness at having to leave them to face the future, and, perhaps the end of life - alone.

One veteran, missing both legs, looked up as we started to leave and said, "You've made my heart glad today." His comment left me searching for a response that never came. Not until later did I realize there was but one appropriate response to give. "No sir, it is you who made *my* heart glad today."

WAKE UP!

Jeff Fischelli

"I liked being in the Marines. They gave me discipline I could live with... sure I was pretty wild - but I had a lot of rough edges knocked off." – Steve McQueen

One week until graduation. One more week and I would finally be a United States Marine. Three months of sweat, pain and hard work were about to make a lifelong dream come true. I had made it - finally.

It was an absolutely gorgeous day aboard Marine Corps Recruit Depot, San Diego, California. If you ever have to endure Marine Corps Boot Camp, do it in San Diego in the early spring months. Gorgeous. I was admiring the city's skyline, the houses on the cliffs, the crisp clean air, and dreaming of home. Life was great. I was going home in a week!

I was doing all of this 'sight-seeing' while my platoon was on the gigantic parade deck, practicing for Final Drill competition. The shouts of our Drill Instructors were echoing across the wide expanse of asphalt – "Co-lumn Left, *Haaaarch!*, Ex-teeeend, *Haaaarch!*, Close, *Haaaarch!*, Port, *Arms!*" Only Marine DIs can march a platoon with such command, such precision. A demand for excellence emanated from them constantly. From their razor-sharp uniforms to their stone cold, piercing eyes, dedication and honor oozed from their pores, and we recruits couldn't get enough.

"Pla-toon, *Halt!*" SNAP! After twelve weeks of Marine Corps training, Platoon 3065 was good, and we knew it.

Not As Lean, Not As Mean, Still a Marine!

Perfect execution of our drill sequence was what we lived for at this point. We had our sights set on being the best in Final Drill - and our DIs would accept nothing less.

"Column of files, from the right! *Haaaarrch!*" Fourth Squad stepped off, then third. I was in second squad, third rank. The third squad leader stepped off behind the last recruit in the second, then the second rank. It was now my turn to step off...

Ahhh, I thought... I can't wait to get home. Brand new pickup truck waiting for me. Strutting around town in my Marine uniform. The respect I will receive. The girls I will meet. Home. I have arrived. I have made it. Rest up now, recruit. Kick back and let that mind of yours wander. Take in the sights. You have made it! I was so busy daydreaming, I had little time for bothersome things like stepping off when it came my turn.

Reality hits. I come to my senses, but it's too late. I just messed up the entire platoon's movement! Fear. Panic. A lump in my throat. Beads of sweat form on my brow. Oh, dear God! Please tell me this isn't happening! I screwed us up! Please let me recover in time to not be noticed. Please! I am in Third Phase! Third Phase recruits don't do this! Stop this nightmare!

Footsteps coming closer and closer. Heart pounding. I am frozen solid at the position of attention. Here it comes. My due punishment has arrived. Bracing myself. Footsteps...

BAM!

Drill Instructor Sergeant Wilson's campaign cover, the famous "Smokey Bear" that all Marine Drill Instructors wear, slams into my forehead. Then his eyeballs. Oh, there's nothing like a Marine Drill Instructor's eyeballs. We're toe to toe. Man to man. DI to recruit. Fear. There are only two people on the earth at this moment - him and me. The hunter and the hunted. Fear. Fear. Fear.

"Wake up, Fischelli!"

It stung. Those words cut deep as they came from the man that had dominated my life for twelve long weeks of training. The man who had taught me so much. The man that embodied everything I ever imagined a Marine to be. He showed me what a Marine was. He was all Marine, and I had let him down. His passion was a well-disciplined platoon. His life was teaching his recruits the art of Close Order Drill - the Marine Corps way.

More than anything, I wanted to beg for forgiveness. From Sergeant Wilson, for failing him. From my platoon, for halting their training. For being the only one responsible for this lack of concentration. But the Marine Corps doesn't want excuses or apologies, and neither does your platoon. They want, and deserve, results.

There's a saying in the Corps – "There's always one." There will always be one who doesn't want to follow the rules. There will always be one who wants to screw everything up for the rest of the unit. There will always be one who gets others killed in battle. For this moment in time, I WAS that one, and it felt terrible.

Luckily, I can say that I was not "the one" in my platoon very often. I was a squared-away recruit, and I desperately wanted to be a Marine. Maybe that's why those three words hurt so badly. "Wake up, Fischelli!" I knew better. I knew the drill movements and when it was time for me to do my part for the platoon, yet I didn't do it that time.

At the time I probably wished the entire incident would be removed from my memory, and that I would never have to dwell on the hard lesson learned that day. Now, though, I am glad it's still very fresh in my mind. Whether you're marching in a platoon, storming a beach, going to college, playing civilian, or wherever you are in life - learn from my mistake and the lesson given to me by one highly dedicated Marine Drill Instructor...

Wake up! Just as a Marine Drill Instructor has a special way of getting your attention, so does life. Live it the way it was intended to be lived. Live it with honor and dignity. Play by the rules. Pay attention. Live your life out of care for those around you - whether it be your platoon, your wife, your children, or your country!

Semper Fi.

THE MEANING OF "IS"

Ed Driscoll

"It depends on what the meaning of the word 'is' is. If 'is' means is and never has been, that is one thing. If it means there is none, that was a completely true statement... Now, if someone had asked me on that day, 'are you having any kind of sexual relations with Ms. Lewinsky,' that is, asked me a question in the present tense, I would have said no. And it would have been completely true."
– President Bill Clinton

President William Jefferson Clinton once famously pointed out that the way we viewed his perjurious testimony during the Monica Lewinsky scandal depended upon our definition of the word "is." How typical of him. He could have learned a lot from a man like John Calhoun, who was willing to take responsibility for his own actions rather than engage in a game of semantics.

Our training had just ended. Our training had just begun. In a few months some of us would be dead, and others crippled and seriously injured. In the parking lot below the barracks waited the wives, girlfriends and beloved family members of the young Marines who in a few days would be fighting for the freedom of a people they did not know in the remote jungles of South Vietnam. We were from all over the United States, but those Marines who had loved ones close enough had this chance to have one last weekend together before we left. The Marine barracks was old but spotless. There were four squad bays in the barracks. All squad bays had been released except ours. And the order had been given

106

Not As Lean, Not As Mean, Still a Marine!

that we would not be released until Lance Corporal John Calhoun's stolen wallet was returned.

Staging Battalion was lonely duty. It was final training before we left for South Vietnam. We came and left not as members of a Marine unit, but as individuals. We were all Marines but were together for only a few weeks. We were trained by Vietnam veterans. Some had long ghostly silent stares. All had the desire to give us the skills needed to come home alive. Unlike boot camp, we were not harassed. We were treated with the respect we had earned in becoming Unites States Marines. In boot camp we learned to shoot straight. Here, we learned to shoot fast from the hip at pop-up targets as we walked along dirt trails. We learned how to avoid capture if separated from our unit, how to trap and kill food. We learned how to identify east and then travel south so as to stay out of North Vietnam. But the most important thing we learned in boot camp, and had reinforced at every duty station, was that the actions of one could get many killed. Therefore we understood that while it seemed totally unfair to the non-military minds of the loved ones waiting in the parking lot on this beautiful California day, we were going nowhere until Lance Corporal Calhoun's stolen wallet was returned.

Wisdom prevailed. The thief did not have to confess. The wallet could show up in the head or in any common area. The order was it simply had to be returned. The method of return was not specified. Tension mounted as the hours passed. The heels of boots hit the clean polished floor just a little harder as if troops were marching. The squad bay doors swung open with more force than necessary as Marines entered and exited. The sudden sound of footlockers slamming shut punctuated the passing minutes. We all wanted to be released for the weekend, but those with loved ones in the parking lot were really uptight.

John Calhoun was my best friend. We left for basic training from the South Boston train station and had been together ever since, partly because his name began with C and mine with D and the importance of order, partly because of chance, but mostly because we grew to love each other. It was not how much money I had, but how much *we* had. Not what I was going to do, but what *we* were going to do. Not if I was going to pass inspection, but were *we* going to pass. Therefore, we volunteered for Vietnam together. John was an award-winning artist, a gentle Marine. I once saw him struck repeatedly by a drunk he could have easily neutralized. He made not a motion to strike back. He was a squared away Marine. He always had starched utilities and spit-shined boots. John Calhoun loved the Marine Corps.

John was not comfortable at the center of this problem. His usually happy face showed the stress. His shoulders, usually straight, slumped forward. Though he had searched his locker a number of times, he searched again. This time he pulled his duffel bag out of the locker and placed it on the floor. When the bag hit the floor his wallet appeared in the back of his locker. I told him his wallet must have been returned. He did not even look at me.

I said, "John, don't be foolish - your wallet has been returned."

His shoulders regained their Marine posture. He walked with purpose toward the sergeant in charge. The sergeant yelled, "Listen up, Lance Corporal Calhoun has something to say to you all."

John spoke softly but deliberately. "My name is Lance Corporal Calhoun. It is my fault you have not been released for the past two hours. I found my wallet. It was in my locker. I am sorry. I will be here in the barracks if any of you want to talk to me more about this. I am very sorry." No one could have put a hand on John Calhoun that day. We all knew what we had seen.

Mrs. Virginia Calhoun later received John's body, an American Flag, and the Navy Cross for John's heroism in battle. Somewhere his courage in the last moments of his life is recorded in an official military citation. Find it and read it if you wish. I don't have to.

WE CAN LEARN FROM THEM

Thomas E. Ricks

"The less secure a man is, the more likely he is to have extreme prejudice." – Clint Eastwood

If every American went through Marine Corps boot camp many of the social problems in our society would be eliminated.

On a hot night in 1992, on my first deployment as a Pentagon reporter, I went on patrol in Mogadishu, Somalia with a squad of Marines led by a twenty-two-year-old corporal. Red and green tracer bullets cut arcs across the dark sky. It was a confusing and difficult time. Yet the corporal led the patrol with a confidence that was contagious.

Ever since that night, I had wanted to see how the Marine Corps turns teenage Americans into self-confident leaders. At a time when the nation seems distrustful of its teenage males - when young black men especially, and wrongly, are figures of fear for many - the military is different. It isn't just that it has done a better job than the larger society in dealing with drug abuse and racial tension - even though that is true. It also seems to be doing a better job of teaching teenagers the right way to live than does, say, the average American high school. And it thrives while drawing most of its personnel from the bottom half of our society, the half that isn't surfing the information superhighway.

I wanted to see how the Marines could turn an undereducated, cynical teenager into that young soldier who, on his second night in Africa, could lead a file of men

110

through the dark and dangerous city. How could a kid we would not trust to run the copier by himself back in my office in Washington become the squad leader addressing questions that could alter national policy. Do I shoot at these threatening mobs in a Third World city? Do I fire when a local police officer points his weapon in my direction? If I am performing a limited peacekeeping mission, do I stop a rape when it occurs fifty yards in front of my position?

To find out how the Marines give young Americans the values and self-confidence to make those decisions, I decided to go to Marine boot camp. I went not as a recruit, but as an observer. I come from the post-draft generation. I majored in English literature at Yale and, like everyone with whom I grew up and went to school, I have no military experience. Yet I learned things at Parris Island that fascinated me - and should interest anyone who cares about where our youth are going. In a society that seems to have trouble transmitting healthy values, the Marines stand out as a successful institution that unabashedly teaches those values to the Beavises and Buttheads of America.

I met Platoon 3086 on a foggy late-winter night in 1995 when its bus arrived on Parris Island, S.C. I followed the recruits intermittently for their eleven weeks on the island, then during their first two years in the Marine Corps.

The recruits arrived steeped in the popular American culture of consumerism and individualism. To a surprising degree, before joining the Corps, they had been living part-time lives - working part-time (and getting lousy grades) and staying dazed on drugs and alcohol part-time. When they arrives at Parris Island, all that was taken away from them. They were stripped of the usual distractions, from television and music to cars and candy. They even lost the right to refer to themselves and "I" or "me." When one confused recruit did so during the first week of boot camp, Sergeant Darren Carey, the platoon's "heavy hat" disciplinarian, stomped his foot on the cement floor and shouted, "You got on the wrong bus, 'cause there ain't no I, me, my's or I's here!"

On Parris Island, for every waking moment during the next eleven weeks, they were immersed in a new, very different world. For the first time in their lives, many encountered absolute standards. Tell the truth. Don't give up. Don't whine. Look out for the group before you look out for yourself. Always do your best - even if you are just mopping the floor, you owe it to yourself and your comrades to strive to be the best mopper at this moment in the Corps. Judge others by their actions, not their words or their race.

The drill instructors weren't interested in excuses. Every day, they transmitted the lesson taught centuries ago by the ancient Greek philosophers. Don't pursue happiness - pursue excellence. Make a habit of that, and you can have a fulfilling life.

These aren't complex ideas, but to persuade a cynical teenager to follow them, they must be painstakingly pursued everyday - lived as well as preached. I have seen few people work as hard as did Platoon 3086's drill instructors in the first few weeks they led the platoon. Sergeant Carey, an intense young reconnaissance specialist from Long Island, routinely put in seventeen hours a day, six and a half days a week. His ability to drive himself at full speed all day long awed and inspired his charges. Recruit Paul Bourassa said of his drill instructor, "When you've gone sixteen hours and you're wiped out and you see him motoring, you say to yourself, 'I've got to tap into whatever he has.'"

Sergeant Carey clearly wasn't doing it for the money. He was paid $1775 a month - a figure that worked out to about minimum wage. Of course, the wages were nearly irrelevant.

Not As Lean, Not As Mean, Still a Marine!

The recruits learned that money isn't the measure of a man, but that a person's *real* wealth is in his character. One of the funniest moments I saw in boot camp came when Sergeant Carey was lecturing the platoon on the importance of knowledge.

"Knowledge is what?" he bellowed.

"Power, sir," responded the platoon.

"Power is what?" he then asked.

That puzzled the platoon. Faces scrunched up in thought. Eventually one recruit hazarded a guess: "Money?"

Sergeant Carey was dumbfounded to find such a civilian attitude persisting in his platoon. "NO!" he shouted. "Power is VICTORY!" (Then, in a whispered aside, he added, "I swear, I'm dealing with aliens.")

The drill instructors didn't try to make their recruits happy. They tried to push members of the platoon harder than they'd ever been pushed, to make them go beyond their own self-imposed limits. Nearly all the members of the platoon cried at one time or another. Yet by the end of eleven weeks almost all had been transformed by the experience - and were more fulfilled than they had ever been. They had subordinated their needs to those of the group, yet almost all emerged with a stronger sense of self. They unembarrassedly used words like "integrity."

I learned more than I expected. One of my favorite moments came when Sergeant Carey ordered a white supremacist from Alabama to share a tent in the woods with a black gang member from Washington D.C. The drill instructor's message to the recruits was clear - if you two are going to be in the Marine Corps, you are going to have to learn to live with each other. Recruits Jonathan Prish and Earnest Winston Jr. became friends during that bivouac. "We stuck up for each other after that," Prish said.

Not As Lean, Not As Mean, Still a Marine!

The recruits generally seemed to find race relations less of an issue at boot camp than in the neighborhoods they'd left behind. If America were more like the Marines, argued Luis Polanco-Medina, a recruit from New Jersey, "there would be less crime, less racial tension among people, because Marine Corps discipline is also about brotherhood."

Two other things surprised me. I didn't hear a lot of profanity. Once notoriously foul-mouthed, today's drill instructors generally are forbidden to use obscenities. Also, I saw very little brutality. "I expected it to be tougher," said recruit Edward Linsky, in a typical comment as he sat on his footlocker.

Platoon 3086 graduated into the Marine Corps in May 1995 and became part of a family that includes 174,000 active-duty members and 2.1 million veterans (there really is no such thing as an "ex-Marine"). Over the last two years, members of the platoon have experiences some disappointments. But, as Paul Bourassa concluded a year after graduating from boot camp, "It pretty much is a band of brothers.'"

I think the Marine Corps represents a counterculture, but the Marines are rebels with a cause. With their emphasis on honor, courage, and commitment, they offer a powerful alternative to the loneliness and distrust that seems so widespread, especially among our youth.

Any American - young or old, pro or anti-military - can learn something from today's Corps. That goes for the corporation as well as the individual. Just listen to Major Stephen Davis describe his approach to leadership. "Concentrate on doing a single task as simply as you can, execute it flawlessly, take care of your people, and go home." Those steps offer an efficient way to run any organization.

Not As Lean, Not As Mean, Still a Marine!

I took away a lot from boot camp myself. I don't talk to my own kids like a drill instructor (and neither do thoughtful drill instructors). But I was struck by the importance of the example the DIs provided. Kids want values, but they are tightly suspicious of talk without action. So while you need to talk to kids about values, your words will be meaningless unless you live them as well. Also, of all things that can motivate people, the pursuit of excellence is one of the most effective - and one of the least used - in our society.

None of this is a revelation. Lots of families live by these standards. But few of our public institutions seem to. "You'd see the drill instructors teach kids who barely made it through high school that they weren't stupid, that they could do things if they had the right can-do attitude," summarized Charles Less of Platoon 3086. "It was all the things you should learn growing up but, for some reason, society de-emphasizes.""

The white supremacist and the black gang member who were thrown together in boot camp went on to happy careers in the Corps. Earnest Winston Jr., the D.C. gangbanger, became a specialist in the recovery of aircraft making emergency landings and was posted to Japan. "It's beautiful," he told me. "Not a lot people on my block get to go to places like this." His friend Jonathan Prish, the Alabaman, became a guard at the American Embassy in London. Prish had his racist tattoos covered. "I've left all that behind," he said. "You go out and see the world, and you see there are cool people in all colors."

This article originally appeared in *Parade* Magazine

MY FAVORITE HOOKER

"All men are created equal - and then some become Marines."

If you are expecting a racy story about exotic 'ladies of the evening' in some far off port of call, well, I'm sorry to disappoint you. This is a story about friendship.

One of the first things to impress me about the Marine Corps was the way my Drill Instructors referred to the black recruits in my platoon as "dark green Marines." They said *all* Marines were green, just in different shades, and that we all bleed the same color - red. We had recruits from all sorts of backgrounds and upbringings, and no doubt many had come to Parris Island filled with some degree of racial bigotry. It was quickly made clear there was no place for those feelings in combat, or in the Corps.

That is not to say things were all peaches and cream. Back in the 1970's there was a lot of racial tension in our nation, and despite the best efforts of my Drill Instructors the Marine Corps was not immune to it. Many Marines tended to hang out exclusively with members of their own ethnic group, and I can remember instances where fights broke out between them for no apparent reason. There were even occasions where Marines walking guard posts were jumped by members of the Black Panthers and had their M-16s stolen, no doubt "for the cause." It was not a good time for America.

One way the Marine Corps combated such racial polarization was through the implementation of the "human relations" program. This consisted of a "touchy-feely" roundtable discussion where we were encouraged to open up and discuss our feelings about, and with, members of other races. I don't know how successful this program was (since I was a peon at the time), but I knew one thing for sure - I hated going to the sessions.

You are probably saying to yourself, "Yeah, yeah, but what does all this have to do with hookers"? Not a thing, other than the fact that a "dark green Marine" named Al Hooker happened to be my best friend during my time with 'A' Company, 1st Recon Battalion back in the early 1980's. "Hook" was one of only three black Marines in the company, and he and I hit it off from the first day I reported aboard. He was, quite simply, a great guy.

One thing that Hook and I used to like doing was tell racial jokes which made fun of each other's heritage. We both knew there was no malicious intent on the other's part, and it was always fun seeing the reaction of strangers who didn't know we were close friends. The politically correct crowd of today would have gone ballistic!

One fine day Hook and I were sent to mainside to attend a briefing, and on the drive over he came up with a few choice jokes about my Italian relatives - and as usual we had a good laugh. I remember one in particular about the most dangerous job in an Italian neighborhood being 'riding shotgun on the garbage truck.' I, of course, had one to throw back at him, but saved it until we were seated in the auditorium and waiting for the briefing to begin.

"Do you know why so many black Marines died in Vietnam?" I suddenly asked.

Hook replied that he didn't know, and as he did so you could see some of the black Marines in the row to our front automatically cock their heads to one side and listen for the answer.

"Because when the sergeant said, 'Get down!' they all started dancing!"

Hook began to laugh his ass off, and the fellows in the next row looked at him like he was crazy. They were obviously taking the comment very seriously, and very personally. And then, a funny thing happened - they started to chuckle too!

The bottom line is this - laughter truly *is* the best medicine!

EYES ON THE PRIZE

Jennifer Brofer

"Winners never quit, and quitters never win."

This Devil Dog will go on to a long and successful career in whatever field he chooses because he understands that the words 'quit, fail, and lose' do not belong in a Marine's vocabulary.

Fourteen years, six months, three weeks and five days ago, eighteen-year-old Recruit Michael A. Smith came to Parris Island and set foot on the infamous yellow footprints for the first time with a goal - to become one of the elite few.

Nearly fifteen years later, thirty-two-year-old Lance Corporal Smith's dream became a reality when he graduated recruit training as the guide and honor graduate for Platoon 3001.

On June 14, 1989 Smith went to Parris Island for the first time to earn the title of Marine, but four weeks later his dream was shattered when a fall rendered him medically unable to continue with training.

"During first phase bayonet training, I dove into a trench and slammed the rifle into my chest - it was severe," Smith explained. It deflated the fluid sack between the rib cage and lungs. When I tried to breathe it was like two pieces of raw meat rubbing. I couldn't breathe, so I hyperventilated. As a result I was medically discharged."

After his discharge, Smith returned home to Wimauma, Florida, where he was consumed by the anguish of his failure.

119

"I cried like a baby," he admits.

Smith tried to cope with the feeling of defeat and move on with his life. He got married, had a child, and had careers at a fire department, juvenile detention center, federal law enforcement agency and a successful insurance agency. But his desire to be a Marine never left him. Ever since he was a toddler, he had wanted nothing more than to pin on the Marine Corps emblem.

"I've always been gung ho on whatever was the best of the best, and I like to be faced with the challenge of doing that," Smith said.

Feeling it was the right time to return, Smith received an age waiver to re-enlist as a Marine Corps Reservist and shipped out to Parris Island for the second time in October of 2003. A lot had changed since his first time getting off the bus at receiving.

"The first time around I was very scared, timid, and did not know what to expect," said Smith, whose green eyes now bear laugh lines, unlike the fresh-faced youth who first went to the island many years ago.

"The second time I knew what to expect, and was much more prepared for it. The second time around I was motivationally driven. I wasn't here to fail again - I came here to complete it.

"The other recruits sort of looked up to him as a father figure," said Staff Sergeant Jamal Cook, Smith's senior drill instructor. "They looked to him for guidance because he's been here before."

Cook added that Smith's "take charge attitude" had the recruits responding to him just as they did to the drill instructors, who all happened to be younger than Smith. For his part, Smith said being older than all of his drill instructors, one of whom was twenty-two, did not bother him in the least. But although Smith had no qualms about taking orders from younger DIs, interacting with and being in charge of recruits who were up to fifteen years younger than him was a whole different story. Even so, he never let his age put limitations on his performance level.

"I still stomped some of the platoon pretty good when it came to physical training," said Smith, who boasted a time in the three mile run of nineteen minutes, five seconds - third fastest in the platoon. "I'm driven to be the fastest one in the platoon. Being the oldest, I felt I had to prove myself as being equal to or better than the others."

Throughout his thirteen weeks on the island, Smith proved to his fellow recruits, as well as his drill instructors, he deserved the role he had been given.

Understandably, Smith was really looking forward to finally receiving his Eagle, Globe and Anchor, the coveted emblem he had worked so hard, and waited so long, to earn.

"It's something that can't be put into words," he said. "Pure emotional feelings of joy, and the success of accomplishing something I had failed at in the past... for doing something a lot of people said I was crazy for trying to do."

When it was over, Smith walked off the parade deck and left Parris Island for the second time. This time he left as a Marine.

ABOVE AND BEYOND

Michael M. Phillips

"I pray that our Heavenly Father may assuage the anguish of your bereavement, and leave you only the cherished memory of the loved and lost, and the solemn pride that must be yours to have laid so costly a sacrifice upon the alter of freedom." - Abraham Lincoln

This story is a follow-up to "Something Special," which appeared in the book "The Only Easy Day Was Yesterday." It told the story of Medal of Honor nominee Jason Dunham, and as a tribute to his bravery I sent a copy to his parents in New York State. Shortly thereafter I had a long telephone conversation with Jason's Mother, and found myself wishing for President Lincoln's wisdom and eloquence. Expressing condolences is such a difficult thing to do. But in the end it didn't matter, because she ended up consoling me:

Early this spring, Corporal Jason Dunham and two other Marines sat in an outpost in Iraq and traded theories on surviving a hand-grenade attack.

Second Lieutenant Brian "Bull" Robinson suggested that if a Marine lay face down on the grenade and held it between his forearms, the ceramic bulletproof plate in his flak vest might be strong enough to protect his vital organs. His arms would shatter, but he might live.

Corporal Dunham had another idea - a Marine's Kevlar helmet held over the grenade might contain the blast. "I'll bet a Kevlar would stop it," he said, according to Second Lieutenant Robinson.

122

Not As Lean, Not As Mean, Still a Marine!

"No, it'll still mess you up," Staff Sergeant John Ferguson recalls saying.

It was a conversation the men would remember vividly a few weeks later when they saw the shredded remains of Corporal Dunham's helmet, apparently blown apart from the inside by a grenade. Fellow Marines believe Dunham's actions saved the lives of two men and recommended him for the Medal of Honor, an award that no act of heroism since 1993 had garnered – and one which he received posthumously two years later.

A six-foot-one star high-school athlete from Scio, New York, Jason Dunham was chosen to become a squad leader shortly after he was assigned to Kilo Company, Third Battalion, Seventh Marine Regiment in September 2003. Just twenty-two years old, he showed "the kind of leadership where you're confident in your abilities and don't have to yell about it," says Staff Sergeant Ferguson. Corporal Dunham's reputation grew when he extended his enlistment, due to end in July, so that he could stay with his squad throughout its tour in the war zone.

During the invasion of Iraq last year, the Third Battalion didn't suffer any combat casualties. But since March, ten of its nine hundred Marines have died from hostile fire, and eighty-nine have been wounded.

April 14 was an especially bad day. Corporal Dunham was in the town of Karabilah, leading a fourteen man foot patrol to scout sites for a new base, when radio reports came pouring in about a roadside bomb hitting another group of Marines not far away.

Insurgents, the reports said, had ambushed a convoy that included the battalion commander, Lieutenant Colonel Matthew Lopez. One rifle shot penetrated the rear of the commander's Humvee, hitting him in the back. His translator and bodyguard, Lance Corporal Akram Falah, had taken a bullet to the bicep which severed an artery.

Corporal Dunham's patrol jumped aboard some Humvees and raced toward the convoy. Near the double-arched gateway of the town of Husaybah, they heard the distinctive whizzing sound of a rocket-propelled grenade overhead. They immediately left their vehicles and split into two teams to hunt for the shooters.

Around 12:15 PM, Dunham's team came to an intersection and saw a line of seven Iraqi vehicles along a dirt alleyway. At Staff Sergeant Ferguson's instruction, they started checking the vehicles for weapons.

Corporal Dunham approached a run-down white Toyota Land Cruiser. The driver, an Iraqi in a black track suit and loafers, immediately lunged out and grabbed the corporal by the throat. Dunham kneed the man in the chest, and the two tumbled to the ground.

Two other Marines rushed to the scene. Private First Class Kelly Miller ran from the passenger side of the vehicle and put a choke hold around the man's neck, but the Iraqi continued to struggle. Lance Corporal William B. Hampton also ran to help.

A few yards away, radio operator Lance Corporal Jason Sanders heard Dunham yell a warning - "No, no, no - watch his hand!"

What was in the Iraqi's hand appears to have been a British-made "Mills Bomb" hand grenade. The Marines later found an unexploded Mills Bomb in the Toyota, along with AK-47 assault rifles and rocket-propelled-grenade launchers.

A Mills Bomb user pulls a ring pin out and squeezes the external lever - called the spoon - until he's ready to throw it. Then he releases the spoon, leaving the bomb armed. Typically, three to five seconds elapse between the time the spoon detaches and the grenade explodes. The Marines later found what they believe to have been the grenade's pin on the floor of the Toyota, suggesting that the Iraqi had the grenade in his hand - on a hair trigger - even as he wrestled with Corporal Dunham.

None of the other Marines saw exactly what Dunham did, or even saw the grenade. But they believe Dunham spotted the grenade - prompting his warning cry - and, when it rolled loose, placed his helmet and body on top of it to protect his squadmates.

The scraps of Kevlar found later, scattered across the street, supported their conclusion. The grenade, they think, must have been inside the helmet when it exploded. His fellow Marines believe Corporal Dunham made an instantaneous decision to try out his theory that a helmet might blunt the grenade blast.

"I deeply believe that given the facts and evidence presented he clearly understood the situation and attempted to block the blast of the grenade from his squad members," Lieutenant Colonel Lopez wrote in a letter recommending Jason Dunham for the Medal of Honor, the nation's highest award for military valor. "His personal action was far beyond the call of duty and saved the lives of his fellow Marines."

Staff Sergeant Ferguson was crossing the street to help when the grenade exploded. He recalls feeling a hollow punch in his chest that reminded him of being close to the starting line when dragsters gun their engines. Lance Corporal Sanders, approaching the scene, was temporarily deafened, he says. He assumed all three Marines and the Iraqi must surely be dead.

In fact, the explosion left Corporal Dunham unconscious and face down in his own blood. He says the Iraqi lay on his back, bleeding from his midsection.

The fight wasn't over, however. To Lance Corporal Sanders' surprise, the Iraqi got up and ran. Sanders raised his rifle and fired twenty-five shots at the man's back, killing him.

The other two Marines were injured, but alive. Lance Corporal Hampton was spitting up blood and had shrapnel embedded in his left leg, knee, arm and face. PFC Miller's arms had been perforated by shrapnel. Yet both Marines struggled to their feet and staggered back toward the corner.

"Corporal Dunham was in the middle of the explosion," PFC Miller told a Marine officer weeks later, after he and Hampton were evacuated to the U.S. to convalesce. "If it was not for him, none of us would be here. He took the impact of the explosion."

At first, mortarman Mark Edward Dean didn't recognize the wounded Marine being loaded into the back of his Humvee. Blood from shrapnel wounds in the Marine's head and neck had covered his face. Then Lance Corporal Dean spotted the tattoo on his chest - an Ace of Spades and a skull - and realized he was looking at one of his closest friends. A volunteer firefighter back home in Owasso, Oklahoma, Dean says he knew from his experience with car wrecks that his friend had a better chance of surviving if he stayed calm.

"You're going to be all right," Dean remembers saying as the Humvee sped back to camp. "We're going to get you home."

When the battalion was at its base in Twentynine Palms, California, the two Marines had played pool and hung out with Dean's wife, Becky Jo, at the couple's nearby home. Once in a while they'd round up friends, drive to Las Vegas and lose some money at the roulette tables. Shortly before the battalion left Kuwait for Iraq, Lance Corporal Dean ran short of cash. He says Corporal Dunham bought him a 550-minute phone card so he could call Becky Jo. He used every minute.

At battalion headquarters in al Qa'im, Chaplain David Slater was in his makeshift chapel - in a stripped-down Iraqi train car with red plastic chairs as pews - when he heard an Army Blackhawk helicopter take off. The Navy chaplain knew that meant the shock-trauma platoon would soon receive fresh casualties.

Shortly afterward, the helicopter arrived. Navy corpsmen and Marines carried Corporal Dunham's stretcher two hundred feet to the medical tent, its green floor and white walls emitting a rubbery scent, clumps of stethoscopes hanging like bananas over olive-drab trunks of chest tubes, bandages and emergency airway tubes.

The bearers rested the corporal's stretcher on a pair of black metal sawhorses. A wounded Iraqi fighter was stripped naked on the next stretcher - standard practice for all patients, according to the medical staff, to ensure no injury goes unnoticed. The Iraqi had plastic cuffs on his ankles and was on morphine to quiet him.

When a wounded Marine is conscious, Chaplain Slater makes small talk - asks his name and hometown - to help keep the patient calm and alert even in the face of often-horrific wounds. Chaplain Slater talked to Dunham, held his hand and prayed. But he saw no sign that the corporal heard a word. After five minutes or so, he moved on to another Marine.

At the same time, the medical team worked to stabilize the wounded Marine. One grenade fragment had penetrated the left side of his skull not far behind his eye. A second entered the brain slightly higher and further toward the back of his head. A third punctured his neck.

Not As Lean, Not As Mean, Still a Marine!

Commander Ed Hessel, an emergency-room doctor, quickly concluded that the corporal was "unarousable." A calm, bespectacled man, he says he wanted to relieve the corporal's brain and body of the effort required to breathe. And he wanted to be sure the corporal had no violent physical reactions that might add to the pressure on his already swollen brain.

Navy Lieutenant Ted Hering, a critical-care nurse, inserted an intravenous drip and fed in drugs to sedate the corporal, paralyze his muscles and blunt the gag response in his throat while a breathing tube was inserted and manual ventilator attached. The Marine's heart rate and blood pressure stabilized. But a field hospital in the desert didn't have the resources to help him any further.

So Corporal Dunham was put on another Blackhawk to take him to the Seventh Marines' base at Al Asad, a transfer point for casualties heading on to the military surgical hospital in Baghdad. During the flight, the corporal lay on the top stretcher. Beneath him was the Iraqi, with two tubes protruding from his chest to keep his lungs from collapsing. Lieutenant Hering stood next to the stretchers, squeezing a plastic bag every four to five seconds to press air into Dunham's lungs. Six or seven minutes before landing, Corporal Dunham's blood-drenched head bandage burst, sending a red cascade through the mesh stretcher and onto the Iraqi's face below.

The Army air crew made the trip in twenty-five minutes, their fastest run ever, according to the pilot, and skimmed no higher than fifty feet off the ground to avoid changes in air pressure that might put additional strain on Corporal Dunham's brain.

When the Blackhawk touched down at Al Asad, Dunham was turned over to new caretakers. The Blackhawk promptly

Not As Lean, Not As Mean, Still a Marine!

headed back to al Qa'im. More patients were waiting - ten Marines from the Third Battalion were wounded on April 14, along with a translator.

At 11:45 PM that day, Deb and Dan Dunham were at home in Scio, a town of 1,900, when they got the phone call all military parents dread. It was a Marine lieutenant telling them their son had sustained shrapnel wounds to the head, was unconscious, and in critical condition.

Mr. Dunham, an Air Force veteran, works in the shipping department of a company that makes industrial heaters, and Mrs. Dunham teaches home economics. She remembers helping her athletic son, the oldest of four, learn to spell as a young boy by playing "PIG" and "HORSE" - traditional basketball shooting games - and expanding the games to include other words. He never left home or hung up the phone without telling his mother, "I love you."

The days that followed were filled with uncertainty, fear and hope. The Dunhams knew their son was in a hospital in Baghdad, and then in Germany, where surgeons removed part of his skull to relieve the swelling inside. At one point doctors upgraded his condition from critical to serious.

On April 21, the Marines gave the Dunhams plane tickets from Rochester to Washington, and put them up at the National Naval Medical Center in Bethesda, Maryland, where their son was going to be transferred. Mrs. Dunham brought along the first Harry Potter novel, so she and her husband could take turns reading to their son, just to let him know they were there.

When Jason Dunham arrived that night, the doctors told the couple he had taken a turn for the worse, picking up a fever on the flight from Germany. After an hour by their son's side, Mr. Dunham says he had a "gut feeling" that the outlook was bleak. Mrs. Dunham searched for signs of hope,

129

planning to ask relatives to bring two more Harry Potter books in case they finished the first one. Doctors urged the Dunhams to get some rest.

They were getting dressed the next morning when the intensive-care unit called to say the hospital was sending a car for them. "Jason's condition is very, very grim," Mrs. Dunham remembers a doctor saying. "I have to tell you the outlook isn't very promising."

Doctors told her the shrapnel had traveled down the side of his brain, and the damage was irreversible. He would always be on a respirator. He would never hear his parents or know they were by his side. Another operation to relieve pressure on his brain had little chance of succeeding, and a significant chance of killing him.

Once he joined the Marines, Jason Dunham put his father in charge of medical decisions and asked that he not be kept on life support if there was no hope of recovery. His son told him, "Please don't leave me like that."

The Dunhams went for a walk on the hospital grounds. When they returned to the room, Corporal Dunham's condition had deteriorated. Blood in his urine signaled failing kidneys, and one lung had collapsed as the other was filling with fluid. The Dunhams took the worsening symptoms as their son's way of telling them they should follow through on his wishes.

At the base in al Qa'im, Second Lieutenant Robinson gathered the men of Corporal Dunham's platoon in the sleeping area - a spread of cots, backpacks, CD players and rifles, its plywood walls papered with magazine shots of scantily clad women. The lieutenant told the Marines of the Dunham's decision to remove their son's life support in two hours time.

Lance Corporal Dean wasn't the only Marine who cried.

Not As Lean, Not As Mean, Still a Marine!

He says he prayed that some miracle would happen in the next 120 minutes. He prayed that God would touch his friend and wake him up so he could live the life he had wanted to lead.

In Bethesda, the Dunhams spent a couple of more hours with their son. Marine Corps Commandant Michael Hagee arrived and pinned the Purple Heart, awarded to those wounded in battle, on his pillow. Mrs. Dunham cried on General Hagee's shoulder. The Dunhams then stepped out of the room while the doctors removed the ventilator. Then, at 4:43 PM, Jason Dunham died.

Six days later, Third Battalion gathered in the parking lot outside the al Qa'im command post for psalms and ceremony. In a traditional combat memorial, one Marine plunged a rifle, bayonet-first, into a sandbag. Another placed a pair of tan combat boots in front, and a third perched a helmet on the rifle's stock. Lance Corporal Dean told those assembled about a trip to Las Vegas the two men and Becky Jo Dean had taken in January, not long before the battalion left for the Persian Gulf. Chatting in a hotel room, the corporal told his friends he was planning to extend his enlistment and stay in Iraq for the battalion's entire tour. "You're crazy for extending," Lance Corporal Dean recalls saying. "Why?"

Jason Dunham responded, "I want to make sure everyone makes it home alive. I want to be sure you go home to your wife alive."

MY CHILD, MY HOME, MY COUNTRY

A Marine Mom Speaks

Cynthia Townley Ewer

"The world has no room for cowards. We must all be ready somehow to toil, to suffer, to die. And yours is not the less noble because no drum beats before you when you go out into your daily battlefields, and no crowds shout about your coming when you return from your daily victory or defeat." - Robert Lewis Stevenson

I wasn't terribly happy the day my seventeen-year-old son told me that he wanted to join the United States Marine Corps. Ryan was a boy from a professional family with many educational options - and he wanted to join the armed forces? I signed the forms permitting him to enlist, but I did so with a heavy heart, fearing he was throwing his future away.

When my son graduated from high school, his gown draped with ribbons for academic and music honors, I envied the proud parents all around me. The program in my hands reflected my feelings. Page after page extolled the college choices of hundreds of graduates - yet there wasn't a single acknowledgment of Ryan or those of his classmates who had chosen to enter military service. Joining the Marine Corps seemed a step backward for my intelligent and talented son.

Boy, was I ever wrong!

I began to glimpse the truth early in my son's military career. Ryan told me of a talk he'd had with his drill

132

instructor during boot camp. The subject was respect. "When I speak," the DI said, "you stand at attention and say 'Yes, sir!' But I've only been tucking you in at night for about six weeks. How do you treat your mother, who's been doing this your whole life? Do you treat her with respect? Do you call her 'Ma'am'?"

I was quick to assure my son that calling me "Ma'am" was completely unnecessary, but a tiny quiet part of my brain began to glow. How long had it been since I had seen or heard public praise of motherhood? As editor of OrganizedHome.com, I could count on one or two e-mails a week objecting to the site's focus on home life, and complaining "I thought we were past all that!" Yet the Marine Corps acted as if motherhood mattered, as if respect mattered, as if even a "good kid" like my son still had a lot to learn about honor and duty and character.

As the months passed, I saw more and more changes in my child. "I used to have to force myself to do my homework in high school," Ryan told me, "but now, I have self-discipline!" When he completed his military occupational specialty school, the first thing he did was visit me, his mother - before he saw his girlfriend, before he saw his former classmates. During that visit, I could see he was still the boy I knew, but he had also become a man, strong and confident, calm and balanced. He had grown inside far more than he had on the outside.

A few weeks later, I received a beautiful letter from the commandant of his training school. Ryan had graduated first in his class, the commandant wrote, adding that his achievement was "possible only because of the parental foundation you have laid; for this, we render the ultimate salute."

The Marine Corps was thanking me? Holding this letter,

the last remnants of resistance to a son in military service crumbled away. The Yuppie parent capitulated, and in her place stood a stand-tall, gung-ho Marine Mom.

In the past few days, this Marine Mom has had good reason to think about my child, my home and my country. Our future may soon lie in the hands of hundreds of thousands of young people just like my son, together with the military leaders who have taught and transmitted the values that have so enriched my child.

Ryan Swain is just twenty years old. But *Corporal* Ryan Swain, USMC, is a man of honor and courage. A man who has pledged to lay down his life for his home, and his country. Together with young men and women from all parts of the United States of America, he is ready to defend us and our way of life.

As his mother, I can't help but think about the possibility that my child could be called upon to make the ultimate sacrifice for our country. I am not afraid. But I do have something to say.

In the past few days, many have asked that I speak out as editor of OrganizedHome.com. Emails urge me to publicize blood drives and fundraisers and memorials. All are worthy efforts, all will make a difference - but none of these pleas have said quite what I want to say.

As a Marine Mom, I would ask, "Will we be worthy?" Will the weeks to come see a flurry of waving flags - but no real changes of heart? Will we dissipate our shock and grief and horror with symbolic acts, or will we use these emotions to fuel new commitment, new idealism, new devotion to the values that have built our nation?

What can we do for our country at this time of trial? Go home and invest ourselves in the lives of our children, our spouses, and our neighbors. If we build strong homes, we

Not As Lean, Not As Mean, Still a Marine!

will build a strong nation. Teach children the virtues of honor and discipline and self-sacrifice. Embrace family, friends and neighbors in a spirit of tolerance and respect, and seek out those who are alone. Be unashamed of standing for the values that my son and his fellow service members have pledged to defend with their lives.

What can we do for our country at this time of trial? Bring a new sense of dedication and service to our homes, schools, churches and communities. Give time and money and talents to make better lives for those around us. If a need is there, meet it. Support charities. Show, by our own sacrifice, that we value the sacrifices which may be asked of our service men and women in the coming months.

What can we do for our country at this time of trial? Prove, by civic participation, that our system of government remains strong and vibrant and relevant to a new century. Vote. Run for office. Speak out on issues. Communicate with our representatives. Fly the flag proudly, and exercise those freedoms of speech and religion that have been hard-bought throughout our history by men and women just like my son.

What can we do for our country at this time of trial? It is not the editor of OrganizedHome.com who answers, but the mother of a Marine who speaks. We can be that nation to which my son has pledged his life's blood.

He believes. Can we do less?

Cynthia Townley Ewer is the Editor of OrganizedHome.com

NEVER SAFER

"The American Marines have it (pride) and benefit from it. They are tough, cocky, sure of themselves and their buddies. They can fight and they know it." – General Mark Clark, US Army

The following letter was sent to former Marine Hugh McLaren by his brother Todd after a visit to Camp Pendleton. Perhaps all Americans should spend a weekend on the beach at Del Mar!

Dear Hugh:

I had the great good fortune to be invited to spend this past weekend on the beach at Camp Del Mar, the family campground for military personnel, present and retired, on the base at Camp Pendleton.

Vehicles coming through the gate were met by a proud young man in fatigues. Courteous, relaxed and yet attentive, he was clearly all business as he directed me toward the beach. It could have been any other oceanfront campground in Southern California, with RV's and tents packed in closely and surrounded by laughter, and scurrying happy kids; except for the dozens of jeeps and armored vehicles parked in perfect rows behind chain link fence on the way to the sand.

It being Saturday, we didn't expect to see any close order drills taking place, and the barracks we passed looked like any typical college dorm complex except that the guys lounging on the lawn chatting all looked the same. Young, ripped, and confident, with their hair shorn "high and tight,"

136

Not As Lean, Not As Mean, Still a Marine!

it was clear that this was no ordinary community.

I work out regularly, and I'll bicycle thirty to fifty miles in a typical week, but I'll tell you this - the beach at Camp Del Mar is no place to be if you're a middle-aged guy with confidence issues. I'm in pretty good shape, but the crowd on the sand made me feel like the Pillsbury Dough Boy in poofy trunks. V-shaped torsos with abs you could scrape paint with, clustered in small groups, with the laughter coming easy and often as they barbecued, played volleyball with the typical vengeance of the invincible, or tackled the serious surf on bodyboards.

But these weren't the perfect pretty-boy physiques of Venice and Huntington. There were no perfect tans, certainly no flowing manes, and no one jogging along the waves showing off. Marines at Pendleton get more than enough "jogging" during the week, I'm guessing, and who are they going to impress anyway, fellow Marines? No, these were the bodies of warriors, crafted carefully and confidently by D.I.'s and their high expectations, honed by two and a quarter centuries of military tradition. And they were taking their "relaxing" seriously.

These are not sophisticated men. They aren't the finishing school elite. They're the sons (and daughters) of farmers, truck drivers, firefighters... and Marines. They're middle-America. They're NFL, not PGA. They're NASCAR, not Wimbledon. One non-military wife pointed out how loud one particular group of guys was, and how much beer they were pounding back. I asked her to try to remember the behavior at a typical frat house, back when she was in college. She agreed it was similar. I then pointed out the big difference. "Every one of those guys," I said, "is willing to take a bullet to protect their flag. Or your children."

And something was missing too - profanity. We all know

137

that Marines know a word or two that isn't in the Sunday Hymnal, but whether from training or tradition it was almost as if they recognized instinctively that there's a proper way to behave when families are present.

Some men too young to be married fawned over too-young wives and babies, and retirees - many wearing caps signifying where they had been deployed these many years ago - and those of us just glad to be there enjoyed the day despite the cool wind and gray marine layer.

As dusk fell campfires started, and the bustle of the beach gave way to the murmur of families grilling dinner, as word started spreading that President Reagan had passed to wherever history's greatest statesmen finally gather. Soon afterwards, the distant call of a bugle signified that the colors were retiring for the night. A hush fell over four acres of campers and beachfront as people stood, removed their hats, and covered their hearts.

I only spoke with a handful of Marines this weekend, mostly to thank them for their service. They were universally respectful, and particularly so with my two young sons. Some of the men on that beach this weekend may have just returned from someplace dangerous. Some are no doubt headed there shortly. Every single one is owed a debt of gratitude by every citizen in this country, and every single one would deny they're owed a thing.

I believe I'll remember this weekend forever. I'll tell you one thing, Hugh - I've never felt safer in my life. Or more proud!

God Bless the Corps & keep up the good work,
Todd McLaren
Lake Arrowhead, CA

I PRAYED WITH A MARINE

Chaplain Shane Dillman

"They just don't give a damn *who* they shoot, do they Chaplain?" - General Lemuel C. Shepherd, USMC while visiting Chaplain Connie Griffin, who had just been wounded during the Korean War

One of the moments frozen in time is the breathtaking and awe-inspiring photograph of the Marines raising the flag atop Mt. Suribachi on Iwo Jima in the gruesome struggle that would claim thousands and forever change the men who took part in this bloodiest of bloody battles. Ministering to the injured Marines who are returning from Iraq and Afghanistan are moments that will be forever frozen in time for *me*. As a staff chaplain at the National Naval Medical Center in Bethesda, Maryland, I am honored to be able to serve the Marines and their families during difficult and trying times.

Every day I am able to see the honor, courage and commitment of these young men and women who have made the U.S. Marine Corps the pride of America's military. I consider it a great honor to be able to care for, support and pray for some of America's greatest heroes. Many of these brave Marines have lost limbs, their sight, and are battle fatigued, but in almost every case their main concern lies with their fellow Marines who are still in harm's way.

As I was talking to one Marine, he told me his greatest regret was that he would no longer be able to serve beside his fellow Marines. The reason this brave young man could no longer serve was that he had lost both arms in combat. As I met with him, his wife, and his parents, he said nothing about the sacrifices he had made. With tears in his eyes, he spoke with grace and poise about the love and sacrifices his family had made for him.

This story of love and strength is not an isolated incident, but is the norm for the injured Marines who are returning from Iraq and Afghanistan. In America, we make movies about heroes and patriots. Some of the finest patriots I have ever met have been Marines who are patients at National Naval Medical Center. Through their valor, they show what it truly means to be one of the few and the proud. When I was growing up, I thought of Marines as super heroes. From talking to members of my family who were Marines, I learned of the intense training and desire that it took to become a devil dog. Whether a Marine is in uniform or in civilian attire, it was always easy to spot them. Even as a child, I could tell that Marines carried themselves differently. They held their heads a little higher, and each step showed their pride.

The young men and women that I am able to visit every day represent everything that is good about America. They have pride in self and country. They do not ask for personal favors, but they are consistently trying to find out information about their fellow Marines. It is very difficult to see people hurting both emotionally and physically. I am privileged to show them God's love and have the opportunity to pray with them, and many times share tears with them. The entire staff of Corpsmen, nurses and doctors who take care of these Marines do so with great proficiency and expertise - but also love.

The image that stands out the most occurred while I was walking down the passageway to my office and heard a voice behind me. I instantly recognized the voice of a young Marine who had lost his left leg in combat. As I turned my

Not As Lean, Not As Mean, Still a Marine!

head, I was astounded to see him walking toward me. He told me that he wanted to come up and thank me for all of the prayers, calling cards and time we had spent talking. He told me that the new prosthetic was really working out well, and that he would be able to carry on.

I wanted to smile and shake his hand, but instead I had to choke back the tears. I told this young man that he did not have to thank me for anything - it was he who had done me a great favor. He had allowed me to stand with him at a very vulnerable time. After a quick nod, he thanked me and walked away.

Whether someone agrees or disagrees with the war in Iraq is inconsequential, because what really matters is the bravery of these young men and women. They are willing to answer the same call that so many before them have heard. With much the same courage their ancestors displayed when they raised the flag at Iwo Jima, these young Americans have raised our flag throughout Iraq. They have given people who have never known freedom the chance to be free. They protect the innocent, and care for the fallen.

They also have allowed this Navy chaplain the highest honor of being able to say, "I prayed with a Marine today."

This article originally appeared in the Baptist Press News on May 28, 2004.

SALTY LANGUAGE

Col James W. Hammond Jr., USMC (Ret)

"By the time the Marines are through with them, the Japanese language will be spoken only in Hell!" – Admiral William F. "Bull" Halsey

In the (not so) Old Corps, the first time a "boot" referred to a vertical partition as a "wall" or said that he had spilled something on the "floor," he incurred the unmitigated wrath of the nearest drill instructor. To gain the attention of the miscreant, the DI would smash his swagger stick on the top of the boot's pith helmet accompanied by a very loud bit of enduring advice, "That's 'bulkhead' [or 'deck']. If you draw the pay, you speak the language!"

Marines are "Soldiers of the Sea," and it is right and proper that conversation be sprinkled with nautical expressions. In *The Leatherneck*, his introduction to *Fix Bayonets*, the late Colonel John W. Thompson Jr. described the many men making up the 4th Marine Brigade about to see action at Belleau Wood in June 1918. "And there were also a number of diverse people who ran curiously to type, with drilled shoulders and a bone-deep sunburn, a tolerant scorn of nearly everything on earth. Their speech was flavored with Navy words, and words culled from all the folk who live on the seas and ports where our warships go." He was describing Marine professionals who, like all professionals, have a language peculiar unto themselves.

A language is a living and evolving thing. As we go to more strange and distant climes, some foreign words creep in. Some are transitory and don't survive. Marines still go to the "head" to "pump bilges," although there was a generation or two who went to the benjo for the same thing. I've always liked the story of the world-traveler Marine sitting in a bar in Athens who politely summoned the waiter and ordered a beer with "Garcon, iddy-wa, una botella de cerveza bitte."

But over the years I have detected not just a lessening of the use of nautical terms among the naval services, but almost a complete lack of them. It was more than twenty-five years ago when my son came home from the United States Naval Academy his Plebe Christmas. He had been raised on "deck," "bulkhead," "overhead," "ladder," "galley," etc. He even called his Boy Scout equipment "782 gear," but was no longer using those descriptive terms because they weren't in use at the Academy.

After he graduated, I spent a dozen years at Annapolis on the staff of the Alumni Association of my alma mater. I was appalled at the lubberly-ness of the staff, faculty and midshipmen at the Academy. Fortunately, the Marines on duty there kept the tradition of nautical language alive. It must be paying off, because every year the allotted "boat spaces" for Marines on graduation are oversubscribed.

But I am not concerned with the Navy per se, but rather our Corps of Marines. I equate it to the reply an old gunnery sergeant gave to the lady who, upon hearing the legend that the quatrefoil on the cover of Marine Officers' frame caps stems from days of sail when Marines in the "fighting tops" could identify their officers on deck by the chalked cross on their caps and not fire on them, asked, "What about the Navy Officers?"

"Who cared?" snapped the Gunny.

Language is both spoken and written. *The Marines' Hymn* says, "We are proud to claim the title of United States Marines." There are Army officers and soldiers, Navy officers and sailors, Air Force officers and airmen, but we are *all* Marines. That is why Marine is always written with a capital "M."

We must be careful not to allow our own professional culture to be corrupted by the words of other services. The Army says 1600 (sixteen hundred) hours. We say 1600 (sixteen hundred). It is a small but subtle difference. Many years ago at a large East Coast Marine base, an overzealous "police sergeant" neatly painted on the "deck" in front of a regimental headquarters building: "NO PARKING AFTER 1600 HOURS."

The commanding general, or "CG," came by and saw the offending sign. He dashed into headquarters, burst into the office of the commanding officer, or "CO," and began holding "school-of-the-boat" (the most basic instruction one can give to the landlubber) on the colonel.

He said, "In the Army, it's 1600 hours; in the Navy, it's eight bells; in the Air Force, I think it is 'when Mickey's big hand is on twelve and his little hand is on four,' but in the Corps it is 1600. Get that abomination corrected immediately!"

Most Marines knew the motto of our Corps before they went to boot camp, or they probably wouldn't have gone. It is "Semper Fidelis" - always faithful. Shortened to "Semper Fi," it is a bond of respectful recognition between and among Marines. One Marine greets another with it. When they part company, each says to the other, "Semper Fi." Informal memos or e-mails between Marines usually are signed "Semper Fi" or just S/F. But there used to be a darker side. Used by Marines to members of the other services or civilians, "Semper Fi, Mac," said with a sneer, had a sinister connotation. It could mean anything from "I got mine; the hell with you!" to "I did fine; how did you do?"

Not As Lean, Not As Mean, Still a Marine!

An old "China Hand" once told me that on payday night in Shanghai cabarets, it meant, "You buy the fifth; my girl is drunk already!" I much prefer the version denoting mutual respect amongst a "band of brothers" to the cynical version.

Some words and phrases have found their way into common American usage through the Marine Corps. Some are of foreign origin. "We have fought in every clime and place." Others were Marine-coined. The best example of a Marine-coined word in widespread use is "gizmo."

"Gung-ho" is of Chinese origin, via Colonel Evans F. Carlson of the World War II Carlson's Raiders. Going back several campaigns, we find that "boondocks" comes from the Tagalog "bundok" or mountain jungles of the Philippines. "Honcho" came back from Korea and Japan.

Another word that is sacred to our Corps is "Doc" - the corpsman who wear our uniform, and who joins with and cares for us in combat. Many years ago I had a "Stateside" battalion during the time that doctors were drafted for two years of service. My battalion surgeon (a billet title since he wasn't really a "cutter") came to me with a complaint. The young Marines were addressing him as "Doc." Since he was a professional man, he felt he deserved the respect of being addressed as "Doctor" I told him that evidently he was not ready to be addressed as "Doc" inasmuch as that is the highest honor that a Marine can bestow upon a "squid."

The language door swings both ways. We have allowed civilian language to corrupt our pure nautical expression. While a landlubber may refer to a ship as "it" a true "soldier of the sea" knows that a ship is a "she." Likewise, it is a real nautical bust, both orally and in writing, to precede the name of a ship with a definite article. A ship is a distinct personality, and referring to *the Lexington* is as improper as referring to me as "the Hammond." She is *Lexington*. Many

145

readers will argue that the definite article is used in professional naval publications, and I invite their attention to the fact that those journals have professional editors and writers, not naval professionals. Finally, one serves in, not on, a ship. If it is the latter, you are in deep trouble. To a precise reader or listener it conjures up the vision of your sitting on the keel of a capsized vessel.

How did this departure from salty language occur? I alluded to the traumatic change to the nautical nature of the Naval Academy, at least in my observation. Emphasis was more on turning out graduates who could go on for advanced degrees. "Techies" and their bastardization of English for computer talk followed. This was compounded by flooding the faculty with academics holding advanced degrees from campuses of the '60s. This sizeable group of civilians avoided being part of the naval culture. Over the past quarter century, the leadership of half the naval service has eroded much of the base of salty-language usage. If those at the top don't lead the way, it is a military axiom that those below won't follow.

But how did the decline of the use of salty language creep into our Corps? Drill Instructors still drill into recruits the use of "deck," "bulkhead," "ladder," etc., although perhaps with a less emphatic way of getting their attention than in the (not so) Old Corps.

For one thing, more Marines are married these days, and many live ashore among the civilian community. These Marines try to blend into the civilian community rather than flaunt their pride in being a Marine. Their use of salty language becomes one of the first casualties.

Even today it is a matter of pride to sport a regulation haircut, spit-shined shoes, proper civilian attire and, of course, salty language. It is quite gratifying when some stranger at a cocktail party says, "You sound like you're a Marine."

Another reason for the decline of salty language is that many young Marines are "cool." Nautical talk is not cool, computer talk and jive talk are. Unlike the Navy with its many technicians, "every Marine is a rifleman" and has the privilege of displaying pride in the language of his profession. It is a privilege not available to others.

How can we restore this eroding tradition? Like everything else in the Corps, it begins at the top. Senior officers should use salty language at every opportunity and hold school-of-the-boat on their subordinates who don't. Top staff noncommissioned officers should do likewise.

Tradition is not something that can be ordered. It must have solid roots to survive. Marines should want to show that they are a different breed and be willing to demonstrate their uniqueness at every opportunity, whether among other Marines or among civilians. That's taking personal pride in being a Marine.

More than fifty years ago, during the Cherry Blossom Pageant in Washington, DC, ten junior officers from the Army, Air Force, Navy, Coast Guard and Marine Corps were detailed as escorts for princesses from forty-eight states and the territories of Alaska and Hawaii. Most of the Marines were strangers to each other.

At the end of the ceremonies a musical tribute to the gallant escorts of the lovely princesses was announced. The band struck up a medley of The Caisson Song, The Air Force Song, Anchors Aweigh and Semper Paratus. At the first note of The Marines' Hymn, the ten Marine lieutenants scattered among the audience were on their feet as twenty heels clicked as one. An officer from another service paid them a high compliment. In a stage whisper audible to all, he said,

Not As Lean, Not As Mean, Still a Marine!

"Those SOBs!"

That's what it is all about - exhibiting your pride in your Corps every time you can.

About thirty years ago there was the tale of an old sergeant major who had retired and gotten a nice job, although he was putting in long hours. He had another problem as well, or at least his boss and co-workers thought so. He still said "deck," "bulkhead, "overhead," etc. The boss made him an appointment with the company psychiatrist. The sergeant major arrived, and the doctor, who was of the Freudian school, directed him to lie on the couch.

Doctor: "Do you lead an active sex life?"

Sergeant Major: "Sure!"

Doctor: "Tell me about it."

Sergeant Major: "What do you want to know?"

Doctor: "Your last affair, when was it?"

Sergeant Major: "About 1950."

Doctor: "You call that active?"

Sergeant Major (looking at his watch): "What do you mean? It's only 2115 now!"

Draw the pay - speak the language. Semper Fi.

Colonel Hammond enlisted in the Corps in 1946, was appointed to the Naval Academy in 1947 and was commissioned as an infantry officer in 1951. He commanded an infantry platoon and company, an artillery battery and battalion, an infantry battalion (2/4) in combat (RVN). He was wounded in action during the Korean War and twice wounded in the Vietnam War. He is the author of more than 50 professional articles in a wide variety of professional publications, including *Marine Corps Gazette, Naval Institute Proceedings, The Hook* and others.

PROFILES IN COURAGE

Rudi Williams

"They summed up and perfected, by one supreme act, the highest virtues of men and citizens. For love of country they accepted death, and thus resolved all doubts, and made immortal their patriotism and virtue." - General James A. Garfield

There was such a hush in the hotel ballroom that one could hear a pin drop in a haystack as Marine Corps Commandant General Michael W. Hagee told short stories of how Marines are respected around the world, and of three heroes from the battlefields of Iraq.

Speaking to the audience at the Marine Corps Law Enforcement Foundation's Tenth Annual Invitational Gala in Atlantic City, Hagee said a recent Gallup poll indicated that the American people recognize what the nation's servicemen and women are doing today. "They stood right at the top as the profession most admired by the American people," Hagee noted. "For those of us wearing the uniform today, that's quite a responsibility that we have to carry on."

That, Hagee said, reminded him of another story having to do with the Battle of Belleau Wood in June 1918, which is a touchstone for Marines. "Marines marching from Paris toward Belleau Wood stopped the Germans about forty-five kilometers from Paris in about a two-week battle that occurred in that small forest," the general noted.

"What most Marines don't know (is that) something else occurred there almost seventy years later," Hagee said. "The battlefield looks today just like it did in June of 1918. During rainstorms, quite often, relics come up from that battle. In the mid-'80s, a Marine came up out of the ground and was to be buried at the American cemetery," specifically the Aisne-Marne American Cemetery south of the village of Belleau, France.

Hagee said about seventy Marines attended the burial. "But what wasn't expected was more than four hundred Frenchmen came to the interment," he said. "They came for one reason - to honor the United States Marine who had given his life in defense of their country. That's the reputation that we have, not only here in the United States, but throughout the world."

When he was in France for the sixtieth anniversary of D-Day, Hagee said, Frenchmen came up and, even though they didn't speak English, got their point across. "We thank you very much for what you do, what you have done for our country, and what you are doing for the world today."

The general then asked all the active duty Marines at the gala to stand up and be recognized, which resulted in thunderous applause from the audience. He then told heartwarming stories about individual Marines who represent all active duty Marines and those who have gone before.

His first story was about the heroism of then-First Lieutenant Brian Chontosh, who was recently promoted to captain.

While serving as a platoon commander in an armored Humvee with a .50-caliber machine gun mounted on top in Iraq, Chontosh was caught in an ambush. His platoon came under heavy enemy fire from AK-47 assault rifles, machine guns, rocket-propelled grenades and mortars. An RPG struck one of his Humvees, killing one Marine and wounding another.

"He was in the kill zone of the ambush," Hagee noted. "He saw the only way out was to drive right toward a .50-caliber machine gun. So he told his driver to attack that machine gun emplacement. The driver drove straight at it, and the machine gunner up top took out the Iraqi machine gun emplacement at point-blank range. He was still receiving fire, so he saw a trench line on his left and told his driver to go into it. The good news is they got to the trench line. The bad news is it was an Iraqi trench line. This lieutenant got out of his vehicle with an M-16 in one hand and a 9mm pistol in the other hand, and he started working his way down the trench line. He ran out of ammunition, so he picked up an AK-47 and continued working down the line. He ran out of ammunition again. He picked up another AK-47 and continued working down the ine. He reached the end of the trench line and there was an Iraqi machine gun emplacement sitting up on top. He picked up an Iraqi RPG and took out that machine gun emplacement."

Someone in the back of the room shouted out, "Ooh-Rah!" and was quickly joined by a chorus of voices.

"He didn't get a scratch - not one scratch," Hagee noted. "I had the honor and pleasure of awarding this nation's second highest award for bravery - the Navy Cross - about three weeks ago. When I gave it to him and thanked him for his service and what he'd done, he said, 'Sir, I was doing it for my Marines, to take care of my Marines.'"

Hagee then told of the heroism of Marine Corporal Jason Dunham, who wasn't so lucky. About three weeks ago, the National Naval Medical Center at Bethesda, Maryland asked Hagee to come to the hospital to pin a Purple Heart on Dunham in the presence of the corporal's parents.

"It had to be done right away because they were afraid he was going to die," Hagee noted.

Not As Lean, Not As Mean, Still a Marine!

When the commandant arrived at Dunham's bedside, the corporal wasn't conscious.

"I was able to pin the Purple Heart on him, and he passed away about forty-five minutes later," Hagee said.

He said all Dunham's parents could talk about was how he felt about the Marine Corps and how he loved and respected the Corps. "They have a fifteen-year-old son who wants to join the Marine Corps," the general said. "And they're going to support him."

The commandant told of how Dunham, a twenty-two-year-old squad leader with the 3rd Battalion, 7th Marine Regiment, was engaged in close combat with an enemy combatant in Iraq when an enemy grenade threatened the safety of Dunham and his fellow Marines. Dunham jumped on the grenade, shielding the blast using his helmet and body, and was severely wounded.

"He was thinking of only one thing - the Marines in his squad," Hagee said.

Hagee's last story was about another twenty-two-year-old squad leader, Corporal Timothy Tardif, who was suffering from grenade fragment wounds and had been evacuated to Germany - but found a way back to the battlefields of Iraq.

"He was in a platoon that was in a very fierce firefight, and he was able to lead his squad across an open road into a village to secure the right flank of the village," Hagee said. "The good news is they made it across. The bad news is they were in a hand grenade-throwing contest."

The battle continued for a couple of hours. Tardif was seriously wounded by shrapnel, but he refused to be evacuated, the general said. "They were successful and secured the village," Hagee noted. "But as they were pulling out of the village, Corporal Tardif passed out due to loss of blood."

Not As Lean, Not As Mean, Still a Marine!

Tardif was evacuated to the Army's Regional Medical Center at Landstuhl, Germany, where most of the wounded servicemen and women go before returning to the United States.

"Somehow, Corporal Tardif convinced the doctors that he needed to be checked out of the hospital," Hagee said. "The doctor checked him out, and Corporal Tardif got hold of a corpsman and borrowed a utility uniform. Then he went to the Air Force base and talked his way onto an aircraft to go back to Iraq."

Hagee said this was in April 2003, and Tardif stayed in Iraq until September, when his squad returned home. Pointing out that Tardif is married, the general said the corporal called his wife from Germany and told her, "Honey, I could come home right now, but I'm a Marine. And I have responsibilities. I'm a squad leader, and my Marines need me. So I'm going to go back."

"Thats the type of young Marines that we have in the Marine Corps today," Hagee said. "Your support of them means much more than you realize."

The Marine Corps Law Enforcement Foundation was formed in 1995 by former Marines and law enforcement personnel and awards scholarship bonds to help finance the education of children who lost parents in the line of duty. Scholarships are now given to various federal law enforcement agencies, and also apply to eligible children of members of the Army, Navy, Air Force and Coast Guard. The foundation also decided to include children of coalition partners in Iraq and Afghanistan, including Great Britain, Poland and Australia.

153

SEMPER FI, DOC

Pamela Grim, M.D.

"Marine basic training attempts to take a kid and turn him into a responsible, disciplined adult - in seventy training days. And it works." – Pamela Grimm, MD

A while ago, before more recent geopolitical disasters, I saw on the news that a "rapid response team" of Marines had landed in Port-au-Prince, Haiti, and I wondered whether any of "my" Marines were there - the recruits I see at the Parris Island training facility in South Carolina. I realized my first morning here that the culture of the "Island" and the "grunts" is worlds away from my own. My first recruit-patient - an eighteen-year-old with pilonoidal abscess - shouted "Yes, Ma'am!" or "No, Ma'am!" whenever I asked him a question. When I was his age, I was out in the streets protesting against a war. Somehow, almost unnoticed, that war has become a long time ago. What did I know about war? About as much as these kids do, I guess.

I was quickly corrected when I called him by name - you call each patient "recruit" and he calls himself "this recruit" - no "I's" are allowed.

Marine basic training attempts to take a kid and turn him into a responsible, disciplined adult - in seventy training days - and it works. You can actually see the transformation from the doorway. On day one, the recruit is lounging on the gurney as if it were a settee. On day sixty-four, he is a taut and toned junior jarhead sitting bolt upright, a cupped hand on each knee. From the very first day, I marveled. How was this possible?

Within a few weeks, I started to get a sense of what I would see clinically. The first thing to ask a recruit is "What training day are you?" You can usually guess the final diagnosis on the basis of this information. Basic training includes two "intake days," five "forming days," and seventy "training days." The kids who come into the emergency room on an intake day are usually there with slapstick stuff. Someone breaks his arm stepping off the bus, another knocks himself out by running into a wall. Not a good beginning.

During the forming days (also known as "*dis*orientation"), the drill instructors introduce themselves and make the first real demands on recruits. This is when the weeding-out process begins. The earliest to go are the kids who've hidden a significant medical history, anything from asthma to bad knees. These are "fraudulent enlistments." When they get into trouble, the DIs send them to us to sort out. One kid sent in for "weakness" told me he would be fine if he could just restart his medications.

"What medications?"

"Zyprexa, Prozac, Buspar, and Ambien for sleep."

"And they let you in here? Did your recruiter know about this?"

"My dad told me not to tell him."

I looked at him. "What does your father do?"

"He's career Navy."

"And he told you not to say anything?"

The kid looked sheepish. "He thought this might make a man out of me."

That first week, the kids meet the "Third Hat" - usually the most junior of the DIs, who has been described as "a maniacal, sadistic, extremist psychopath whose name you, the recruit, will never forget." His job is to ensure that once a recruit becomes a Marine, he will not crack up, become insubordinate, or "go postal" at a critical moment. Obviously, the Third Hat doesn't accomplish this feat by being soft-spoken. And it's because of him, I presume, that I see the other common complaints of early training - chest pain, shortness of breath, dizziness, weakness. The diagnosis invariably is "panic attack," but these are *ferocious* panic attacks. Heart rates of 180, respiratory rates of fifty, carpopedal spasm, and - worst of all - tears. Seeing a 6-ft 4-in., 250-lb former high school football star hyperventilating, sobbing, and begging to be sent home is an unsettling experience. And what exactly should I do for him?

I have two roles here – doctor, and member of the Marine training team. My usual remedies, benzodiazepines and reassurance, aren't really adequate for this situation. Six months from now, any one of these kids could be dying in a ditch somewhere in a country he first heard of ten minutes before he got there. How do I help someone deal with that kind of stress?

I tell the recruit, "What you are feeling is normal fear. It's totally understandable." The recruit, say, has just come from a drill in which he's required to sit in a chamber filled with CS gas with his gas mask off for a certain period. A fair number can't handle it. They bolt out of the chamber, gasping and vomiting. We get the ones with worrisome symptoms - chest pain, severe dyspnea. Usually, it's just nerves. "It's normal to be scared," I tell the sobbing kid. "But your job now is to learn how to deal with these perfectly normal feelings. Your job as a recruit is to learn how to think even though you are frightened." Most, given time, manage to pull themselves together, but a few try to convince me that it is their constitutional right to quit basic training that very instant. (It's not.) The DI rolls his eyes. "This is the gnarliest set of recruits that has ever come through this hole," he mutters.

The DI is the catalyst that transforms recruits into Marines, and his job may have its own psychological sequelae. Recently, I saw a DI whose chief complaint was "I want to kill the recruits."

"We all want to kill the recruits," I said solicitously.

"No," he said, giving every word equally ponderous weight, "I. Want. To. Kill. The. Recruits." He buried his head in his hands. "Just send me back to Iraq. I didn't have any trouble with Iraq."

After the first few weeks, unsuitable recruits are sent home for "failure to adapt," and the long grind begins. From the endless hours of physical training, we get the traditional diseases of foot soldiers - shin splints, stress fractures, hernias, pneumonia. "Combat simulation" drills bring us shoulder dislocations, nasal fractures, and on one occasion, a mandibular fracture.

The final stage of boot camp, the Crucible, is a fifty-four-hour mental and physical gauntlet. It consists of combat exercises, forced marches, and "warrior stations." Each station is dedicated to a great Marine of the past, and as the recruits maneuver under barbed wire and over the mud flats of the Beaufort River, they are expected to relive these warriors' golden moments - Marines like Gunnery Sergeant Dan Daly, who in 1918 led the Marine charge into Belleau Woods with the cry, "Come on, you sons of bitches, do you want to live forever?"

Oddly enough, we don't get too many injuries at this stage. Most of the kids are smarter about dodging blows. What we do see are kids who are end-stage sick, with double pneumonia, grapefruit-size abscesses, appendicitis. These guys will do anything now to see this thing through. By this time, a recruit has become invested - invested in making it with his fellow recruits, invested in proving the Third Hat wrong, invested in just getting the whole damn thing over with. One kid came in with fulminating Guillain–Barré and dropped out only when he became apneic.

The final stage of the Crucible, a nine-mile hike, is dedicated to the men of Easy Company who in 1944 fought their way to the top of Mount Suribachi on Iwo Jima and planted an American flag.

"Wear the Corps' emblem with pride and honor not only on your uniform but in your heart," these new Marines are told. "Remember - once a Marine, always a Marine. Semper Fi!"

Clausewitz, the great strategist on war, says there is only one means to war - combat. And with combat come casualties. The wounded from Iraq have started to make their way back home. The first we see are those with head injuries. The scuttlebutt is that we are going to see a lot of these. Most of these injuries are from roadside bombs - "improvised explosive devices" - which differ from traditional antipersonnel devices in that they shoot shrapnel and dirt up rather than the more traditional out, making a Kevlar helmet merely a bucket that collects ordnance.

Last night a middle-aged couple came in, with the wife complaining of shortness of breath. They had gotten the news that afternoon that their only son had been killed in Iraq. The man was retired from the military, and he stood ramrod straight and expressionless. But the woman was a basket case, a bottomless pit of sorrow. Her son supposed to have come home a month ago, she told me, but his tour had been extended because of the ongoing insecurity. I called the chaplain. I talked to her for a while. I gave her some lorazepam. What else could I do?

The Marines are in the news every morning now as I get

ready for work, the anchor talking about "taking casualties" and "hearts and minds." When I go outside, I can hear the shouts floating across the water, the young recruits out there sounding off in unison as they go out for their morning run, flat-out gung-ho at six AM. The shouting sounds as if it is coming not just across the marshes but across the decades, and I swear sometimes that I can hear what they are shouting - all that Marine tough-guy talk:

Lock and load!

Ready on the right!

Ready on the left!

Ready on the firing line!

Failure is not an option!

Good to go…

THANK YOU VIETNAM VETS
From a Marine in Iraq

Major Brian P. Bresnahan

"Thousands of Vietnam Veterans earned medals for bravery every day. A few were even awarded."

John Kerry, Jane Fonda and their cohorts were a prime reason our valiant troops were spat upon and called baby-killers when they returned from Vietnam, and they will never be forgiven by the men they dishonored with their lies. This letter represents the feelings of many who have followed in the footsteps of those brave warriors, and it comes not a moment too soon – because it is about time they got their due!

A guy gets time to think over here, and I was thinking about all the support we get from home. Sometimes it's overwhelming. We get care packages at times faster than we can use them. There are boxes and boxes of toiletries and snacks lining the center of every tent. The generosity has been amazing. So I was pondering the question, "Why do we have so much support?"

In my opinion, it comes down to one thing - Vietnam. I think we learned the lesson, as a nation, that no matter what, you have to support the troops who are on the line, who are risking everything. We treated them so poorly back then. When they returned was even worse. The stories are nightmarish of what our returning warriors were subjected to. It is a national scar, a blemish on our country, an embarrassment to all of us.

Not As Lean, Not As Mean, Still a Marine!

After Vietnam, it had time to sink in. The guilt in our collective consciousness grew. It shamed us.

However, we learned from our mistake. Somewhere during the late 70's and into the 80's we realized that we can't treat our warriors that way. So, starting during the Gulf War, when the first real opportunity arose to stand up and support the troops we did. We did it to support our friends and family going off to war. But we also did it to right the wrongs from the Vietnam era. We treated our troops like the heroes they were, acknowledged and celebrated their sacrifice, and rejoiced at their homecoming, instead of spitting on them.

And that support continues today for those of us in Iraq. Our country knows it must support us, and it does. That lesson was learned in Vietnam, and we are a better nation because of it.

Everyone who has gone before is a hero. They are celebrated in my heart. I think admirably of all those who have gone before me. From those who fought to establish this country in the late 1770's to those I serve with here in Iraq - they have all sacrificed to ensure our freedom.

But when I get back, I'm going to make it a personal mission to specifically thank every Vietnam Vet I encounter for their sacrifice. Because if nothing else good came from that terrible war, one thing did. It was the lesson learned on how we treat our warriors. We as a country learned from our mistake, and now treat our warriors as heroes - as we should. I am the benefactor of their sacrifice. Not only for the freedom they, like veterans from other wars, ensured, but for how well our country now treats my fellow Marines and I. We are the benefactors of their sacrifice.

THE NASTY RECRUIT

Bill Cahir

"I'd rather be a Marine Private than a civilian executive." – Major H.G. "Dunk" Duncan, *Fiction and Fact From Dunk's Almanac*

Stripped naked in the office shower room, I was appalled. I had been jogging every other day for several months. Still, when I looked in the mirror, the man I saw was fat and soft, almost unbelievably so. I wondered, 'Was there a United States Marine in there somewhere?'

* * *

The recruiter was ignoring my calls. Apparently the Marine Corps wasn't dying to sign up a thirty-four-year-old reporter from Washington, D.C. Ordinarily, the Marines recruit young men and women seventeen to twenty-seven, and college graduates as old as twenty-nine. I was far past the regular cutoffs.

Diligence produced a meeting with an officer in charge of recruiting in the Baltimore-Washington region. The major was intrigued. He had me take the Marine Corps physical fitness test. I ran the three-mile track in 21:10, did six pull-ups and eighty-four crunches. A perfect score was eighteen minutes, twenty pull-ups and one hundred crunches. My run time was decent. The recruiters took up my cause.

I met with a sergeant and a captain at the 4th Civil Affairs Group, a Marine Corps reserve unit headquartered at Bolling Air Force Base in Washington. Assured I would take orders from younger Marines, they signed their names to an age-waiver application.

162

Not As Lean, Not As Mean, Still a Marine!

The paperwork, sent up the chain of command, was approved with bracing speed. The offer:

- Go to Parris Island for thirteen weeks and survive basic training;

- Enroll in Marine combat training at Camp Geiger, N.C., and complete the second stage of combat education; and

- Attend a school in Norfolk, Virginia, and learn to become a Marine Air-Ground Task Force planner.

If I signed, I would ship out in just twenty-two days. Visiting Fort Meade, Maryland, I deliberated. I would enter as a private first class, not an officer. I would lose thousands of dollars in civilian salary. I probably would be activated and sent to the Middle East.

There it was - my last, best chance to serve. I had one final opportunity to be a Marine, to learn martial arts, to shoot, to speak a new language, to make whatever contribution I could to the war on terrorism. I had nearly enlisted after graduating from college, after working a few years, and after the terrorist attacks of September 11, 2001. Each time I hesitated.

In October of 2003, the recruiter asked the decisive question. In the future, would I look back and regret my inaction if I didn't enlist?

I signed.

* * *

I charged at the eight-foot wooden wall, leapt up and grabbed the flat plank on top. To my surprise, I managed to hoist myself up and roll my body over. I fell into the sawdust below, ready for the next challenge on the Parris Island obstacle course.

"Get back, Ca-heer!" my drill instructor bellowed, deliberately mispronouncing my name, which actually sounds like 'care.' "Get back and do it again!"

Arms leaden, I wondered why the DI was forcing me to scale the wall a second time? It didn't matter. I hollered, "Aye, sir!"

I took a second run at the wall, leapt up and stalled. I didn't have the arm strength.

"Yeah, yeah!" the DI, crouching atop the wall, shouted into my face. "Some things don't get easier with age, do they, Ca-heer?"

That did it. I wasn't going to be labeled the lazy old man in front of several platoons. Again I pulled, this time shuffling over the top plank and plunging into the sawdust. I wasn't setting any speed records. But I hadn't quit.

"Nasty recruit!" another DI shouted as I trudged past.

* * *

I stood up from my meal and started the walk along the tables, hoping to make it to the milk dispenser.

One of the four DIs erupted: "No f---ing way! No f---ing way!"

A second DI joined the chorus. "In some countries, that's a crime against the dead!" He was pointing at my food. I had stuck a fork in my baked chicken, and left the utensil sticking straight up in the air.

"Get back! Get back, and sit down!" shouted the second DI.

"Aye sir!" I shouted.

But I forgot to give the greeting of the day. I had not shouted, "Good afternoon, gentlemen!" Immediately I was surrounded by three DIs from my platoon.

"You haven't learned a thing here, have you, Ca-heer?"

"You're too stupid to get it right, aren't you, college boy?"

"I guess we just walk away from DIs and don't give them the courtesy of a greeting! That's what you've been taught!"

My senior drill instructor, the fourth non-commissioned officer in my platoon and a staff sergeant by rank, interrupted the storm.

"All right," he said. "Get your milk."

* * *

The DI grabbed my M16A2 service rifle, pushed the plastic hand guard against my forehead and bent me backwards until I was pinned against my bunk, also known as a rack.

"Ca-heer, I've been waiting for you to show one ounce of intensity in your f---ing body, and you can't do it, can you, you motherf---ing communist p---y!"

I made a mental note of the insult. The epithet was the most creative I'd heard to date. I was a college-educated reservist. I was older than the DIs, and in my civilian job I earned more money than they did.

Later, the DIs made it clear they were worried about what I might write about them. "You don't know my specialty, do you?" one raged. "Counterintelligence! You'll never see me coming!"

But I admired their toughness. At three required points during training, I signed paperwork saying the DIs hadn't abused me verbally or physically. I didn't believe they had. The drill instructors worked more than one hundred hours each week. They performed the workouts required of the recruits, and more. They had mastered several military trades - marksmanship, first aid, land navigation - and practiced the best methods for teaching those skills. It was a fighting man's world. The DIs thrived in it. They had earned their stripes, and they were preparing us for ours.

* * *

It was my third day on the rifle range. I had nearly qualified twice, shooting a 186 and a 175. But the minimum score was 190. If I failed again, I probably would be dropped to another platoon. That would mean falling back to an earlier phase of training, getting lumped in with another bunch of recruits, and getting hollered at by a new set of DIs. It would mean writing home to tell relatives of a new graduation date. It would mean staying longer in the drill instructors' universe.

There I sat, hoping to qualify on my third try, carrying the wrong weapon. I didn't have my own rifle. Earlier, my platoon was ordered to unlock all rifles from our racks. Several of us were absent, having been sent to medical, to dental or to pick up laundry. I unlocked a weapon belonging to a neighboring recruit who was absent. That part I got right - I was supposed to take his rifle from his bunk. But before being hustled to the range, I had passed off my own weapon to another recruit and held onto my neighbor's. What a mistake!

I kept mum. My neighbor had qualified as a rifle expert. Maybe I could do the same. I shot, but the wind and elevation settings on this M16A2 were different than mine. I couldn't figure it out. I was spraying bullets far above the target.

"Let me see that rifle," the marksmanship instructor said. "Why, this isn't even your weapon! Why didn't you say anything?"

I didn't have an answer. I was supposed to be more mature than the other recruits. I was terrified of being dropped.

The instructor called over a DI from another platoon, and

the two men pulled me from the rifle range. They escorted me to the warrant officer's tower and called one of the drill instructors with my platoon. To my amazement, the DI from my platoon showed up in a van and disembarked with my rifle in his hands.

"I guess that's what you've been taught? Walk off with the wrong weapon!" he shouted.

"No, sir!" I replied.

"Hey, Ca-heer!" shouted the DI who had taken me to the tower. He was waving his hands over his head as if doing jumping jacks. "This is you tonight!"

I knew I'd do a furious bout of calisthenics as punishment for my error. But the marksmanship instructor took it in stride. He had me try again with recruits taking part in the afternoon session. I shot a 199.

"You qualified, journal," the instructor said, using his nickname for journalist.

* * *

We survived physical fitness drills, obstacle and confidence courses, martial arts training, the rifle range, rappelling from a fifty-foot tower, swim week, and the chamber in which we were exposed to tear gas.

Finally it was time for the Crucible, the fifty-four-hour march and series of military challenges that marked the culmination of our training. It was late January. It was cold - above freezing, but not much. It rained.

We saw other recruits in twenty-man teams who had completed the daytime infiltration course with bayonets fixed. They had crawled through puddles of water, slid under barbed wire and thrust their bayonets into tires mounted on wooden dummies. We too completed the course and, panting and sore, found ourselves soaked from bellies to shins.

I had shed eighteen pounds since arriving at Parris Island.

Not As Lean, Not As Mean, Still a Marine!

I was thirty-eight pounds lighter than when I had first started getting into shape. I knew I could take it.

We learned we would have to complete the same course again that night, in the dark. As darkness fell, we were ordered to take off our sweatshirts and any other cold weather gear. We would wear only green cotton T-shirts and damp camouflage utility uniforms.

The DIs marched us to an abandoned airstrip. They ordered us to sit on the asphalt and wait for the opportunity to start. Fogs of breath rose above our formations. The cold penetrated the swollen joints in our hands.

"We'll be watching," the DIs hollered. "Anyone who tries to go around the puddles will be sent back! You'll do it over!"

Ordered to advance, my team of twenty walked through the trees that constituted the first part of the course. Flares lingered overhead. Shadows made by the burning phosphorous danced through the forest. Simulated explosions and machine-gun fire blasted from our right and left.

We came to an open field and a series of sandy trails that led under barbed wire fences. We dropped to our chests and crawled into the puddles. Water soaked our shirts and trousers.

"Yeah, yeah!" shouted the DIs. "Hurry up, Ca-heer! Go through it!"

They followed us throughout the course, which was maybe 250 yards in length. I advanced through every puddle, including one at the end that might have been twelve feet long. I helped another recruit drag an ammunition can full of sand.

We finished. Another recruit looked at me and cursed. I was dirtier and wetter than anyone else. But I had stayed with my team, and we had finished together.

* * *

My entire family came to Parris Island for graduation. All my relatives and my girlfriend had sent letters to keep up my spirits. Their best wishes had helped steel me against the insults and failures.

We walked to our cars after the ceremony. I was a Marine. Free to take ten days off before reporting to Camp Geiger, I heard a familiar voice.

"Good job, Ca-heer," shouted a DI.

I looked over. It wasn't one of the non-commissioned officers from my platoon. It was the one who had taunted me with the jumping-jacks motion on the rifle range. He and the marksmanship instructor had saved me when I took the wrong weapon out to shoot.

"Aye, sir," I shouted back.

PFC Bill Cahir, a reporter at Newhouse News Service, joined the Marine Corps at age 34. He was killed by enemy gunfire on August 13, 2009 while on active duty in Afghanistan. He married the former Rene Browne in 2006, and she was pregnant with twin girls at the time of his death. A memorial fund was established to pay for the family's needs at Bill Cahir Memorial Fund, Box 268, Alexandria, Va. 22313

NO INSIGNIFIGANCE HERE

Author Unknown

"In the Army, shock troops are a small minority supported by a vast group of artisans, laborers, clerks, and organizers. In the Marines, there are practically *nothing* but shock troops." – Combat correspondent John Lardner, Iwo Jima, 1945

Sometimes it's hard for some Marines, especially those in support roles, to remember that we are all part of the same team. Force Recon and the infantry may be out at the "tip of the spear," but without someone to feed, clothe and supply them they would all be hungry, naked and unarmed (although, no doubt, still highly motivated!). Remember, it only took one failed two-dollar bolt to bring down the Space Shuttle. No matter how insignificant you may feel at times, you are an important cog in the machine.

Since arriving in Iraq, Master Sergeant Adams just didn't feel like himself physically. He had apparently developed some kind of upper respiratory infection, but like most Marines he just passed it off and hoped it would subside. He was in great shape, and usually had no problem exercising his way through such minor setbacks. Little did he know that the progression of his illness would bring him to an experience which would have extraordinary meaning for him, as well as all Marines who would be privileged enough to hear about it.

A few months had passed and Top Adams found himself on a trip from Al Asad to Taqaddum, Iraq, a base in close proximity to the town of Fallujah. On his second day there, some down time gave him the opportunity to finally get checked out medically. After walking into the sick call tent, greetings came from a nearby corpsman asking "What's the problem?" After some discussion, the Master Sergeant removed his gear, sat, and waited his turn. Shortly thereafter another young corpsman escorted him to a makeshift exam room with a field gurney and a poncho liner for a curtain. Vital signs were taken, and the corpsman left the room. On the way out the corpsman closed the curtain, leaving it slightly open.

The situation had slightly shifted in the tent. Through the opening in the curtain, Marines in their body armor paced to and fro. The sound of incoming casualties began to fill the air. Top Adams knew that constant clashes with insurgents were all too common for Marines located at Fallujah, and he began to sense there were Marines who needed much more medical attention that he did. Suddenly the faint sound of a medical officer's voice asked a young Marine, "What is your name?" The Marine replied, "Lance Corporal Phillips, sir." Next came a series of questions and answers that could only be described as far too common.

First, the doctor asked Phillips how he sustained a deep burn on his lower back. The young leatherneck replied that he and his team were receiving small arms fire when a rocket impacted the area close to him and a piece of hot shrapnel became lodged under his body armor, which cut and burned him. Unfortunately, the doctor was not done.

The second question inquired about the Lance Corporal's broken arm. Again, the young Marine told his story. After having recovered from the first impact, another rocket had come zooming in and killed a buddy to his left and knocked him to the ground. By this time Master Sergeant Adams was feeling pretty selfish. The Top completely expected a

'General Patton' type of Marine to walk into his field hospital and kick him out saying that his hospital is for fighting Marines, not Marines with a runny nose! As the Master Sergeant was preparing to walk out, the doctor asked about Lance Corporal Phillips third injury.

Continuing with his description, Phillips exclaimed, "After the corpsman patched me up and put my arm in a sling, another rocket or RPG impacted near me, killed another buddy, and projected shrapnel into my hand." Finally Top Adams, filled with guilt, got up and started to make his way toward the hatch. Just at that moment a Navy Lieutenant greeted him and he asked, "Where are you going, Master Sergeant?" The Top then explained to him that there were Marines here that needed his attention much more. The lieutenant then told him to sit down so he could have a look.

The lieutenant quickly went through the examination of the Marine's ears, nose and throat and, just to be sure, they went outside away from the noisy generator so he could get a listen to his lungs. The doctor confirmed a bronchial infection that required medication. The lieutenant quickly returned with a prescription, while Master Sergeant Adams humbly thanked him and exited the cubicle. While departing, the Top caught a glimpse of Lance Corporal Phillips laying with his arm in a sling with a six-inch-wide bandage around his midsection, and another on his hand.

The Top soon had his gear on and was headed out of the tent when he suddenly stopped, turned around, and walked quickly back to the injured Lance Corporal's cubicle. He stuck his head in and startled him slightly. When Phillips made eye contact, he attempted to dismount his gurney and stand up. The Master Sergeant told him to relax, and that he just couldn't help overhearing the incredible account of the actions from the previous night. The young Marine went on

Not As Lean, Not As Mean, Still a Marine!

to give a few other horrific details that left the Top again shaking his head in utter disbelief. At a loss for words, Master Sergeant Adams said he just wanted to thank him for what he does and for the bravery he displayed. After a well deserved "Semper Fi" and "good luck," once again the Master Sergeant attempted to leave the area.

Phillips then stopped him in his tracks by asking, "What do you do, Top?" After hearing his story, followed by seeing and talking to this young man, his response was simply "Nothing important." That day the Master Sergeant felt insignificant compared to this Marine, and to his ordeal. Then the young Marine inquired again, "No, really Master Sergeant, what do you do?" The Top then explained that he was an Aviation Supply Chief. Phillips went on to ask if he had anything to do with making sure that the Cobras fly and have ordnance?

The Top replied that the Marines he works with issue parts to the squadrons, and the ordnance Marines issue and load rockets onto the Cobras. It was then that the young Lance Corporal could have stopped time with his profound statement. He said, "If it were not for the Cobra helicopter that zoomed in about ten minutes after the third impact, I would probably not be here." He went on to say that two helicopters wiped out a bunch of the "bad guys" that were encroaching upon them as well. Phillips then thanked the Master Sergeant and shook his hand. As the Top left the tent he was amazed, shocked, and proud all at the same time. He could only think and be reminded of what a great institution the Marine Corps is, and of every Marine it took to put that Cobra Helicopter on target. His thoughts rang an anthem of our Corps' ethos.

There is nothing like a true story to get our attention. Just a few days ago, the words and actions, respectively, of

Not As Lean, Not As Mean, Still a Marine!

Master Sergeant Adams and Lance Corporal Phillips solidified and confirmed every Marine's worth to the institution, and more so, to each other. In this case, an account like this brings us all back to reality and tells us to bloom where we are planted and sustain our individual link in the chain. From the last Marine in the last squad to the Commandant of the Marine Corps, our collective importance cannot be underestimated. In a Corps where every Marine must contribute, let this anecdote guide your conscience and keep your mind right. Take the time this week and remember to stay focused on being the best Marine you can be, whatever the task you're given. Your actions equal reaction which will prove to be significant - I guarantee it.

THANK MARINE MOM
Eva Savage

Tim Chavez

"He was just a kid, as was I. He confided to me that he had never even kissed a girl before... unfortunately, he never got the chance. I think his mother would be happy to know that only she and God ever knew the tenderness of his kiss." – A friend of PFC Bruce E. Cunningham, KIA in Vietnam

I sometimes wonder how my mom would have handled losing me in combat. I always made it a point to remind her that I loved the Corps and what it stood for, because I have always believed it lightens the load somewhat if your parents know you are doing something in which you strongly believe.

To honor this country and celebrate its freedoms on the 4th of July, don't just watch fireworks or make vacation plans to visit a national monument. Send an e-mail to Eva Savage.

No matter how many times we've read the Declaration of Independence or have pledged allegiance to the flag and its ideals, the freedom this country embodies is merely a concept to most of us. Freedom is like the air we breathe - it is what we've always known. It's what we've always had.

Eva Savage, however, lives it. She knows it. She bears its burden and cherishes its value each and every day.

And on this Fourth of July, Eva Savage is one of freedom's newest mothers - another in a long line of heroic Americans who endure the continuing sacrifice that our liberty demands.

"Freedom isn't free, and unfortunately most people don't

175

understand that," the Livingston, Tennessee, woman said. "My family and I have paid the ultimate price for freedom. My son died for what he believed in. He died with honor. The only thing I can say is red, white and blue, those are colors worth fighting for. Stand up and be counted."

Twenty-one-year-old Lance Corporal Jeremiah E. Savage was killed on May 12, 2004 in Iraq. And the previous Fourth of July was the final time Eva Savage held her son, during his pre-deployment day leave.

Some people would dispute Eva Savage's contentions or her place in this nation's history. They believe her son died for nothing. They argue that the Iraq war is not about freedom and honor at all, or anything good for that matter. They're wrong - by the most basic measure of what it means to be an American and to live in America. And today is the proper time to reiterate the lesson.

Here is how Ellen Garrison explains it. She is an associate professor of history at Middle Tennessee State University. She also is the mother of Army Captain John Neal, who lead an artillery unit in Iraq.

"When we were going through the 2000 election controversy, I asked one of my classes, 'How many of you guys are asking what is the Army going to do?'"

Her point - Americans didn't have to worry. Just like the freedom we take for granted, the belief in the people of this nation remaining in control came naturally despite the controversy. Everything was going to be all right.

"There are very few countries where you can say the Army is not a factor politically," Garrison said. "So when people ask 'Do you support the war?' I say that's an irrelevant question. My son is there because civilian control of our military is the cornerstone of our country."

The Declaration of Independence echoes Garrison's

interpretation: "We hold these Truths to be self-evident, that all Men are created equal, that they are endowed by their Creator with certain unalienable Rights, that among these are Life, Liberty and the Pursuit of Happiness - That to secure these Rights, Governments are instituted among Men, deriving their just Powers from the Consent of the Governed, that whenever any Form of Government becomes destructive of these Ends, it is the Right of the People to alter or to abolish it, and to institute a new Government..."

The Army didn't make the decision to go to Iraq. Our elected leaders did - from the White House to Congress, from George Bush to John Kerry. The war in Iraq is emblematic of our way of governance, that power or force can only be exerted through our consent. And that principle preserves our freedom - as long as there are Eva Savages willing to live with the ultimate sacrifice often required.

Read her story about freedom's cost, then send her an e-mail at eva@twlakes.net.

"Hi, my name is Eva Savage. My Marine, my hero, was Lance Corporal Jeremiah Savage. He was my oldest child, and my best friend. As a child, all he ever wanted to be was a Marine. He grew up playing G.I. Joe with tanks and guns. That was who he was. At age eleven, he knew what he wanted to be. The last three things on a school paper telling about himself were:

> *8. I like the B-2 Bomber*
> *9. I like to blow things up (he was mortarman in the Marines)*
> *10. I wanna be a MARINE!*

My son lived his dream. He joined the Marines his junior year on the delayed entry program. He graduated high school in May, and three days later was on his way to Parris Island for boot camp. For three months he questioned his decision, as I am sure all Marines do. But graduation at Parris Island on August 19, 2001, changed our lives forever.

Then September 11 happened. Once again our country was changed. The red, white and blue was proudly displayed. In November 2001, Jeremiah was sent to his duty station two thousand miles from home - Camp Pendleton, California.

He received his first tour orders for Japan and left in July of 2002. In June 2002, I flew out to spend a week with him in California. Japan was supposed to be a six-month duty, which turned into eleven and a half months. His daughter Madison was born in October while he was there.

Jer and I talked often while he was overseas, and we shared many stories, concerns, fears, thoughts. In June 2003 he returned home to Camp Pendleton, and then came home to Tennessee for twenty-one days. We went as a family back home to Illinois for the Fourth and celebrated being together. This year on the Fourth will be very hard for me as I remember the last time we were together, with joy and love and watching him hug his dad bye and with tears in his eyes as he left. Who knew that was the last time we would see him, hold him?

In November it was announced that Marines from Camp Pendleton were going to Iraq. I cannot explain the feelings at that time. I remembered Jer and my conversations:

'Mom, they are my brothers. I need to be there with them, not sitting here.'

I asked Jer if his was one of the Marine units going.

'No, Mom. We are going to Japan.'

No matter what he told me, I knew he would be going to Iraq. The week before Christmas when he called, he was talking about night-vision goggles and a different type of gun than what he normally carried. It was then that I asked him why he had that gear?

He said, 'I'm going to Iraq, Mom. Don't worry, just going to rebuild. My skills in welding will come in handy.'

In January of 2004, I wanted to go see him before he left. This, too, I can't explain, the need. But it was not to be. In February, he went to Iraq. There were many calls from the airport in Jersey. And E-mails.

He was having some problems that only Mom was able to help him with. We talked as often as possible. It seemed like every time something would happen, I happened to be sitting at the computer searching for information and the phone would ring.

'Hey mom, what's up?'

Then my world was right once again.

He would call us when he had the chance on Friday nights and Saturdays, and everyone would have to talk to him. Then along came the Internet. Yeah! We were able to talk to him via Yahoo Messenger, and I even turned on the Web cam, and he was able to see us.

On a Monday I talked to him for two hours, went to practice with the Praise Band at church, came home and talked to him for two more hours. Those were the last conversations we had, filled with joking and lots of laughter.

Now I try to fill my days spending time with his brother Jonathan, who is nineteen and was married on April 3rd - the same day Jer's son Wyatt was born. Jonathan, before the trip to Arlington National Cemetery, went and had an eagle, globe and anchor tattoo put on his back in loving memory of his brother.

Chelsea is fifteen and going on thirty-five. Her faith is such a blessing to me as she has professed that until God tells her otherwise, she is going to be a minister.

Not As Lean, Not As Mean, Still a Marine!

Me, I am a Marine Mom learning to live without my Marine. Between the immense pride and the pain, my love is unfailing."

May our gratitude to this mother of our freedom, and others like her, *also* be unfailing.

Tim Chavez is a columnist for *The Tennessean*

BILLY WILSON'S BLUES

James L. Garrahy

"The only thing bigger than a Marine's mouth is his heart." - Major H.G. "Dunk" Duncan

Marine Corporal Billy Wilson was severely injured in Viet Nam in 1969. One afternoon in 1988, I was having a beer with Billy at the "Hillside," a country tavern where Billy has worked since he got out of the Philadelphia Naval Hospital in 1970. Over these beers, Billy asked if I had ever had a set of Marine Corps Dress Blues. I answered him no, because like him, a corporal in those years did not require a dress uniform. Billy then said, "It would be neat to be buried in a set of Dress Blues!"

I thought that if ever a Marine had earned a set of Dress Blues, it was Corporal Wilson, so I set out to find Billy Wilson's Blues. I thought I would ask a pair of recruiters from the Harrisburg Recruiting Station to bring the uniform to the Hillside on a busy Friday night, call everyone to attention, and present Billy with his new uniform.

As word got around Gettysburg that this was going to soon happen, more and more people asked me to be sure to let them know when the date was to be scheduled. Soon the Hillside Restaurant was not big enough to handle the number of people interested in attending this presentation, so I had to find another location.

During this time, along with then Captain Brad Shultis (now a Lieutenant Colonel) and Mark Nesbit, a local Civil War author, I wrote a letter to the Commandant of the Marine Corps, General A.M. Gray, about our upcoming

Not As Lean, Not As Mean, Still a Marine!

ceremony honoring a Viet Nam veteran.

Dear General Gray,

On 27 Jan69, on Hill 55, six miles north of Da Nang, Quanong Province, Republic of Vietnam, Corporal Joseph William Wilson, USMC, was wounded by an enemy booby trap while entering a bunker. In this action he lost both his legs above the knees, was blinded in one eye, and partially blinded in the other. He was awarded the Bronze Star with Combat V and the Purple Heart.

In a recent conversation with myself and other Marines, Corporal Wilson expressed his desire to one day be buried in Marine Corps Dress Blues. We are purchasing this uniform for him. Everyone in the Gettysburg area knows of Billy and his remarkable courage, both on the battlefield and in everyday life.

It is our desire to have a ceremony to honor Corporal Wilson by presenting him with this uniform and by having his Bronze Star and Purple Heart pinned to it. The ceremony will take place somewhere on the Gettysburg Battlefield - an appropriate venue for such an occasion.

We respectfully request the honor of the General's presence at a date and time of his choosing to present Corporal Wilson with his medals and to help his fellow Marines and neighbors thank him, after twenty years, for what he gave for his country. The General's presence would mean a great deal to him.

A response, at the General's convenience, with regard to a time and date for this brief but meaningful ceremony would be greatly appreciated.

Semper Fi Sir,
Seamus Garrahy

Not As Lean, Not As Mean, Still a Marine!

On 10 June, 1989 General Al Gray came to the Gettysburg National Cemetery and pinned a Bronze Star with combat 'V' and a Purple Heart on Billy Wilson's new Dress Blues. During this ceremony, the General said he was going to do something he had only done eight times in his entire career as a Gunfighter in the Marine Corps. He said he was going to salute an enlisted Marine! Billy started to stand up and General Gray bellowed, "You sit down! I will do the standing and saluting!" – and when the Commandant of the Marine Corps saluted Corporal Billy Wilson, there wasn't a dry eye in the entire crowd.

James "Seamus" Garrahy is the President of Gettysburg-based Jim Garrahy's Fudge Kitchen, makers of the world famous Gung-Ho Steak Sauce (www.gunghosauce.com).

THE FOUR CHAPLAINS

"By his patient, sympathetic labors with the men, day in, day out, and through many a night, every chaplain I know contributed immeasurably to the moral courage of our fighting men. None of the effort appears in the statistics. Most of it was necessarily secret between pastor and his confidant. It is for that toil in the cause both of God and country that I honor the Chaplain most."
- Fleet Admiral Chester W. Nimitz, USN May 1946

In the Marine Corps we have a special place in our hearts for our chaplains - and that includes those Marines who are not "believers." They are there for us when the going gets the roughest, and in the back of our minds we know a chaplain may well be the last person we see on this earth. In a world where differences have all too often created conflict and separated brothers, the Four Chaplains found a special kind of unity, and in that unity they found strength. Despite their differences, they became "brothers" - for they had one unseen characteristic in common that overshadowed everything else.

In November of 1942 four young men "found each other" while attending the Chaplains' School at Harvard University. They had enough in common to bond them together. At age forty-two, George Fox was the "older brother." The youngest was thirty-year old Clark Poling, and less than three years separated him from the other two, Alexander Goode and John Washington. A common cause had brought them together - the desire to render service to their Nation during the critical years of World War II.

Not As Lean, Not As Mean, Still a Marine!

Between the early days of May to late July, the four had entered military service from different areas of the country. Reverend Fox enlisted in the Army from Vermont the same day his eighteen-year old son Wyatt enlisted in the Marine Corps. During World War I, though only seventeen years old, Fox had convinced the Army he was actually eighteen and enlisted as a medical corps assistant. His courage on the battlefield earned him the Silver Star, the Croix de Guerre, and the Purple Heart. When World War II broke out he said, "I've got to go. I know from experience what our boys are about to face. They need me." This time, however, he didn't enlist to heal the wounds of the body. As a minister he was joining the Chaplains Corps to heal the wounds of the soul.

Reverend Clark V. Poling was from Ohio and pastoring in New York when World War II threatened world freedom. He determined to enter the Army, but not as a Chaplain. "I'm not going to hide behind the church in some safe office out of the firing line," he told his father when he informed him of his plans to serve his country. His father, Reverend Daniel Poling, knew something of war - having served as a Chaplain himself during World War I. He told his son, "Don't you know that chaplains have the highest mortality rate of all? As a chaplain you'll have the best chance in the world to be killed. You just can't carry a gun to kill anyone yourself." With a new appreciation for the role of the Chaplains Corps, Clark Poling accepted a commission and followed in his father's footsteps.

Like Clark Poling, Alexander Goode had followed the steps of his own father in ministry. His first years of service were in Marion, Indiana, and then he moved on to York, Pennsylvania. While studying and preparing to minister to the needs of others, "Alex" had joined the National

Guard. Ten months before Pearl Harbor he sought an assignment in the Navy's Chaplains Corps, but wasn't initially accepted. When war was declared, he wanted more than ever to serve the needs of those who went in harm's way to defend freedom and human dignity. He chose to do so as a U.S. Army Chaplain.

One look at the be-speckled, mild mannered John P. Washington, would have left one with the impression that he was not the sort of man to go to war and become a hero. His love of music and beautiful voice belied the toughness inside. One of nine children in an Irish immigrant family living in the toughest part of Newark, New Jersey, he had learned through sheer determination to hold his own in any fight. By the time he was a teenager he was the leader of the South Twelfth Street Gang. Then God called him to ministry, returning him to the streets of New Jersey to organize sports teams, play ball with young boys who needed a strong friend to look up to, and inspire others with his beautiful hymns of praise and thanksgiving.

Upon meeting at the Chaplains' school, the four men quickly became friends. One of Clark Poling's cousins later said, "They were all very sociable guys, who seemed to have initiated interfaith activities even before the war. They hit it off well at chaplains' school. Sharing their faith was not just a first-time deal for them. They were really very close. They had prayed together a number of times before that final crisis."

The observation pointed out by Clark's cousin is of note, for the men of whom he spoke were unique. Their close bond might easily have marked them as "The Four Chaplains" long before a fateful night three months after they first met, when their actions would forever make the title synonymous with the names George L. Fox, Alexander

Not As Lean, Not As Mean, Still a Marine!

D. Goode, Clark V. Poling, and John P. Washington. The differences in their backgrounds and personalities could have been easily outweighed by their common calling to ministry, had it not been for one major difference.

U.S.A.T. *Dorchester* was an aging, luxury coastal liner that was no longer luxurious. In the nearly four years from December 7, 1941 to September 2, 1945 more than sixteen million American men and women were called upon to defend human dignity and freedom on two fronts, in Europe and the Pacific. Moving so large a force to the battlefields was a monumental effort, and every available ship was being pressed into service. Some of these were converted into vessels of war, others to carrying critical supplies to the men and women in the field. *Dorchester* was designated to be a transport ship. All non-critical amenities were removed, and cots were crammed into every available space. The intent was to get as many young fighting men as possible on each voyage. When the soldiers boarded in New York on January 23, 1943 *Dorchester* certainly was filled to capacity. In addition to the Merchant Marine crew and a few civilians, young soldiers filled every available space. There were 902 lives about to be cast to the mercy of the frigid North Atlantic.

As *Dorchester* left New York for an Army base in Greenland, many dangers lay ahead. The sea itself was always dangerous, especially in this area known for ice flows, raging waters, and gale force winds. The greatest danger, however, was the ever present threat of German submarines, which had recently been sinking Allied ships at the rate of one hundred every month. *Dorchester* would be sailing through an area that had become infamous as "Torpedo Junction."

Most of the men who boarded for the trip were young,

frightened soldiers. Many were going to sea for the first time and suffered sea-sickness for days. They were packed head to toe below deck, a steaming human sea of fear and uncertainty. Even if they survived the eventual Atlantic crossing, they had nothing to look forward to, only the prospect of being thrown into the cauldron of war on foreign shores. They were men in need of a strong shoulder to lean on, a firm voice to encourage them, and a ray of hope in a world of despair. In their midst moved four men, Army Chaplains, called to put aside their own fears and uncertainties to minister to the needs of others.

Perhaps Chaplain Fox thought of his own eighteen-year old son, who was serving in the Marine Corps, as he walked among the young soldiers aboard *Dorchester*, giving strength and spiritual hope to those he could. Before leaving he had said goodbye to his wife and seven year old daughter Mary Elizabeth. It was Chaplain Fox's second war, for the "war to end all wars" ... HADN'T!

In other parts of the ship Father Washington likewise did his best to soothe the fears of those about him. As a Catholic Priest he was single and hadn't left behind a wife or children, but there were eight brothers and sisters at home to fear for him and pray for his safety. Now his closest brothers were the other three Chaplains on *Dorchester*. They leaned on each other for strength, as they tried daily to mete that strength out to others. Surely as he prayed for his make-shift parish, Father Washington also whispered a prayer for Chaplain Fox, Chaplain Poling and Rabbi Goode. Not only had Chaplain Fox left a son and daughter behind, Rabbi Goode had left behind a loving wife and three-year-old daughter. Chaplain Poling's son Corky was still an infant, and within a month or two his wife would be giving birth to their second child. In time of war, perhaps being single had its advantages.

With so many men crammed into so small a space, all of them so much in need of the ray of hope spiritual guidance could afford, differences ceased to be important. All of the soldiers shared the same level of misery and fear, whether Protestant, Catholic, or Jew. The title "Rabbi," "Father," or "Reverend" was of little consequence when a man needed a chaplain. A prayer from Rabbi Goode could give strength to the Catholic soldier as quickly as a hymn from the beautiful voice of Father Washington could warm the heart of a Protestant. The Jewish soldier facing an uncertain future on foreign shores could draw on the strength of a Protestant to help him face tomorrow. When sinking in the quicksand of life one doesn't ask for the credentials of he who offers the hand of hope, he is simply thankful for the helping hand.

The crossing was filled with long hours of boredom and misery. Outside, the chilly Arctic winds and cold ocean spray coated *Dorchester's* deck with ice. Below deck the soldiers' quarters were hot from too many bodies, crammed into too small a place, for too many days in a row. Finally, on February 2nd, *Dorchester* was within 150 miles of Greenland. It would have generated a great sense of relief among the young soldiers crowded in the ship's berths, had not the welcomed news been tempered by other news of grave concern. One of their three Coast Guard escorts had received sonar readings during the day, indicating the presence of an enemy submarine in "Torpedo Junction."

Hans Danielson, *Dorchester's* captain, listened to the news with great concern. His cargo of human lives had been at sea for ten days, and was finally nearing its destination. If he could make it through the night, air cover would arrive with daylight to safely guide his ship home. The problem would be surviving the night. Aware of the potential for disaster, he instructed the soldiers to sleep in their clothes and life jackets... just in case. Below deck however, it was hot and sweaty as too many bodies lay down, closely packed in the cramped quarters. Many of the men, confident that tomorrow would dawn without incident, elected to sleep in their underwear. The life jackets were also hot and bulky, so many men set them aside as an unnecessary inconvenience.

Outside it was another cold, windy night as the midnight hour signaled the passing of February 2nd and the beginning of a new day. In the distance a cold, metal arm broke the surface of the stormy seas. At the end of that arm, a German U-Boat captain monitored the slowly passing troop transport. Shortly before one in the morning he gave the command to fire three torpedoes.

Quiet moments passed as silent death reached out for the men of *Dorchester*, then the early morning was shattered by the flash of a blinding explosion and the roar of massive destruction. The "hit" had been dead on, tossing men from their cots with the force of its explosion. A second torpedo followed the first, instantly killing one hundred men in the hull of the ship. Power was knocked out by the explosion in the engine room, and darkness engulfed the frightened men below decks as water rushed through gaping wounds in *Dorchester's* hull. The ship tilted at an unnatural angle as it began to sink rapidly, and piles of clothing and life jackets were tossed about in the darkness where no one would ever find them. Wounded men cried out in pain, frightened survivors screamed in terror, and all groped frantically in the darkness for exits they couldn't find. Somewhere in that living hell, four voices of calm began to speak words of comfort, seeking to bring order to panic and bedlam. Slowly soldiers began to find their way to the deck of the ship, many still in their underwear, where they were confronted by the cold winds blowing down from the arctic. Petty Officer John J. Mahoney, reeling from the cold, headed back towards his cabin. "Where are you going?" a voice of calm in the sea of distress asked.

"To get my gloves," Mahoney replied.

"Here, take these," said Rabbi Goode as he handed a pair of gloves to the young officer who would never have survived the trip to his cabin and then back to safety.

"I can't take those gloves," Mahoney replied.

"Never mind," the Rabbi responded. "I have two pairs." Mahoney slipped the gloves over his hands and returned to the frigid deck, never stopping to ponder until later when he had reached safety, that there was no way Rabbi Goode would have been carrying a spare set of gloves. As that thought finally dawned on him he came to a new understanding of what was transpiring in the mind of the fearless Chaplain. Somehow, Rabbi Goode suspected that he would himself never leave *Dorchester* alive.

Before boarding ship back in January, Reverend Poling had asked his father to pray for him, "Not for my safe return, that wouldn't be fair. Just pray that I shall do my duty... never be a coward... and have the strength, courage and understanding of men. Just pray that I shall be adequate." He probably never dreamed that his prayer request would be answered so fully. As he guided the frightened soldiers to their only hope of safety from the rapidly sinking transport, he spoke calm words of encouragement, urging them not to give up. In the dark hull of *Dorchester*, he was more than adequate. He was a hero.

Likewise Reverend Fox and Father Washington stood out within the confines of an unimaginable hell. Wounded and dying soldiers were ushered into eternity to the sounds of comforting words from men of God more intent on the needs of others than in their own safety and survival. Somehow, by their valiant efforts, the Chaplains succeeded in getting many of the soldiers out of the hold and onto *Dorchester's* slippery deck.

In the chaos around them, life boats floated away before men could board them. Others capsized as panic continued to shadow reason and soldiers loaded the small craft beyond limit. The strength, calm, and organization of the Chaplains had been so critical in the dark hull. Now on deck, they found their mission had not been fully accomplished. They organized the effort, directed men to safety, and left them with parting words of encouragement. In little more than twenty minutes, U.S.A.T. *Dorchester* was almost gone. Icy waves broke over the railing, tossing men into the sea, many of them without life jackets. In the last moments of the transport's existence, the Chaplains were too occupied opening lockers to pass out life jackets to note the threat to their own lives.

In less than half an hour, water was beginning to flow across the deck of the sinking ship. Working against time, the Chaplains continued to pass out the life vests from the lockers as the soldiers pressed forward in a ragged line. And then... the lockers were all empty... the life jackets gone. Those still pressing in line began to realize they were doomed - there was no hope. And then something amazing happened, something those who were there would never forget. All Four Chaplains began taking their own life jackets off... and putting them on the men around them. Together they sacrificed their last shred of hope for survival, to ensure the survival of other men... most of them total strangers. Then time ran out. The Chaplains had done all they could for those who would survive, and nothing more could be done for the remaining...including themselves.

Not As Lean, Not As Mean, Still a Marine!

Those who had been fortunate enough to reach lifeboats struggled to distance themselves from the sinking ship, lest they be pulled beneath the ocean swells by the chasm created as the transport slipped into a watery grave. Then, amid the screams of pain and horror that permeated the cold dark night, they heard the strong voices of the Chaplains. "Shma Yisroel Adonai Elohenu Adonai Echod."... "Our Father, which art in Heaven, Hallowed be Thy name. Thy kingdom come, Thy will be done."

Looking back they saw the slanting deck of *Dorchester*, her demise almost complete. Braced against the railings were the Four Chaplains... praying... singing, giving strength to others by their final valiant declaration of faith. Their arms were linked together as they braced against the railing and leaned into each other for support, Reverend Fox, Rabbi Goode, Reverend Poling, and Father Washington. Said one of the survivors, "It was the finest thing I have ever seen this side of heaven."

And then, only twenty-seven minutes after the first torpedo struck, the last vestige of U.S.A.T. *Dorchester* disappeared beneath the cold North Atlantic waters. In its death throes the stricken ship reached out to claim any survivors nearby, while also taking to its grave the four ministers of different faiths who learned to find strength despite their diversity.

The Chapel of the Four Chaplains was built at Temple University in Pennsylvania and became one of the most enduring tributes to Reverend Fox, Rabbi Goode, Reverend Poling, and Father Washington. Time has dimmed the memory of the four great men, and with that fading memory the chapel itself has slipped into the background of the American conscience.

DESPERATE VOLUNTEERS

Susan Percy

"I had the unpleasant opportunity to view the new movie 'Fahrenheit 9/11' by Michael Moore last night. I have never been so offended in my life." - Corporal W.M. Howard II, Iraq

The following is a letter sent to the Washington Post in July of 2004 in response to an article which called into question the "fairness" of our all-volunteer professional military. It appeared around the same time Michael Moore asked interviewer Bill O'Reilly, "Would you send your son to fight in Iraq?" My answer to that question would have been no - I wouldn't "send" him (or her) anywhere. But I would respect and support their choice to serve, if that's what they wanted to do. I don't know about anybody else, but my mother didn't "send" me to Parris Island, anymore than she volunteered me for recon, jump school or demolitions training. I also resent Moore and Kinsley's assertion that those who join the armed forces are poorly educated, destitute, and have no other options. Perhaps they should travel to Camp Lejeune or Camp Pendleton and try telling that to some Marines!

Michael Kinsley wrote in *What's Fair About a Draft* that draft proponents cite fairness as a criterion for their argument, "...asking young people to disrupt their lives and risk dying for their country, that burden ought to be spread across society, not concentrated among those desperate enough to volunteer," and then proceeds to make the case that the draft is, in essence, unfair.

As the widow of a Viet Nam era serviceman, remarried to

Not As Lean, Not As Mean, Still a Marine!

a career serviceman now retired, mother to two who have served or are still serving, and mother-in-law to a current military member, I take issue with the absurdity of nearly every point Kinsley made, but the one that rankled most also revealed Kinsley's cluelessness to anything military, as he characterized military volunteers as "desperate," as if the only plausible motive for entering military service is the dearth of other opportunities open to them in the civilian world. Likening soldiers, sailors and Marines to the dregs of the earth, employment wise. "Hey," he intimates, "they aren't cut from the cloth of investment bankers after all."

It must be inconceivable to Kinsley, high priest to snotty liberal elites who wouldn't touch the idea of military service for themselves or their children with a ten foot pole, that bright, promising youths might have other motives. Perhaps they're afflicted with lofty, spine tingling ideals (of course that requires a spine in the first place to recognize it, Mr. Kinsley) and volunteer to serve for reasons *other* than "desperation." How condescending of him, and how untrue. Kinsley actually tries to sell us mothers of stretched thin service members on the idea that it would be unfair if the progeny of his ilk, who really don't want to prosecute a war anyhow, much less die in one (so who does want to die in war, Mr. Kinsley?) had to participate in the defense of our way of life. Why? *Because they don't want to.* Besides, they might deny those poor desperate fools who actually see value in putting their lives on the line for this nation a shot at having their dream come true. To make America safe for Mike and Company... who would rather pass the Merlot than the ammunition.

I'm a freelance writer who focuses on being an advocate for military families. I have had articles published in *The*

195

Not As Lean, Not As Mean, Still a Marine!

Marine Gazette and *Naval Proceedings*. My first husband, Lieutenant Commander Barton Creed, was lost in Laos in '71, my second husband was a career Marine aviator, my older son is a Marine aviator, and my daughter served five years in the Navy and is now married to a naval officer.

Michael Kinsley's column was supremely offensive to me.

WARRIORS BY CHOICE

Nathaniel Fick

"Let him who desires peace prepare for war."
– Vegetius, Roman military strategist

I went to war as a believer in the citizen-soldier. My college study of the classics idealized Greeks who put down their plows for swords, returning to their fields at the end of the war. As a Marine officer in Afghanistan and Iraq however, I learned that the victors on today's battlefields are long-term, professional soldiers. Thus the increasing calls for reinstating the draft - and the bills now before Congress that would do so - are well intentioned but misguided. Imposing a draft on the military I served in would harm it grievously for years.

I led platoons of volunteers. In Afghanistan, my Marines slept each night in holes they hacked from the rocky ground. They carried hundred-pound packs in addition to their fears of minefields and ambushes, their homesickness, loneliness and exhaustion. The most junior did it for $964.80 per month. They didn't complain, and I never wrestled with discipline problems. Each and every Marine wanted to be there. If anyone hadn't, he would have been a drain on the platoon and a liability in combat.

In Iraq I commanded a reconnaissance platoon, the Marines' special operations force. Many of my enlisted Marines were college-educated, and some had been to graduate school. All had volunteered once for the Marines, again for the infantry, and a third time for recon. They were proud to serve as part of an elite unit. Like most demanding professionals, they were their own harshest critics, and intolerant of peers whose performance fell short.

The dumb grunt is an anachronism. He has been replaced by the strategic corporal. Immense firepower and improved technology have pushed decision-making with national consequences down to individual enlisted men. Modern warfare requires that even the most junior infantryman master a wide array of technical and tactical skills.

Honing these skills to reflex, a prerequisite for survival in combat, takes time - a year of formal training and another year of on-the-job experience were generally needed to transform my young Marines into competent warriors. The Marine Corps demands four-year active enlistments because it takes that long to train troops and ensure those training dollars are put to use in the field. One or two-year terms, the longest that would be likely under conscription, would simply not allow for this comprehensive training.

Some supporters of the draft argue that America's wars are being fought primarily by minorities from poor families who enlisted in the economic equivalent of a Hail Mary pass. They insist that the sacrifices of citizenship be shared by all Americans. The sentiment is correct, but the outrage is misplaced. There is no cannon-fodder underclass in the military. In fact, front-line combat troops are a near-perfect reflection of American male society.

Yes, some minority men and women enlist for lack of other options, but they tend to concentrate in support jobs where they can learn marketable skills like driving trucks or fixing jets, not throwing grenades and setting up interlocking fields of machine gun fire. African-Americans, who comprise nearly thirteen percent of the general population, are overrepresented in the military at more than nineteen percent - but they account for only 10.6 percent of infantry soldiers, the group that suffers most in combat. Hispanics, who make up 13.3 percent of the American population, are underrepresented at only eleven percent of those in uniform.

The men in my infantry platoons came from virtually every part of the socio-economic spectrum. There were prep-school graduates and first-generation immigrants, blacks and whites, Muslims and Jews, Democrats and Republicans. They were more diverse than my class at Dartmouth, and far more willing to act on their principles.

The second argument most often advanced for a renewed draft is the military is too small to meet its commitments. Absolutely true. But the armed forces are stretched thin not from a lack of volunteers, but because Congress and the Pentagon are not willing to spend the money to expand the force. Each of the services met or exceeded its recruiting goals in 2003, and the numbers have increased across the board so far this year. Even the Army National Guard, often cited as the abused beast of burden in Iraq, has seen re-enlistments soar past its goal of 65 percent to 141 percent (the figure is greater than 100 because many guardsmen are re-enlisting early).

Expanding the military to meet additional responsibilities is a matter of structural change. If we build it, they will come. And build it we must. Many of my Marines are already on their third combat deployment in the global war on terrorism - and they will need replacing. Increasing the size of the active-duty military would lighten the burden on every soldier, sailor, airman and Marine. Paradoxically, a larger military becomes more sustainable than a smaller one. Fewer combat deployments improves service members' quality of life and contributes to higher rates of enlistment and retention. For now, expanding the volunteer force would give us a larger military without the inherent liabilities of conscription.

And while draft supporters insist we have learned the lessons of Vietnam and can create a fair system this time around, even an equitable draft would lower the standards for enlistees. Defense Secretary Donald Rumsfeld was once chastised for saying Vietnam-era draftees added no value to the armed forces. But his error was semantic - the statement was true of the system, if not of the patriotic and capable individuals who served.

The current volunteer force rejects applicants who score poorly on its entrance aptitude exam, disclose a history of significant drug use, or suffer from any of a number of orthopedic or chronic injuries. Face it, any unwilling draftee could easily find a way to fail any of these tests. The military would then be left either to abandon its standards and accept all comers, or to remain true to them and allow the draft to become volunteerism by another name. Stripped of its volunteer ideology, but still unable to compel service from dissenters, the military would end up weaker and less representative than the volunteer force - the very opposite of the draft's intended goals.

Renewing the draft would be a blow against the men and women in uniform, a dumbing down of the institution they serve. The United States military exists to win battles, not to test social policy. Enlarging the volunteer force would show our soldiers that Americans recognize their hardship and are willing to pay the bill to help them better protect the nation. My view of the citizen-soldier was altered, but not destroyed, in combat. We cannot all pick up the sword, nor should we be forced to - but we owe our support to those who do.

Nathaniel Fick, a former Marine Captain, is the author of *One Bullet Away – The Making of a Marine Officer.*

WE HONOR YOU HERE

By Barbara Simpson

"I am a Mexican-American and we have a tradition. We're supposed to be *men*, not sissies." - Medal of Honor winner Silvestre S. Herrera

I am as perturbed by the lax immigration policies of this country as anyone else, and am tired of the flood of illegals pouring across our borders on a daily basis. That said, I have absolutely no problem with those who come here legally to try and make a better life for themselves and their families - provided, of course, they learn to speak English! After all, it does say, "Give me your tired, your hungry, your poor, etc," on the Statue of Liberty. This is especially true in the case of those willing to serve in our military, and who make sacrifices in defense of the liberties they are seeking:

Mexican President Vicente Fox owes big-time apologies to a deceased U.S. Marine and his family, to every member of the United States Marine Corps, to the U.S. military, the Pentagon, President Bush and the people of the United States. It's a big order, but then Mr. Fox is a big man. Isn't he? Or is the unconscionable delay in his good-neighbor good-manners a reflection of the fact that he is, in reality, a very small man who, perhaps because of his "macho" image, just can't handle saying, "I'm sorry. We were wrong." They *were* wrong. Consider: a full military funeral for a U.S. Marine disrupted by Mexican soldiers, armed with automatic weapons. They not only demanded the honor guard turn over their (fake) weapons but ordered them back to their car, later surrounding the vehicle and refusing to allow it to leave.

Not As Lean, Not As Mean, Still a Marine!

It was as good as spitting on the grave of twenty-two-year-old Juan Lopez, a Mexican born U.S. Marine who was killed in Iraq. But it's more than that. By avoiding this moral obligation, Vicente Fox shows Americans just what he thinks of this country. Apparently, not much. He plays the good neighbor, but in the case of the funeral of Lance Corporal Lopez, there isn't a scintilla of decency. Juan Lopez was born in the small Mexican farming town of San Luis de la Paz. He immigrated to Dalton, Georgia as a teen, and joined the Marines. His assignment took him to Iraq, where he was killed. His wife and family wanted him buried in his hometown with full military honors, and arrangements were made for a July 4th funeral. That's when everything began to hit the fan - at least as far as the Mexican government and military were concerned. It seems Mexico doesn't take kindly to "foreign military forces" on their land, so the presence of U.S. Marines in uniform and carrying firearms got them all in a snit. *But it was a funeral!* No matter. Assurances that the weapons were part of the uniform and that some form of weapon was needed for the ceremonial military firing detail didn't hold any water. Finally, a compromise was reached with the Mexican government. The salute was banned, and no weapons would be fired into the air. Also, any "weapons" carried by the Marine honor guard would be ceremonial - in reality, fake guns. They would not be operational. That should have done it. But it didn't. Family and friends gathered, and the Marine honor guard and pallbearers were there. The flag-draped casket was ready for the ceremony, and burial in the tiny cemetery in the village. Four Marines marched toward the grave - two of them carrying the ceremonial rifles. Suddenly, their path was blocked. Four armed Mexican soldiers demanded the Marines return to their vehicle. It remained a standoff until a trumpet player began the music of the ceremony, which then proceeded over the objections of the Mexican troops. When the proceedings were over and the Marines returned to their vehicle, some fourteen Mexican troops turned up to "guard" the area and prevented their car from leaving for a period of time. Lopez's family was outraged that the Mexican government disrupted their requested military funeral. The reaction was the same in this country, although the story didn't get the media play it should have. Apparently, it isn't politic to criticize the Mexican government. Three days later, the Mexicans issued an apparent defense of the incident. According to the statement, it all happened because the honor guard violated Mexican law by carrying rifles. So much for prior agreements. Even though the story quickly disappeared from any news coverage, the U.S. Defense Department remained furious. According to a Defense Department memo, the incident was "deplorable," the Mexican response didn't satisfy U.S. concerns about the funeral's disruption, and the department was still waiting to hear from Mexico about the situation. I'm glad the Pentagon was furious. I hope the Marines were. I know I was. We all should be. We needed a full, public apology. We should have a long memory. Tell the Mexican government no more free passes. Stop letting them tell this country how to run our immigration policies. Ignore demands to accept their poorest people so they can rid himself of financial drains on the Mexican economy. Ignore demands for driver's licenses and votes for illegals. Stop honoring ID's issued by Mexican consulates. Ignore demands and criticisms of our justice system. Secure our borders and fire on Mexican troops who cross *our* border illegally. And send home all Mexican citizens who are here illegally.

Following Lance Corporal Lopez's burial his family was

Not As Lean, Not As Mean, Still a Marine!

presented with his official U.S. citizenship, which he earned following his military service and death. Welcome, Lance Corporal Juan Lopez. Your adopted country honors you. Semper Fi!

Barbara Simpson, "The Babe in the Bunker" as she's known to her KSFO 560 radio talk-show audience in San Francisco, has a twemty-year radio, television and newspaper career in the Bay Area and Los Angeles.

THE MEANING OF SEMPER FI

"Today, all Americans are united in anguish and anger. But we must also be united in purpose and in will. While the immediate task of vanquishing freedom's enemies will fall to our military men and women, all of us - particularly those like you who understand the price of freedom - will be called upon to strengthen our national resolve." - Secretary of Defense Donald Rumsfeld

On September 11, 2001at the Pentagon, one of today's generation of the proud and the few showed all of us the true meaning of "Semper Fidelis."

A corporal from 8th & I standing guard duty at the Pentagon on that fateful Tuesday morning was close to the point of impact of the jetliner which crashed into the building, and when his uniform caught on fire he peeled off his clothes and in his skivvies rushed into hell to rescue victims of the disaster along with one of his Marine buddies.

While trying to pull a lady from the rubble, something fell upon his hands and broke his fingers. Even so he continued his desperate work until his buddy grabbed him by the shoulders to restrain and get him medical help. When his fellow Marine touched his shoulders and arms, the skin came off the corporal onto his friend's hands.

I wanted to give you his name and address at Bethesda Naval Hospital at that time, but his sister said he was not ready to receive cards and letters. He was angry. He wanted to be a warrior and already knew his career in the Corps was over. Third degree burns over his upper body and numerous wounds from flying debris pretty well decided that.

God bless the young men who wear our uniform.

LAST TO LET YOU DOWN

Mary D. Karcher

"For those beneath the wooden crosses, there is nothing we can do, except perhaps to pause and murmur, 'Thanks pal, thanks.'" - Ernie Pyle

Ronald Reagan, whom I consider to be the greatest President to serve during my lifetime, was recently laid to rest with full military honors. As I watched his funeral I could not help but be impressed by the professionalism of the various honor guards and, in particular, the body bearers who carried his casket during each leg of the long journey to the President's final resting place. The news commentators frequently discussed the preparation involved in a state funeral, but few of them realize that each of us who serve will receive similar (although certainly less grandiose) treatment when we go on to our final roll call.

Six gloved hands grip the flag-draped casket bearing one of their own. With ramrod posture and synchronized steps, the Marine Corps Body Bearers ceremoniously carry the Marine veteran to his final resting place. At the grave site, the body bearers stand perfectly still, holding the flag taut above the casket while the chaplain speaks, sometimes for more than an hour. Then silently the six Marines begin to fold the flag. Their slow, deliberate motion magnifies the honor and appreciation reflected in this final act for a fellow Marine.

This ceremony will be executed with the same degree of dignity and expertise more than five-hundred times a year by

Not As Lean, Not As Mean, Still a Marine!

the U.S. Marine Body Bearer Section. This small but vital group of Marines, called the "World Famous Body Bearers," is composed of sixteen Marines from one of the ceremonial drill companies at Marine Barracks 8th&I in Washington, D.C.

Their mission is to conduct funerals for Marines, Marine veterans, and Marine dependents at Arlington National Cemetery and other cemeteries in the Washington, D.C. area. They also are called upon to perform funerals for senators, members of Congress, heads of state and Presidents. They have earned their reputation and, as all Marines do, they set high standards and train hard to exceed them.

Funerals are just one of the duties assigned to the Body Bearer Section. It also is responsible for firing salutes with the 40mm cannons on the parade deck at 8th&I to render honors to visiting dignitaries and foreign military personnel. Every year on the Marine Corps Birthday, body bearers lay wreaths on the Arlington National Cemetery grave sites of former Commandants of the Marine Corps and former Sergeants Major of the Marine Corps. Between the funerals, cannon firing and wreath laying, the body bearers, who are all infantrymen, must maintain their military occupational specialty proficiency by attending classes and going to the field for training.

There are also occasionally some high profile assignment which put the unit in the public eye. In 2001 it participated in a two-day ceremony burying the remains of thirteen "Makin Island Raiders" of the 2nd Marine Raider Battalion who were killed during a raid on Butaritari Island in 1942. When Central Intelligence Agency agent and former Marine officer Mike Spann was killed in Afghanistan at the hands of pro-Taliban prisoners in late November 2001, the body bearers escorted his body in a full honors burial at. Also in 2001, the

207

body bearers traveled to New York City to participate in a memorial service for Sergeant Major Michael Curtin, USMCR (Ret), a member of the New York City Police Department who perished in the World Trade Center terrorist attack. Then in 2003 the unit provided the funeral detail for Felix de Weldon, the creator of the iconic Marine Corps War Memorial sculpture.

Every Marine is handpicked for body bearer duty because of the unusual standards which must be met. There are three initial criteria for candidates - they must be infantrymen, they must pass an initial strength test, and they must have a recommendation from their command. Once these are met, the command looks at the Marine's character. These young Marines shoulder an enormous responsibility to represent the Marine Corps in an atmosphere of respect and honor, and being able to maintain ceremonial composure is critical to their success.

Since body bearers must carry caskets ranging in weight from 350 to 700 pounds with precision, physical strength is critically important in performing their mission. The initial strength test requires that Marines bench press 225 pounds for ten repetitions, do a military press (behind-the-neck seated shoulder press with a barbell) of 135 pounds for ten repetitions, and do ten barbell curls with 115 pounds. These are the *minimum* strength requirements. Once the Marine passes the test, he is expected to continue to progress. There also is a height range requirement, between five-feet, eleven-inches and six-feet, two-inches, to enable the body bearers to carry the casket level.

Once a Marine has been accepted into the unit, he attends Body Bearer Ceremonial Drill School for four months. The training targets the three main aspects of being a body bearer - learning the proper techniques necessary to conduct a funeral, working as a team, and weight training. By the end of the third month, a new body bearer is ready to participate in funerals. Although the school lasts four months, the training never ends. The body bearers drill for fifteen hours a week in humble surroundings on the lower level of the Marine Barracks parking garage. Overhead, amber lights cast a dull glow on suspended industrial pipes. In a corner there is an assortment of caskets and a caisson used for practice. A wooden platform, which simulates the area around the grave site, is placed in the center amidst the parked cars.

During a funeral Marines often have to adjust to unexpected circumstances. They may need to navigate around a large gravestone, be wary of uneven surfaces around the grave site, or adjust to a flag that a funeral home has placed on the casket incorrectly. All six Marines must react to these anomalies in a heartbeat, often without commands. The training is designed to hone their situational awareness so they can inconspicuously adjust to these challenges while maintaining their military bearing.

Flag folding is a very precise and poignant procedure occurring at the end of the funeral ceremony, and it is a tedious and time-consuming task to learn because it requires many complicated movements which must be executed in tandem with the Marine on the opposite side of the flag. The slow, exaggerated movement must be fluid from the first fold to the final triangular-shaped flag that is presented to the next of kin.

Teamwork and dedication to drill are common among Marines, but the third aspect of body bearer training, intense weightlifting, is an additional requirement critical to the success of their mission. Unlike the other services that mostly use eight men, the Marine Corps always uses only six to bear the weight of a casket which can be as much as seven hundred pounds. Additionally, Marines honor the deceased by lifting the casket head-high, a move no other service does, which requires great strength. Consequently weightlifting is an integral part of these Marines' training, averaging ten hours a week.

The average body weight of a Marine body bearer is 230 pounds. This necessitates specially altered uniforms that are tailored to fit, yet flexible enough to allow for the range of motion necessary to lift the caskets. Marines must monitor their weight training to meet the strength requirements, but still present the smart appearance required of every Marine. Strength training is coupled with health and nutrition classes to help the body bearers achieve their weightlifting goals safely.

The Body Bearer unit is a professional group of Marines who honor fallen comrades with respect and dignity – and judging by the letters received from grateful families, the World Famous Marine Body Bearers do indeed uphold the Marine Corps traditions of honor and excellence. David S. Wininger penned the following words in appreciation to the body bearers who laid to rest his father-in-law, Robert K. Dore: "As former Marine myself, I cannot express the pride and honor I felt as the funeral procession pulled into the cemetery and the Body Bearer Detail came into view... I'm sure the last thing these Marines wanted to do on Christmas weekend was to stand in cold wind and bury an old man. Express to them that they gave this old Marine the greatest farewell he could have asked for."

TAKING CHANCE

Lieutenant Colonel Mike Strobl

"I do not approve of a word you say, but will defend to the death your right to say it." - Voltaire

Chance Phelps was wearing his Saint Christopher medal when he was killed on Good Friday. Eight days later, I handed the medallion to his mother. I didn't know Chance before he died. Today, I miss him.

Over a year ago, I volunteered to escort the remains of Marines killed in Iraq should the need arise. The military provides a uniformed escort for all casualties to ensure they are delivered safely to the next of kin and are treated with dignity and respect along the way.

Thankfully, I hadn't been called on to be an escort since Operation Iraqi Freedom began. The first few weeks of April, however, had been a tough month for the Marines. On the Monday after Easter I was reviewing Department of Defense press releases when I saw that a Private First Class Chance Phelps had been killed in action outside Baghdad. The press release listed his hometown - the same town I'm from. I notified our Battalion adjutant and told him that, should the duty to escort PFC Phelps fall to our Battalion, I would take him.

I didn't hear back the rest of Monday and all day Tuesday until 1800. The Battalion duty NCO called my cell phone and said I needed to be ready to leave for Dover Air Force Base at 1900 in order to escort the remains of PFC Phelps.

Before leaving for Dover I called the major who had the task of informing Phelps's parents of his death. The major

211

said the funeral was going to be in Dubois, Wyoming. It turned out that PFC Phelps had only lived in my hometown for his senior year of high school. I had never been to Wyoming, and had never heard of Dubois.

With two other escorts from Quantico, I got to Dover AFB at 2330 on Tuesday night. First thing on Wednesday we reported to the mortuary at the base. In the escort lounge there were about half a dozen Army soldiers and about an equal number of Marines waiting to meet up with "their" remains for departure. PFC Phelps was not ready, however, and I was told to come back on Thursday. Now, at Dover with nothing to do and a solemn mission ahead, I began to get depressed.

I was wondering about Chance Phelps. I didn't know anything about him - not even what he looked like. I wondered about his family, and what it would be like to meet them. I did pushups in my room until I couldn't do any more.

On Thursday morning I reported back to the mortuary. This time there was a new group of Army escorts, and a couple of the Marines who had been there on Wednesday. There was also an Air Force captain there to escort his brother home to San Diego.

We received a brief covering our duties, the proper handling of the remains, the procedures for draping a flag over a casket, and of course the paperwork attendant to our task. We were shown pictures of the shipping container and told that each one contained, in addition to the casket, a flag. I was given an extra flag, since Phelps's parents were divorced. This way they would each get one. I didn't like the idea of stuffing the flag into my luggage, but I couldn't see carrying a large flag, folded for presentation to the next of kin, through an airport while in my Alpha uniform. It barely fit into my suitcase.

Not As Lean, Not As Mean, Still a Marine!

It turned out that I was the last escort to leave on Thursday. This meant that I repeatedly got to participate in the small ceremonies that mark all departures from the Dover AFB mortuary.

Most of the remains are taken from Dover AFB by hearse to the airport in Philadelphia for air transport to their final destination. When the remains of a service member are loaded onto a hearse and ready to leave the Dover mortuary, there is an announcement made over the building's intercom system. With the announcement, all service members working at the mortuary, regardless of service branch, stop work and form up along the driveway to render a slow ceremonial salute as the hearse departs. Escorts also participated in each formation until it was their time to leave.

On this day there were some civilian workers doing construction on the mortuary grounds. As each hearse passed, they would stop working and place their hard hats over their hearts. This was my first sign that my mission with PFC Phelps was larger than the Marine Corps, and that his family and friends were not grieving alone.

Eventually I was the last escort remaining in the lounge. The Marine Master Gunnery Sergeant in charge of the Marine liaison there came to see me. He had Chance Phelps' personal effects. He removed each item - a large watch, a wooden cross with a lanyard, two loose dog tags, two dog tags on a chain, and a Saint Christopher medal on a silver chain. Although we had been briefed that we might be carrying some personal effects of the deceased, this set me aback. Holding his personal effects, I was starting to get to know Chance Phelps.

Finally we were ready. I grabbed my bags and went outside. I was somewhat startled when I saw the shipping container, loaded three-quarters of the way in to the back of

213

a black Chevy Suburban that had been modified to carry such cargo. This was the first time I saw my "cargo," and I was surprised at how large the shipping container was. The Master Gunnery Sergeant and I verified that the name on the container was Phelps' and then they pushed him the rest of the way in and we left. Now it was PFC Chance Phelps' turn to receive the military - and construction workers' - honors. He was finally moving towards home.

As I chatted with the driver on the hour-long trip to Philadelphia, it became clear that he considered it an honor to be able to contribute in getting Chance home. He offered his sympathy to the family. I was glad to finally be moving, yet apprehensive about what things would be like at the airport. I didn't want this package to be treated like ordinary cargo, yet I knew that the simple logistics of moving around a box this large would have to overrule my preferences.

When we got to the Northwest Airlines cargo terminal at the Philadelphia airport, the cargo handler and hearse driver pulled the shipping container onto a loading bay while I stood to the side and executed a slow salute. Once Chance was safely in the cargo area, and I was satisfied that he would be treated with due care and respect, the hearse driver drove me over to the passenger terminal and dropped me off.

As I walked up to the ticketing counter in my uniform, a Northwest employee started to ask me if I knew how to use the automated boarding pass dispenser. Before she could finish, another ticketing agent interrupted her. He told me to go straight to the counter, then explained to the woman that I was a military escort. She seemed embarrassed. The woman behind the counter already had tears in her eyes as I was pulling out my government travel voucher. She struggled to find words, but managed to express her sympathy for the family and thank me for my service. She also upgraded my

Not As Lean, Not As Mean, Still a Marine!

ticket to first class.

After clearing security, I was met by another Northwest Airline employee at the gate. She told me a representative from cargo would be up to take me down to the tarmac to observe the movement and loading of PFC Phelps. I hadn't really told any of them what my mission was, but they all knew.

When the man from the cargo crew met me, he too struggled for words. On the tarmac, he told me stories of his childhood as a military brat and repeatedly told me that he was sorry for my loss. I was starting to understand that, even here in Philadelphia, far away from Chance's hometown, people were mourning with his family.

On the tarmac, the cargo crew was silent except for occasional instructions to each other. I stood to the side and saluted as the conveyor moved Chance to the aircraft. I was relieved when he was finally settled into place. The rest of the bags were loaded, and I watched them shut the cargo bay door before heading back up to board the aircraft.

One of the pilots had taken my carry-on bag himself and had it stored next to the cockpit door so he could watch it while I was on the tarmac. As I boarded the plane, I could tell immediately that the flight attendants had already been informed of my mission. They seemed a little choked up as they led me to my seat.

About forty-five minutes into our flight I still hadn't spoken to anyone except to tell the first class flight attendant that I would prefer water. I was surprised when the flight attendant from the back of the plane suddenly appeared and leaned down to grab my hands. She said, "I want you to have this" as she pushed a small gold crucifix, with a relief of Jesus, into my hand. It was her lapel pin, and it looked somewhat worn. I suspected it had been hers for quite some time. That was the only thing she said to me the entire flight.

When we landed in Minneapolis, I was the first one off the plane. The pilot himself escorted me straight down the side stairs of the exit tunnel to the tarmac. The cargo crew there already knew what was on this plane. They were unloading some of the luggage when an Army sergeant, a fellow escort who had left Dover earlier that day, appeared next to me. His "cargo" was going to be loaded onto my plane for its continuing leg. We stood side-by-side in the dark and executed a slow salute as Chance was removed from the plane. The cargo crew at Minneapolis kept Phelps' shipping case separate from all the other luggage as they waited to take us to the cargo area. I waited with the soldier, and we saluted together as his fallen comrade was loaded onto the plane.

My trip with Chance was going to be somewhat unusual in that we were going to have an overnight stopover. We'd had a late start out of Dover, and there was just too much traveling ahead of us to continue on that day. We still had a flight from Minneapolis to Billings, Montana, then a five-hour drive to the funeral home, followed by a ninety-minute drive to Chance's hometown.

I was concerned about leaving him overnight in the Minneapolis cargo area. My ten-minute ride from the tarmac to the cargo holding area eased my apprehension. Just as in Philadelphia, the cargo guys in Minneapolis were extremely respectful and seemed honored to do their part. While talking with them, I learned that the cargo supervisor for Northwest Airlines at the Minneapolis airport is a Lieutenant Colonel in the Marine Corps Reserves. They called him for me and let me talk to him.

Once I was satisfied that all would be okay for the night, I asked one of the cargo crew if he would take me back to the terminal so that I could catch my hotel's shuttle. Instead, he drove me straight to the hotel himself. At the hotel, the Lieutenant Colonel called me and said he would personally pick me up in the morning and bring me back to the cargo area.

Before leaving the airport, I had told the cargo crew that I wanted to come back to the cargo area in the morning rather than go straight to the passenger terminal. I felt bad for leaving Chance overnight, and wanted to see the shipping container where I had left it for the night. It was fine.

The Lieutenant Colonel made a few phone calls, then drove me around to the passenger terminal. I was met again by a man from the cargo crew and escorted down to the tarmac. The pilot of the plane joined me as I waited for them to bring Chance from the cargo area. The pilot and I talked of his service in the Air Force, and how he missed it.

I saluted as Chance was moved up the conveyor and onto the plane. It was to be a while before the luggage was to be loaded, so the pilot took me up to board the plane where I could watch the tarmac from a window. With no other passengers yet on board, I talked with the flight attendants and one of the cargo guys. He had been in the Navy and one of the attendants had been in the Air Force. Everywhere I went, people were continuing to tell me their relationship to the military. After all the baggage was aboard I went back down to the tarmac, inspected the cargo bay, and watched them secure the door.

When we arrived at Billings, I was again the first off the plane. This time Chance's shipping container was the first item out of the cargo hold. The funeral director had driven five hours up from Riverton, Wyoming to meet us. He shook my hand as if I had personally lost a brother.

We moved Chance to a secluded cargo area. Now it was

time for me to remove the shipping container and drape the flag over the casket. I had predicted that this would choke me up, but I found I was more concerned with proper flag etiquette than the solemnity of the moment. Once the flag was in place, I stood by and saluted as Chance was loaded onto the van from the funeral home. I was thankful that we were in a small airport, and the event seemed to go mostly unnoticed. I picked up my rental car and followed Chance for five hours until we reached Riverton. During the long trip I imagined how my meeting with Chance's parents would go. I was very nervous about that.

When we finally arrived at the funeral home, I had my first face-to-face meeting with the Casualty Assistance Call Officer. It had been his duty to inform the family of Chance's death. He was on the Inspector/Instructor staff of an infantry company in Salt Lake City, Utah and I knew he'd had a difficult week.

Inside I gave the funeral director some of the paperwork from Dover and discussed the plan for the next day. The service was to be at 1400 in the high school gymnasium up in Dubois, population about nine hundred, some ninety miles away. Eventually, we had covered everything. The CACO had some items that the family wanted to be inserted into the casket, and I felt I needed to inspect Chance's uniform to ensure everything was proper. Although it was going to be a closed casket funeral, I still wanted to ensure his uniform was squared away.

Earlier in the day I wasn't sure how I'd handle this moment. Suddenly, the casket was open and I got my first look at Chance Phelps. His uniform was immaculate - a tribute to the professionalism of the Marines at Dover. I noticed that he wore six ribbons over his marksmanship badge - the senior one was his Purple Heart. I had been in the

218

Corps for over seventeen years, including a combat tour, and was wearing eight ribbons. This Private First Class, with less than a year in the Corps, had already earned six.

The next morning I wore my dress blues and followed the hearse for the trip up to Dubois. This was the most difficult leg of our trip for me. I was bracing for the moment when I would meet his parents, and hoped I would find the right words as I presented them with Chance's personal effects.

We got to the high school gym about four hours before the service was to begin. The gym floor was covered with folding chairs neatly lined in rows. There were a few townspeople making final preparations when I stood next to the hearse and saluted as Chance was moved out of the hearse. The sight of a flag-draped coffin was overwhelming to some of the ladies.

We moved Chance into the gym to the place of honor. A Marine sergeant, the command representative from Chance's battalion, met me at the gym. His eyes were watery as he relieved me of watching Chance so that I could go eat lunch and find my hotel.

At the restaurant, the table had a flier announcing Chance's service. Dubois High School gym - two o' clock. It also said that the family would be accepting donations so that they could buy flak vests to send to troops in Iraq.

I drove back to the gym at a quarter after one. I could've walked - you could walk to just about anywhere in Dubois in ten minutes. I had planned to find a quiet room where I could take his things out of their pouch and untangle the chain of the Saint Christopher medal from the dog tag chains and arrange everything before his parents came in. I had twice before removed the items from the pouch to ensure they were all there - even though there was no chance anything could've fallen out. Each time the two chains had been quite tangled, and I didn't want to be fumbling around trying to untangle them in front of his parents. Our meeting, however, didn't go as expected.

I practically bumped into Chance's step-mom accidentally, and our introductions began in the noisy hallway outside the gym. In short order I had met Chance's step-mom and father, followed by his step-dad and, at last, his mom. I didn't know how to express to these people my sympathy for their loss, and my gratitude for their sacrifice. Now, however, they were repeatedly thanking me for bringing their son home and for my service. I was humbled beyond words.

I told them that I had some of Chance's things and asked if we could try to find a quiet place. The five of us ended up in what appeared to be a computer lab - not what I had envisioned for this occasion.

After we had arranged five chairs around a small table, I told them about our trip. I told them how, at every step, Chance was treated with respect, dignity, and honor. I told them about the staff at Dover, and all the folks at Northwest Airlines. I tried to convey how the entire Nation, from Dover to Philadelphia, to Minneapolis, to Billings, and Riverton expressed grief and sympathy over their loss.

Finally, it was time to open the pouch. The first item I happened to pull out was Chance's large watch. It was still set to Baghdad time. Next were the lanyard and the wooden cross. Then the dog tags and the Saint Christopher medal. This time the chains were not tangled. Once all of his items were laid out on the table, I told his mom that I had one other item to give them. I retrieved the flight attendant's crucifix from my pocket and told its story. I set that on the table and excused myself. When I next saw Chance's mom, she was wearing the crucifix on her lapel.

Not As Lean, Not As Mean, Still a Marine!

By 1400 most of the seats on the gym floor were filled and people were finding seats in the fixed bleachers above. There were a surprising number of people in military uniform. Many Marines had come up from Salt Lake City. Men from various VFW posts and the Marine Corps League occupied multiple rows of folding chairs. We all stood as Chance's family took their seats in the front.

It turned out the Chance's sister, a Petty Officer in the Navy, worked for a Rear Admiral - the Chief of Naval Intelligence - at the Pentagon. The Admiral had brought many of the sailors on his staff with him to Dubois to pay respects to Chance and support his sister. After a few songs and some words from a Navy Chaplain, the Admiral took the microphone and told us how Chance had died.

Chance was an artillery cannoneer, and his unit was acting as provisional military police outside of Baghdad. Chance had volunteered to man a .50-caliber machine gun in the turret of the leading vehicle in a convoy. The convoy came under intense fire, but Chance stayed true to his post and returned fire with the big gun, covering the rest of the convoy, until he was fatally wounded.

Then the commander of the local VFW post read some of the letters Chance had written home. In letters to his mom he talked of the mosquitoes and the heat. In letters to his stepfather he told of the dangers of convoy operations and of receiving fire.

The service was a fitting tribute to this hero. When it was over, we stood as the casket was wheeled out with the family following. The casket was placed onto a horse-drawn carriage for the mile-long trip from the gym, down the main street, then up the steep hill to the cemetery. I stood alone and saluted as the carriage departed the high school. I found my car and joined Chance's convoy.

Not As Lean, Not As Mean, Still a Marine!

The town seemingly went from the gym to the street. All along the route, the people had lined the street and were waving small American flags. The flags that were otherwise posted were all at half-staff. For the last quarter mile up the hill, local boy scouts, spaced about twenty feet apart, all in uniform, held large flags. At the foot of the hill, I could look up and back and see the enormity of our procession. I wondered how many people would be at this funeral if it were in, say, Detroit or Los Angeles - probably not as many as were here in little Dubois, Wyoming.

The carriage stopped about fifteen yards from the grave and the military pall bearers and the family waited until the men of the VFW and Marine Corps league were formed up and schools buses had arrived carrying many of the people from the procession route. Once the entire crowd was in place, the pallbearers came to attention and began to remove the casket from the caisson. As I had done all week, I came to attention and executed a slow ceremonial salute as Chance was being transferred from one mode of transport to another.

From Dover to Philadelphia, Philadelphia to Minneapolis, Minneapolis to Billings, Billings to Riverton, and Riverton to Dubois we had been together. Now, as I watched them carry him the final fifteen yards, I was choking up. I felt that, as long as he was still moving, he was somehow still alive.

Then they put him down above his grave. He had stopped moving.

Although my mission had been officially complete once I turned him over to the funeral director at the Billings airport, it was his placement at his grave that really concluded it in my mind. Now he was home to stay, and I suddenly felt at once sad, relieved, and useless.

The chaplain said some words that I couldn't hear, and two Marines removed the flag from the casket and slowly folded it for presentation to his mother. When the ceremony was over, Chance's father placed a ribbon from his service in Vietnam on Chance's casket. His mother approached the casket and took something from her blouse and put it on the casket. I later saw that it was the flight attendant's crucifix. Eventually, friends of Chance's moved closer to the grave. A young man put a can of Copenhagen on the casket, and many others left flowers.

Finally, we all went back to the gym for a reception. There was enough food to feed the entire population for a few days. In one corner of the gym there was a table set up with lots of pictures of Chance and some of his sports awards. People were continually approaching me and the other Marines to thank us for our service. Almost all of them had some story to tell about their connection to the military. About an hour into the reception, I had the impression that every man in Wyoming had, at one time or another, been in the service.

It seemed like every time I saw Chance's mom she was hugging a different well wisher. As time passed, I began to hear people laughing. We were starting to heal.

After a few hours at the gym, I went back to the hotel to change out of my dress blues. The local VFW post had invited everyone over to "celebrate Chance's life." The Post was on the other end of town from my hotel, and the drive took less than two minutes. The crowd was somewhat smaller than what had been at the gym, but the Post was packed.

Marines were playing pool at the two tables near the entrance and most of the VFW members were at the bar or around the tables in the bar area. The largest room in the Post was a banquet/dinning/dancing area and it was now called "The Chance Phelps Room." Above the entry were two items - a large portrait of Chance in his dress blues, and the

223

Eagle, Globe, & Anchor. In one corner of the room there was another memorial to Chance. There were candles burning around another picture of him in his blues. On the table surrounding his photo were his Purple Heart citation and his Purple Heart medal. There was also a framed copy of an excerpt from the Congressional Record. This was an eloquent tribute to Chance Phelps delivered on the floor of the United States House of Representatives by Congressman Scott McInnis of Colorado. Above it all was a television that was playing a photo montage of Chance's life from small boy to proud Marine.

I did not buy a drink that night. As had been happening all day, indeed all week, people were thanking me for my service and for bringing Chance home. Now, in addition to words and handshakes, they were thanking me with beer. I fell in with the men who had handled the horses and horse-drawn carriage. I learned that they had worked through the night to groom and prepare the horses for Chance's last ride. They were all very grateful that they were able to contribute.

After a while we all gathered in the Chance Phelps Room for the formal dedication. The Post commander told us of how Chance had been so looking forward to becoming a Life Member of the VFW. Now, in the Chance Phelps Room of the Dubois, Wyoming post, he would be an *eternal* member. We all raised our beers and the Chance Phelps Room was christened.

Later, as I was walking toward the pool tables, a Staff Sergeant form the Reserve unit in Salt Lake grabbed me and said, "Sir, you gotta hear this." here were two other Marines with him and he told the younger one, a Lance Corporal, to tell me his story. The Staff Sergeant said the Lance Corporal was normally too shy and modest to tell it, but now he'd had enough beer to overcome his usual tendencies.

Not As Lean, Not As Mean, Still a Marine!

As the Lance Corporal started to talk, an older man joined our circle. He wore a baseball cap that indicated he had been with the 1st Marine Division in Korea. Earlier in the evening he had told me about one of his former commanding officers - a Colonel named Puller.

So, there I was, standing in a circle with three Marines recently returned from fighting with the 1st Marine Division in Iraq and one not so recently returned from fighting with the 1st Marine Division in Korea. I, who had fought with the 1st Marine Division in Kuwait, was about to gain a new insight into our Corps.

The young Lance Corporal began to tell us his story. At that moment, in this circle of current and former Marines, the differences in our ages and ranks dissipated - we were all simply Marines.

His squad had been on a patrol through a city street. They had taken small arms fire and had literally dodged an RPG round that sailed between two Marines. At one point they received fire from behind a wall and had neutralized the sniper with a SMAW round. The back blast of the SMAW, however, kicked up a substantial rock that hammered the Lance Corporal in the thigh, and only missed his groin because he had reflexively turned his body sideways at the shot.

Their squad had suffered some wounded and was receiving more sniper fire when suddenly he was hit in the head by an AK-47 round. I was stunned as he told us how he felt like a baseball bat had been slammed into his head. He had spun around and fell unconscious. When he came to he had a severe scalp wound, but his Kevlar helmet had saved his life. He continued with his unit for a few days before realizing he was suffering the effects of a severe concussion.

As I stood there in the circle with the old man and the

other Marines, the Staff Sergeant finished the story. He told of how this Lance Corporal had begged and pleaded with the Battalion surgeon to let him stay with his unit. In the end, the doctor said there was just no way - he had suffered a severe and traumatic head wound and would have to be medevaced.

The Marine Corps is a special fraternity. There are moments when we are reminded of this. Interestingly, those moments don't always happen at awards ceremonies or in dress blues at Birthday Balls. I have found, rather, that they occur at unexpected times and places - next to a loaded moving van at Camp Lejeune's base housing, in a dirty CP tent in northern Saudi Arabia, and in a smoky VFW post in western Wyoming.

After the story was done, the Lance Corporal stepped over to the old man, put his arm over the man's shoulder and told him that he, the Korean War vet, was his hero. The two of them stood there with their arms over each other's shoulders and we were all silent for a moment. When they let go, I told the Lance Corporal that there were recruits down on the yellow footprints tonight that would soon be learning his story.

I was finished drinking beer and telling stories. I found Chance's father and shook his hand one more time. Chance's mom had already left, and I deeply regretted not being able to tell her goodbye.

I left Dubois in the morning before sunrise for my long drive back to Billings. It had been my honor to take Chance Phelps to his final post. Now he was on the high ground overlooking his town.

I miss him.

Taking Chance was made into an award-winning 2009 HBO movie starring Kevin Bacon.

BURIAL AT SEA

Lieutenant Colonel George Goodson

"You will never know how much it has cost my generation to preserve your freedom. I hope you will use it wisely." – John Adams

In my seventy-sixth year, the events of my life appear to me, from time to time, as a series of vignettes. Some were significant. Most were trivial.

War is the seminal event in the life of everyone who has endured it. Though I fought in Korea and the Dominican Republic and was wounded there, Vietnam was my war.

Now thirty-seven years have passed, and thankfully I rarely think of those days in Cambodia, Laos, and the panhandle of North Vietnam where small teams of Americans and Montangards fought much larger elements of the North Vietnamese Army. Instead I see vignettes - some exotic, some mundane:

- The smell of Nuc Mam.

- The heat, dust, and humidity.

- The blue exhaust of 'cyclos' clogging the streets.

- Elephants moving silently through the tall grass.

- Hard eyes behind the servile smiles of the villagers.

- Standing on a mountain in Laos and hearing a tiger roar.

- A young girl squeezing my hand as my medic delivered her baby.

- The flowing Ao Dais of the young women biking down Tran Hung Dao.

- My two years as Casualty Notification Officer in North Carolina, Virginia, and Maryland.

It was late 1967. I had just returned after eighteen months in Vietnam. Casualties were increasing. I moved my family from Indianapolis to Norfolk, rented a house, enrolled my children in their fifth or sixth new school, and bought a second car.

A week later, I put on my uniform and drove ten miles to Little Creek, Virginia. I hesitated before entering my new office. Appearance is important to career Marines. I was no longer, if ever, a poster Marine, and I had returned from my third tour in Vietnam only thirty days before. At 5'9," I now weighed one hundred and twenty-eight pounds, which was thirty-seven pounds below my normal weight. My uniforms fit ludicrously, my skin was yellow from malaria medication, and I think I had a twitch or two.

I straightened my shoulders, walked into the office, looked at the nameplate on the Staff Sergeant's desk and said, "Sergeant Jolly, I'm Lieutenant Colonel Goodson. Here are my orders and my Qualification Jacket."

Sergeant Jolly stood, looked carefully at me, took my orders, stuck out his hand and as we shook said, "How long were you there, Colonel?" I replied "Eighteen months this time. "Jolly breathed, "Jesus, you must be a slow learner Colonel." I smiled.

Jolly said, "Colonel, I'll show you to your office and bring in the Sergeant Major. I said, "No, let's just go straight to his office." Jolly nodded, hesitated, and lowered his voice, "Colonel, the Sergeant Major. He's been in this Goddamn job two years. He's packed pretty tight. I'm worried about him." I nodded.

Jolly escorted me into the Sergeant Major's office. "Sergeant Major, this is Colonel Goodson, the new Commanding Office. The Sergeant Major stood, extended his hand and said, "Good to see you again, Colonel." I responded, "Hello Walt, how are you?" Jolly looked at me, raised an eyebrow, walked out, and closed the door.

I sat down with the Sergeant Major. We had the obligatory cup of coffee and talked about mutual acquaintances. Walt's stress was palpable. Finally, I said, "Walt, what's the hell's wrong?" He turned his chair, looked out the window and said, "George, you're going to wish you were back in Nam before you leave here. I've been in the Marine Corps since 1939. I was in the Pacific thirty-six months, Korea for fourteen months, and Vietnam for twelve months. Now I come here to bury these kids. I'm putting my letter in. I can't take it anymore." I said, "Okay, Walt. If that's what you want, I'll endorse your request for retirement and do what I can to push it through Headquarters Marine Corps."

Sergeant Major Walt retired twelve weeks later. He had been a good Marine for twenty-eight years, but he had seen too much death and too much suffering. He was used up.

Over the next sixteen months, I made twenty-eight death notifications, conducted twenty-eight military funerals, and made thirty notifications to the families of Marines that were severely wounded or missing in action. Most of the details of those casualty notifications have now, thankfully, faded from memory. Four, however, remain.

My third or fourth day in Norfolk, I was notified of the death of a nineteen-year-old Marine. This notification came by telephone from Headquarters Marine Corps. The information detailed:

- Name, rank, and serial number.

- Name, address, and phone number of next of kin.

- Date of and limited details about the Marine's death.

- Approximate date the body would arrive at the Norfolk Naval Air Station.

- A strong recommendation on whether the casket should be open or closed.

The boy's family lived over the border in North Carolina, about sixty miles away. I drove there in a Marine Corps staff car. Crossing the state line into North Carolina, I stopped at a small country store/service station/post office and went in to ask directions.

Three people were in the store. A man and woman approached the small Post Office window. The man held a package. The storeowner walked up and addressed them by name, "Hello John. Good morning Mrs. Cooper."

I was stunned. My casualty's next-of-kin's name was John Cooper!

I hesitated, then stepped forward and said, "I beg your pardon. Are you Mr. and Mrs. John Copper of (address)?"

The father looked at me - I was in uniform - and then, shaking, bent at the waist, and vomited. His wife looked horrified at him and then at me. Understanding came into her eyes, and she collapsed in slow motion. I think I caught her before she hit the floor.

The owner took a bottle of whiskey out of a drawer and handed it to Mr. Cooper, who drank. I answered their questions for a few minutes. Then I drove them home in my staff car. The storeowner locked the store and followed in the Cooper's truck. We stayed an hour or so until the family began arriving.

I returned the storeowner to his business. He thanked me and said, "Mister, I wouldn't have your job for a million dollars." I shook his hand and said, "Neither would I."

I vaguely remember the drive back to Norfolk. Violating about five Marine Corps regulations, I drove the staff car straight to my house. I sat with my family while they ate dinner, went into the den, closed the door, and sat there all night, alone.

My Marines steered clear of me for days. I had made my first death notification.

Weeks passed with more notifications and more funerals. I borrowed Marines from the local Marine Corps Reserve and taught them to conduct a military funeral - how to carry a casket, how to fire the volleys, and how to fold the flag.

When I presented the flag to the mother, wife, or father, I always said, "All Marines share in your grief." I had been instructed to say, "On behalf of a grateful nation," but I didn't think the nation was grateful, so I didn't say that.

Sometimes my emotions got the best of me and I couldn't speak. When that happened, I just handed them the flag and touched a shoulder. They would look at me and nod. Once a mother said to me, "I'm so sorry you have this terrible job." My eyes filled with tears and I leaned over and kissed her.

Six weeks after my first notification, I had another. This was a young PFC. I drove to his mother's house. As always, I was in uniform and driving a Marine Corps staff car. I parked in front of the house, took a deep breath, and walked towards the house. Suddenly the door flew open, and a middle-aged woman rushed out. She looked at me and ran across the yard, screaming "NO! NO! NO! NO!"

I hesitated. Neighbors came out. I ran to her, grabbed her, and whispered stupid things to reassure her. She collapsed. I picked her up and carried her into the house. Eight or nine neighbors followed. Ten or fifteen minutes later, the father came in followed by ambulance personnel. I have no recollection of leaving.

The funeral took place about two weeks later. We went through the drill. The mother never looked at me. The father looked at me once and shook his head sadly.

One morning, as I walked in the office, the phone was ringing. Sergeant Jolly held the phone up and said, "You've got another one, Colonel." I nodded, walked into my office, picked up the phone, took notes, thanked the officer making the call - I have no idea why - and hung up. Jolly, who had listened, came in with a special Telephone Directory that translates telephone numbers into the person's address and place of employment.

The father of this casualty was a Longshoreman. He lived a mile from my office. I called the Longshoreman's Union Office and asked for the Business Manager. He answered the phone, I told him who I was, and asked for the father's schedule.

The Business Manager asked, "Is it his son?" I said nothing. After a moment, he said, in a low voice, "Tom is at home today." I said, "Don't call him. I'll take care of that." The Business Manager said, "Aye, Aye Sir," and then explained, "Tom and I were Marines in WWII."

I got in my staff car and drove to the house. I was in uniform. I knocked, and a woman in her early forties answered the door. I saw instantly that she was clueless. I asked, "Is Mr. Smith home?" She smiled pleasantly and responded, "Yes, but he's eating breakfast now. Can you come back later?" I said, "I'm sorry. It's important, I need to see him now."

She nodded, stepped back into the beach house and said,

"Tom, it's for you."

A moment later a ruddy man in his late forties appeared at the door. He looked at me, turned absolutely pale, steadied himself, and said, "Jesus Christ man, he's only been there three weeks!"

Months passed. More notifications and more funerals. Then one day while I was running, Sergeant Jolly stepped outside the building and gave a loud whistle, two fingers in his mouth - I never could do that - and held an imaginary phone to his ear.

Another call from Headquarters Marine Corps. I took notes, said, "Got it," and hung up. I had stopped saying "Thank You" long ago.

Jolly asked, "Where?"

"Eastern Shore of Maryland. The father is a retired Chief Petty Officer. His brother will accompany the body back from Vietnam."

Jolly shook his head slowly, straightened, and then said, "This time of day, it'll take three hours to get there and back. I'll call the Naval Air Station and borrow a helicopter. And I'll have Captain Tolliver get one of his men to meet you and drive you to the Chief's home."

He did, and forty minutes later I was knocking on the father's door. He opened the door, looked at me, then looked at the Marine standing at parade rest beside the car, and asked, "Which one of my boys was it, Colonel?"

I stayed a couple of hours, gave him all the information, including my office and home phone number, and told him to call me anytime.

He called me that evening at about 11:00 PM. "I've gone through my boy's papers and found his will. He asked to be buried at sea. Can you make that happen?" I said, "Yes I can Chief. I can, and I will."

My wife, who had been listening, said, "Can you do that?" I told her, "I have no idea. But I'm going to break my ass trying."

I called Lieutenant General Alpha Bowser, Commanding General, Fleet Marine Force Atlantic, at home to explain the situation, and asked, "General, can you get me a quick appointment with the Admiral at Atlantic Fleet Headquarters?" General Bowser said, "George, you be there tomorrow at 0900. He will see you."

I was, and the Admiral did. He said coldly, "How can the Navy help the Marine Corps, Colonel." I told him the story. He turned to his Chief of Staff and said, "Which is the sharpest destroyer in port?" The Chief of Staff responded with a name.

The Admiral called the ship, "Captain, you're going to do a burial at sea. You'll report to a Marine Lieutenant Colonel named Goodson until this mission is completed."

He hung up, looked at me, and said, "The next time you need a ship, Colonel, call me. You don't have to sic Al Bowser on my ass." I responded, "Aye Aye, Sir" and got the hell out of his office.

I went to the ship and met with the Captain, Executive Officer, and the Senior Chief. Sergeant Jolly and I trained the ship's crew for four days. Then Jolly raised a question none of us had thought of. He said, "These government caskets are air tight. How do we keep it from floating?"

All the high-priced help including me sat there looking dumb. Then the Senior Chief stood and said, "Come on Jolly. I know a bar where the retired guys from World War II hang out."

They returned a couple of hours later, slightly the worse for wear, and said, "It's simple. We cut four twelve-inch holes in the outer shell of the casket on each side, and insert

234

three hundred pounds of lead in the foot end of the casket. We can handle that, no sweat."

The day arrived. The ship and the sailors looked razor sharp. General Bowser, the Admiral, a U.S. Senator, and a Navy Band were on board. The sealed casket was brought aboard and taken below for modification. The ship got underway to the twelve-fathom depth.

The sun was hot. The ocean flat. The casket was brought aft and placed on a catafalque. The Chaplin spoke. The volleys were fired. The flag was removed, folded, and I gave it to the father. The band played "Eternal Father Strong to Save." The casket was raised slightly at the head, and it slid into the sea.

The heavy casket plunged straight down about six feet. The incoming water collided with the air pockets in the outer shell. The casket stopped abruptly, rose straight out of the water about three feet, stopped, and slowly slipped back into the sea. The air bubbles rising from the sinking casket sparkled in the in the sunlight as the casket disappeared from sight forever.

The next morning I called a personal friend, Lieutenant General Oscar Peatross, at Headquarters Marine Corps and said, "General, get me the fuck out of here. I can't take this shit anymore." I was transferred two weeks later.

I was a good Marine, but after seventeen years I had seen too much death and too much suffering. I was used up.

Vacating the house, my family and I drove to the office in a two-car convoy. I said my goodbyes. Sergeant Jolly walked out with me. He waved at my family, looked at me with tears in his eyes, came to attention, saluted, and said, "Well Done, Colonel. Well Done."

I felt as if I had received the Medal of Honor!

THE PROTESTER

"When you men get home and face an anti-war protester, look him in the eyes and shake his hand. Then, wink at his girlfriend, because she knows she's dating a pussy."
- Attributed to General Tommy Franks

I never cease to be amazed by the hypocrisy of "anti-war protesters" in this country. They claim to abhor violence and call themselves pacifists, yet they are usually the first ones to become confrontational. And I say that from personal experience.

During the 2004 Presidential race I was across the street from a rally being held in St. Petersburg, Florida for the Democratic candidate with a friend of mine who happens to be a decorated veteran of the Vietnam War. The friend, Wayne Ridgley, had served three tours of duty in Southeast Asia and had, ironically, received the exact same decorations as John Kerry - a Silver Star, a Bronze Star, and three Purple Hearts. In the process, he had also lost one of his legs.

Wayne was very vocal in his dislike of Senator Kerry, mainly due to the candidate's less than truthful testimony about atrocities supposedly committed in Vietnam, so it wasn't long before he had gotten into an argument with one of the union "goons" on the other side of the low chain link fence which separated our two groups. Now, I personally think a bit of discourse is healthy for our democracy - but when the union guys began pointing at Wayne's USMC ballcap and calling him a "baby killer" I began getting a bit agitated myself.

That's when things got out of hand. One of the "union activists" reached across the fence and shoved Wayne in an

236

attempt to knock him down (I know that was his intent because Wayne was wearing shorts, and you could clearly see that he had a prosthetic leg and was therefore unstable). I had seen enough by that point, so I reached out and slapped a Kerry sign out of the guy's hand and asked if he'd like to try that with someone who has *two* legs. He flipped out and started climbing over the fence, and as I prepared for his arrival on my side some of his union cohorts realized what was about to happen to their buddy and held him back. You can imagine my disappointment!

I think the truth of the matter is most of the so-called "conscientious objectors" out there don't so much object to the idea of killing another human being, as they do to putting themselves in a situation where they *themselves* could get killed. Why not just be honest and say "I'm scared," instead of pretending to have lofty ideals? Just be honest!

And that incident in St. Pete was certainly not the only time I found myself in such a situation. In October of 2003 I was in Washington, D.C. on the weekend the Marine Corps Marathon was to be run. Prior to making the trip I had made plans to have dinner with the parents of a friend who had been killed in a helicopter accident at Camp Pendleton a couple of years earlier. As I drove along the Capitol Mall I came upon a police roadblock, and was diverted down a side street. As I made the turn I looked further up the Mall and saw the reason - there were thousands of people marching down the street. Upon closer inspection I saw that many of them were wearing tie-dyed clothes and looked like, for lack of a better word, hippies. It was as if I was caught in a time warp!

They were, of course, there to protest the war in Iraq. One fellow was standing on a corner handing out signs that said "impeach now" and "liar," and when he offered me one I reflexively asked if the signs were left over from the Clinton years. He didn't appreciate my humor, and I thought the guy was going to throw down with me then and there - but I guess he thought better of it when he noticed the USMC pin on my lapel.

I then turned my attention to the marchers. It was quite a show. As one particularly odd group went by I couldn't help but shake my head in amusement, and it didn't go unnoticed. One of the protesters, who was carrying a large "peace" symbol on a long pole, apparently took exception to my body language and shouted, "What the f**k are you looking at, a**hole?" over his shoulder.

I looked back at him and replied, in all honesty, "That's what *I'm* trying to figure out!"

Well, you would have thought I had insulted his mother or something. The fellow thought for a second, and then responded with a brilliantly phrased verbal onslaught which had obviously been painstakingly planned and rehearsed over the course of many months for just such a moment as this. He said, "F**k you!"

Not to be outdone, I fired back with the equally eloquent, "F**k *with* me, dirtbag!"

That is when the *fit*, as they say, hit the *shan*. The "peace activist" threw his sign to the ground (remember, it was a "peace" symbol), turned, and charged directly at me with blood in his eye. I have to admit I was a bit surprised by this, and as I spun on my heel to face the charging peacenik I had all of three seconds to consider my options. I could run (which is never really an option for a Marine), negotiate (in three seconds?), or fight. All in all, not really a tough call.

I didn't want to hurt the guy. Really. But I also didn't want to ruin the nice suit I was wearing. Just as he reached me my subconscious took over, and I flashed back to a time twenty years earlier when I had been a sergeant at 1st Recon Battalion and had taken a few judo lessons from a lieutenant named Hideo Sato, who was a black belt. I had the dubious distinction of being probably the worst student he ever taught, but Lieutenant Sato would have been proud of me on this day. I stepped in just as my opponent reached me and executed a textbook right hip throw, and the fellow landed on the pavement with a heavy thud - with his head (fortunately) just missing the curb.

I heard a "whoosh" as the air was expelled from his lungs, and even though he was momentarily neutralized I prepared myself to "repel boarders" in the event the suddenly "inactive activist" was to get up and foolishly continue what he had started. Just then I noticed there were half a dozen police motorcycles parked in a nearby intersection to block it off, and as several of the cops were sprinting in my direction. I thought to myself, "That's just great - I'm going to get arrested!"

When the police officers reached us the one closest to me looked down at my assailant, who by now was struggling to get up, and put his hands on his hips. He then turned to me and, instead of reading me my rights, said, "Would you like to press charges, sir? We had a front row seat for the whole thing, and this guy was clearly the aggressor."

I looked at the protester, who by now had managed to get himself into a sitting position, and let the possibility of his going to jail sink in for a few moments. Then I replied to the officer, "Nah, this guy already has *enough* problems, and I believe in taking pity on *stupid* people."

The cops then indicated that I could go, and as I stepped off the officer who had been doing the talking stopped me, looked at the Marine Corps pin on lapel of my suit jacket, and quietly said, "Semper Fi, Devil Dog."

FLY THE FRIENDLY SKIES

"If man was meant to fly we would have been born with wings – and a parachute!"

Whenever someone finds out I made a couple of hundred parachute jumps during my time in the Marine Corps, the typical reaction is, "Oh, my, that sounds awfully dangerous. You'd never catch *me* doing that!" It's all I can do to keep from laughing. Granted, throwing oneself from a perfectly good airplane is not a natural act, and yes, it can be quite exhilarating... and of course there *is* the occasional unfortunate accident... but all-in-all the idea of jumping scares me far less than many other things. Take driving for instance. Have you *seen* some of the people out on the roads these days? It's downright frightening! And almost as frightening is the prospect of taking off and landing in some of those "perfectly good" airplanes mentioned earlier. Think about it for a second. You are entrusting your life to a pilot you have never even *met!* And odds are the aircraft's maintenance has been performed by a high school dropout whose uncle got him into the union in exchange for a kickback to the shop steward. Not too encouraging, is it?

In all fairness though, the safety record of U.S. flag airlines is pretty good - although not perfect. I am reminded of the autistic character played by Dustin Hoffman in the film *Rainman*, who will only fly on Qantas Airlines because they have never had an accident resulting in a fatality. Unfortunately, the Aussies don't fly to all destinations, and for that matter neither do U.S. airlines. It is therefore occasionally necessary to fly on foreign flag carriers, which can sometimes be quite an adventure.

My first experience with third world airlines came when I was traveling from Camp Lejeune to my first Embassy posting in the Republic of the Congo. I had been warned by those in the know to avoid flying Air Afriqué at all costs, and I made it a point to specifically request a ticket on one of the two other airlines serving Brazzaville, namely SwissAir and Sabena. Naturally, my request was ignored. When I changed planes at Charles De Gaulle Airport for the flight from Paris to Southwest Africa I was greeted by the ugliest puke green jet I had ever seen, and knew immediately it was going to be a long, long flight.

The thing about that flight which sticks out most clearly in my mind was the food they served. I remember we had a choice between fish, and something else which I could not identify. The fish smelled like it had been rotting in the sun for a week, and the other choice looked like a piece of roadkill. I declined both.

As if the menu wasn't bad enough we had not one, but two, stops enroute - in places not known for their amenities. The first, N'djamena, Chad, was a charming example of North African hospitality. From the air the place looked like nothing more than a collection of poorly constructed mud huts, and the desert stretched in all direction for as far as I could see. When we landed our aircraft was immediately surrounded by a hoarde of AK-47 toting troops, and for a time it looked as if we were going to be boarded. After a tense hour or so in the middle of the runway we finally deplaned a few people, took on a couple of passengers, and departed. The next stop was Bangui, capitol of the Central African Republic - a world class sh*thole to be sure, but a lush tropical paradise in comparison to N'Djamena. From there it was on to Brazzaville.

Not As Lean, Not As Mean, Still a Marine!

Our flight finally arrived in the Congo late in the evening, and although I was initially glad to finally be in Brazzaville and at journey's end, that soon changed. They packed us onto a bus for the trip from the plane to the terminal (there were no jetways), and I got my first real taste of "olfactory overload." That is what happens when one's sense of smell is overwhelmed by a particularly repugnant odor - in this case a busload of people who think good personal hygiene means bathing once a month (whether they need it or not). I fought to get a window open, but to no avail.

Upon arriving at the terminal (by this time it was the middle of the night) I discovered it was the custom in that part of the world to pay the AK-47 toting customs official a bribe in order to get your passport stamped. At least that's what I found out once the "expediter" arrived from the Embassy and translated for me. It was a harbinger of things to come for the next two years.

A few months later I was traveling on an Air Cameroon flight from Nairobi, Kenya back to Brazzaville, with a stopover in Bujumbura, Burundi. I expected it to be pretty much like any other flight - right up until the moment one of the other passengers tied the leash of his goat to the armrest of my seat. That's right... I said GOAT. I asked what the heck was going on, and was politely informed that passengers were allowed to travel with a domesticated animal in lieu of a piece of carry-on baggage. "How cosmopolitan," I thought to myself.

When it came time to eat, the flight attendant came around with a tray of sandwiches from which we could choose. To say they were unappetizing would be a gross understatement. The sandwiches they served were reminiscent of a scene from *The Odd Couple*, where Oscar's friends are rummaging through his refrigerator during their weekly poker game and

Not As Lean, Not As Mean, Still a Marine!

discover there is a choice between brown sandwiches and green sandwiches. When asked to identify the green sandwiches, Oscar tells them they are either "very new cheese, or very old meat." Naturally, they select the brown ones - and I did the same. I ended up feeding it to the goat. Then came our stop in Burundi. We picked up a few passengers, which is not unusual. What *was* unusual was the cargo we took on. It was an SUV. When the plane began to rock violently back and forth I peeked through a crack in the bulkhead and saw that they had actually opened the side of the airplane to put it in. The allotted space was just large enough to hold the vehicle, and several laborers in loincloths were trying to slide it in sideways by picking up first one end, and then the other, over and over. The weight distribution was enough to make the loadmaster on a C-130 cringe. I wasn't too confident about the airworthiness of the plane at this point, but just as I was contemplating getting off and making my way back to the Congo through the jungle (and the warring Hutu and Tutsi tribes) we buttoned up and took off. For the remainder of the trip, I drank heavily.

When I finally completed my tour in the Congo I was in a position to make my *own* reservations, and my trip out was a darn sight better than the trip in on Air Afriqué. I was given a seat in first class by my friend Francois, the local representative for the Belgian airline, Sabena. To this day it remains the only time I have flown in a class other than cattle car economy, and I was determined to enjoy it. As I sat back in my plush, oversized seat and sipped a celebratory glass of champagne it suddenly occurred to me that even though there was no goat tied to my seat and the brown and green sandwiches of Air Cameroon had been replaced with fine Continental cuisine, there was still the possibility that we could end up in a twisted mass of wreckage...

BEN STEIN GETS IT!

"A real star... is the U.S. Marine in Baghdad who saw a little girl playing with a piece of unexploded ordnance on a street... He pushed her aside and threw himself on it just as it exploded." – Ben Stein

For many years Ben Stein wrote a biweekly column for an online website called "Monday Night at Morton's," in which he told glitzy, if irrelevant, tales of the Hollywood elite who were out on the town. He has recently had a change of heart about whom he considers a "star," and it is quite refreshing. Here is his final column.

I no longer think Hollywood stars are terribly important. They are uniformly pleasant, friendly people, and they treat me better than I deserve to be treated. But a man or woman who makes a huge wage for memorizing lines and reciting them in front of a camera is no longer my idea of a shining star we should all look up to.

How can a man or woman who makes an eight-figure wage and lives in insane luxury really be a star in today's world, if by a "star" we mean someone bright and powerful and attractive as a role model? Real stars are not riding around in the backs of limousines or in Porsches or getting trained in yoga or Pilates and eating only raw fruit while they have Vietnamese girls do their nails. They can be interesting, nice people, but they are not heroes to me any longer.

A real star, the kind who haunts my memory night and day, is the U.S. Marine in Baghdad who saw a little girl playing with a piece of unexploded ordnance on a street near where he was guarding a station. He pushed her aside and threw himself on it just as it exploded. He left a family desolate in California, and a little girl alive in Baghdad.

The stars who deserve media attention are not the ones who have lavish weddings on TV, but the ones who patrol the streets of Mosul even after two of their buddies were murdered and their bodies battered and stripped for the sin of trying to protect Iraqis from terrorists. Yet we put couples with incomes of a hundred million a year on the covers of our magazines.

The noncoms and officers who barely scrape by on military pay, but stand guard in Afghanistan and Iraq and on ships and in submarines and near the Arctic Circle, are anonymous as they live and die.

I am no longer comfortable being a part of the system that has such poor values, and I do not want to perpetuate those values by pretending that who is eating at Morton's is a big subject. There are plenty of other stars in the American firmament... the policemen who go off on patrol in South Central and have no idea if they will return alive, the orderlies and paramedics who bring in people who have been in terrible accidents and prepare them for surgery, the teachers and nurses who throw their whole spirits into caring for autistic children, the kind men and women who work in hospices and in cancer wards. Think of each and every fireman who was running up the stairs at the World Trade Center as the towers began to collapse.

Now you have my idea of a real hero.

PISS AND VINEGAR

"Genuine empathy reaps untold rewards."
– Major H. G. "Dunk" Duncan

General Carl Mundy was the Commandant of the Marine Corps from '91 to '95. His son, to whom he sent the following quotes, is an infantry battalion commander in Iraq. One of the Marines the now retired General visited in the hospital said that he was a "Magnificent Bastard" (for the benefit of the uninitiated, that is the 2nd Battalion of the 4th Marine Regiment), and the attitudes described below are indeed magnificent. They make a mockery of the words that emanate from Capitol Hill and elsewhere. These Marines all reflect the same selfless attitude. They are amazed at the attention that they receive, and are more concerned with having left their fellow Marines behind than the extent of their own injuries. They are magnificent - bastards or not!

General Mundy wrote his son, "I spent part of today visiting some piss and vinegar young Marines on the wards at Bethesda Naval Hospital."

One said to him, "What the hell, Sir... it's only a leg!"

Another commented, "The RPG blew off both my arms, and my Mom here has the bungy cord they tied off one of them with, because the corporal in the back seat of the Humvee couldn't find the first aid kit after the RPG hit. I kept yelling at him that I couldn't fire my SAW with my goddamned hands blown off! Do you think I'll be able to stay in the Corps with two artificial arms?"

A third said, "I'd have shot that low-life son-of-a-bitch if the blood hadn't been running down in my eyes."

And when a fourth was asked, "What outfit were you in?" he replied, "Sir, I'm a Magnificent Bastard," as he struggled to climb from his hospital bed.

General Mundy put up a hand and said, "Lie back down, Marine. I'm just here to say hello."

The Marine continued to get up, saying, "I know Sir, but I'm a Marine, and you're an officer!"

The General closed by saying, "I am so filled with pride and admiration for these fine young men, I could burst."

THE GUNNY'S DOMAIN

Colonel Sam Grant

"Those of us who have had the privilege of serving in the Marine Corps value our experience as among the most precious of our lives. The fellowship of shared hardships and dangers in a worthy cause creates a close bond of comradeship. It is the basic reason for the cohesiveness of Marines and for the pride we have in our Corps and our loyalty to each other." - Senator and Former Marine Paul H. Douglas

This is a personal story about Colonel Grant, who was probably a lieutenant at the time:

Behind the low berm, with sweat and dust mingling in a red muddy river down his back, the Gunny grunted as he threw a shovel full of dirt from his newly formed foxhole. I watched wearily as I collected my thoughts and wondered how I could face the day after another almost sleepless night. The image of the Gunny quickly faded with the heat of Vietnam as I began my day, which was not due to end until tomorrow. Later, much later, when I finally was able to crawl under my blanket, sleep came quickly and heavily.

The dull thump of grenades contrasted with the sharp crack, crack of automatic rifle fire from attacking Viet Cong dragged me from my first true slumber in many nights. Instinctively, I reached for my weapon and moved in the black night towards that vague memory of the Gunny's foxhole. As I neared it, the flash bang of a nearby grenade spurred me to dive forward.

Instead of landing in the foxhole or even behind the

relative shelter of the berm, I found myself eagle-spread on loops of concertina barbed wire, the barbs penetrating my legs and chest. As I gingerly tried to extract myself, a fragment from a second grenade cut into my wrist. Without a conscious thought and an impetus provided by pure adrenaline, I found myself in the Gunny's foxhole firing at the VC. Within seconds the Gunny arrived, stood, and questioned MY presence in HIS foxhole, impervious to the danger around him. As graciously as possible, I thanked him for his foresight in digging the foxhole big enough for two and moved to one side, continuing to fire.

Grumbling passionately, he refused and threw himself on the face of the berm and began to fire his M-16. Within minutes the VC broke off the attack and I returned to my cot, bleeding slightly from the cut on my wrist and several punctures from the barbed wire, but more exhausted than hurt.

As I awoke early the next morning, the Vietnam heat was already rising in waves and my eyes caught the sunlight reflecting off a new sign driven into fresh red dirt beside the foxhole:

STAFF NCO QUARTERS ONLY
NO OFFICERS ALLOWED

THE WEENIE ROAST

"Ours is a world of nuclear giants and ethical infants. If we continue to develop our technology without wisdom or prudence, our servant may prove to be our executioner."
- General Omar Bradley

During the height of the Cold War, at an undisclosed, highly sensitive location, a group of Marines were moved into a series of hardened underground bunkers as the United States braced for the possibility of nuclear war. The Marines' mission was to defend the compound against ground attack by manning a series of outposts and checkpoints. Although all were grunts by trade, those selected for this duty were required to undergo extensive psychological screenings before being assigned - and it soon became apparent why.

News broadcasts piped into the compound, mixed with official situational updates, painted a somber picture of the deteriorating world situation. The United States and the Soviet Union were on the brink of war, and as the clouds of conflict gathered, the mood of the troops became somber. Then the unthinkable happened. The Marines were notified that the Soviets had launched an undetermined number of missiles at the United States. Needless to say, the "pucker factor" went through the roof!

The heavy blast doors were closed, and while they afforded some protection against anything other than a direct hit it was still necessary to man the posts on the compound's exposed perimeter. For a time things were quiet as the men thought about their families above-ground and wondered if they were safe, but those thoughts were soon interrupted by the job at hand. It wasn't long before the shift ended for the

Marines outside, and it was time to change the guard.

As the new section gathered their gear and prepared to exit the bunker the tension was palpable. These young men were heading out to an almost certain death, and they knew it. Just before they cleared the door the Commanding Officer stopped them, and announced he wanted volunteers to man the exposed posts. Every Marine present raised his hand, and the NCO in charge of the relief immediately spoke up and said, "What do you mean, sir? It's *our* watch!" The CO visibly swelled with pride, and the guard was changed on the normal rotation.

Although those Marines were brave, they were by no means stupid. They knew going outside to man their posts would almost certainly put them in the middle of a huge nuclear fireball. But Marines are also famous for their gallows humor - they somehow manage to find something to laugh about under the worst of circumstances, and this was no exception. Once they got outside one of the PFCs turned to the Corporal of the Guard and asked, "So, corporal... do you have any marshmallows"?

Since the United States has never been hit by nuclear weapons you have probably figured out by now that the scenario I just described was just a drill designed to evaluate how the Marines assigned to this special duty would handle such a stressful situation - but of course *they* didn't know that. Their conduct, while not known to many, serves as one more testament to the dedication and esprit of those special individuals who wear the Eagle, Globe and Anchor.

SEÑOR ROBERTO
Is That You?

Captain Robert Melchionda

"In Italy for thirty years under the Borgias they had warfare, terror, murder and bloodshed but they produced Michelangelo, Leonardo da Vinci and the Renaissance. In Switzerland, they had brotherly love; they had five hundred years of democracy and peace, and what did that produce? The cuckoo clock!" - Orson Welles

A humorous tale from the first Gulf War:

Please bear in mind that I am of Italian ancestry, as you can tell by my long last name. My Grandparents emigrated from Italy to America in the 1930s. My Grandfather Paul was an accomplished Electrical Engineer, and paid his way through college as a concert musician. Once in America, he played the French Horn in the New York Philharmonic until he had learned enough technical English to work as an "EE." He was hired by Westinghouse, and earned an Army/Navy "E" award during WWII for helping to develop ground-air radar for the United States. So I have family over there to this day, and in fact they came over for my wedding.

I made more trips from Germany and Spain to Saudi Arabia during Gulf War I than I can count. One night we were returning to Ramstein AFB, and the radio was quiet as we headed Northwest up "Upper Amber 1" - the 'highway in the sky' up Italy's west coast. We were talking to Roma Control. I asked the controller if he had time for a favor. He said yes, and what was it. I asked him to call my Aunt and

Uncle (Zia & Zio in Italian) and tell them I was alive and well and not to worry and send my love. He asked my name (Señor Roberto Giovanni Melchionda), and Zio's name (Giovanni Mechionda). The controller started to get choked up on the radio. I gave the address and phone number in Genoa. Next thing that happens is he sends all the other aircraft traffic to another frequency. The mike is keyed, and I hear this emotional conversation between the controller and my uncle. They were crying in Italian as they talked about the family and who I was and my father in America. We were getting close to Genoa and I was given radar vectors to my Uncle's penthouse! Then I was given clearance to descend! Lower and lower we went. I was told "Señor Roberto, turn on all your lights" - and we did. "Roberto! Giovanni sees your airplane." My uncle had the entire apartment building on the roof to see this C-5 fly over. We then climbed back up to altitude and were given a shortcut to Germany, courtesy of Roma Control. He even got the French to help out - truly a miracle!!!!! My uncle immediately got on the phone and called my father and they had another emotional conversation.

The next day I was heading back down to Saudi again - this time with the squadron commander of the 9th Airlift Squadron out of Dover, Delaware. I told the Lieutenant Colonel to let me work the radios to see if I could get some preferred routing to Italy from the French. I used my best 'Bon Jour' and it worked. It saved us twenty minutes! Next came Roma Control. "Bon Giorno Roma Control, MAC 31285 checking in Flight Level 290."

"Bon Giorno MAC, is this Señor Roberto?"

"Si!"

"Bon Giorno Señor Roberto, cleared DIRECT LORNO." Direct to the end of Italian Airspace where it meets

Greece!!!! The Lieutenant Colonel looked over at me and said, "Who are you?"

I said, "I don't have this alphabet soup name for nothing. I've got family down there, and I talked with the controllers last night - and my family too!"

He said, "You're kidding?"

"NO!"

"Nobody gets direct here!"

"I DO!"

We made it to Saudi, dropped the cargo and headed back. I was asleep in the back when we came up to LORNO again.

The boss woke me up and dragged me to the jump seat. "Rob, you gotta talk to the Italians again for us."

"Buono Sera Roma, MAC 31285 checking in Flight Level 310 over LORNO."

"Buono Sera MAC, Señor Roberto, you are cleared DIRECT TORINO!"

"Gratzi!"

" Prego!" Rob thanks again. No problem sir. Back to bed.

We arrived back in Germany and the Colonel goes to the Stage Manager who was running all the crews (I was a pool pilot, a group of pilots used to augment to crew for the 24-hour duty day down and back).

"Colonel Black, I want Captain Melchionda here as my permanent pool pilot."

"I'm sorry sir, but we can't do that."

"He is the 'Italian Connection' - nobody gets direct, but this guy does. Do you know how much time we saved?"

"That's great sir, but you'll have to see what happens tomorrow."

So, this Squadron Commander calls my Squadron Commander. Something I didn't know about. Well, the next day I show up to fly, and guess who it's with. Yep... my BOSS.

"All right Bob, what's this 'Italian Connection' stuff?"

I tried to explain, but he had to be shown. So we did another Saudi shuttle and you guessed it. "Señor Roberto, is that you?"

"Si!"

"Cleared DIRECT LORNO." He was a believer. I had direct routings for the next six months!

Back at home, every time the boss saw me in the hallway it was always "Señor Roberto, is that you?" I always responded with "Si, Sir!"

Captain Melchionda closed out his C-5 career with about 3,500 hours in the big machine.

AN AMERICAN IN SPARTA

Pamela Hess

Upon being told that when the Persians loosed their arrows the sky went black, a Spartan warrior named Dienekes rejoined, "Then we shall fight in the shade."

If you have ever seen the movie "300 Spartans" it will be pretty clear why the author titled this piece the way she did. If you missed it, here's the deal: In 480 B.C. a small force of Spartans and other Greek warriors held up the advance of King Xerxes and his huge Persian army at the narrow pass of Thermopylae, and in doing so saved Greece and changed the course of western civilization. The Spartans were arguably the greatest warriors of their time, just as Marines are the greatest of ours!

Living on a Marine base on the edge of restive Ramadi is a shock to a civilian's senses. It's endlessly dusty and loud. The latrines smell. It's beastly hot. There is no color other than brown, and everyone is armed. But mostly you marvel at how they go about their days. Runs with M-16s flapping against their backs for miles at high noon when it's topping 115 degrees - just for the exercise. How they wear long sleeves, pants, suede desert boots, thirty pounds of armor and man a gun on top of a Humvee, faces encrusted with dust. How they work at least twelve hours a day, every day, with no days off, under a constant threat of mortars and rockets.

You wonder where they find the energy to play basketball at midnight (the military police do, reliably, every night, sometimes listening to rap, sometimes heavy metal and once to Michael Jackson's greatest hits.) How they detach themselves sufficiently from the danger to teach fellow Marines to salsa after dinner. How in the dark of night they practice martial arts to a hypnotic drum beat, lit only by pale green chemlights broken at their feet. It probably has something to do with the fact most of them seem to be around twenty years old, and many are in a combat zone for the first time - something they actually *relish*. "Marines run *toward* gunfire, not away from it," a senior commander told me.

And the worse conditions are, the better Marines seem to like it. Marines at a dusty outpost on the Syrian border take great pride they are not serving instead at "Camp Chocolate Cake," as they refer to Al Asad, home of the 7th Regimental Combat Team. Everything here is relative. To an American eye it is downright bleak. But inside row upon row of plywood buildings it is cool. A Marine doesn't care how hot he gets as long as he knows he has a cool place to sleep, I'm told. An air conditioned place to sleep is one of the things 1st Marine Division Commander Major General Jim Mattis requires for his troops.

It's a change from some previous practices in the military. In Afghanistan in the blistering hot summer of 2002, Army soldiers were chided for complaining to me about their rudimentary tents. Once the sun came over the mountains, they heated up quickly and it was impossible to sleep - a bad situation for soldiers mostly carrying out night missions.

Mattis has also introduced the notion of making the regimental command headquarters a psychological safe haven for battle-weary Marines. If they get jittery at the front, they can fall back on the RCT headquarters where they can get cleaned up, a shower, sleep, counseling from other Marines, and medical attention. "The regiment is safe in his mind. It allows him to catch his breath. When he's ready to go (he returns to his unit) and he regains his manhood, right there with his buddies," Mattis explained, over breakfast at Camp Chocolate Cake, where he has come by helicopter to welcome a new set of Marines to the front.

"We never want to evacuate a combat stress (Marine) behind the regiment," Mattis said. The approach is paying dividends, according to Mattis' statistics. "We've only had one guy leave in a division of twenty thousand (in the last six months) and that was a preexisting psychiatric disorder," he said proudly. Last year only three left of the twenty-five thousand in the 1st Marine Division in Iraq, a testament to what Mattis calls a humanistic approach to keeping military personnel healthy in both mind and body.

Some of his success in maintaining morale so far may be attributable to Mattis' policy of assigning every Marine a "combat buddy" - someone they trained with at home and with whom they are deployed, so a Marine is never alone in a unit as the new guy. "People fight better when they know each other," he said. "The more stability we give them, the more anchors they have, the better. (At this age) they don't have the emotional shock absorbers that you and I do." He derides the experience in Vietnam when the newest guy - FNG, in profane military parlance - was sent out his first night to walk point to see if he'd get shot. "You don't do that with human beings. You bring them in and let them be part of a team," he said.

A recent report on military mental health showed an alarming number of combat veterans from Iraq are suffering from post-traumatic stress disorder, something Mattis believes can be mitigated, albeit not wiped out, by hands-on commanders who watch for signs of stress and help troops deal with it. "I don't have any use for the strong silent type,"

258

he said.

Mattis commands a powerful loyalty and respect from his troops. "He leads from the front," one Marine noted in the cool and noisy morale, welfare and recreation tent at Camp Blue Diamond. It has a pool table, a ping pong table, foosball, Nintendo, a large-screen TV, twenty Internet monitors, a library filled with cast off magazines and paperbacks, and a seemingly perpetual dominos game that somehow the Marines have turned into a full contact sport.

When Mattis' "jump platoon" goes out in a convoy - it is regularly attacked and has been hit by improvised explosive devices at least twice - it is not uncommon for the general to have his head out the turret, assuming the same risk as the gunners, say Marines. A lieutenant colonel gave a more specific example of leading from the front - when the Iraqi-led Fallujah Brigade was created, Mattis decided it needed a test run to see if the native force could actually keep order in the city after weeks of fighting. He sent a Marine convoy through town to see if it would be shot at. He was in the convoy.

For all his tenderness to his Marines - whom he usually addresses as "gents" - he clearly enjoys a battle. "The first time you blow someone away is not an insignificant event," he tells about two hundred Marines, sitting on the ground under a metal windbreak against a cliff in Al Asad. "That said, there are some assholes in the world that just need to be shot. But you go on and find your next victim, or he's gonna kill you or your buddy. It's kill or be killed," he said. "There are hunters and there are victims. By your discipline, cunning, obedience and alertness, you will decide if you are a hunter or a victim... It's really a hell of a lot of fun. You're gonna have a blast out here!" he said, with marked glee. "I feel sorry for every son of a bitch that doesn't get to serve with you."

He is also icily clear with what he expects of the new Marines in the theater, who are much needed reinforcements and relief for departing troops. "You must know the commander's intent. (Our motto) is 'no better friend, no worse enemy.' But I have added, 'first do no harm.' No harm to the innocent. No harm to a prisoner, ever. This is the Marine Corps, not the National Guard," he barked, referring to the prison abuse at Abu Ghraib by an Army National Guard unit. "They were undisciplined, sorry-ass excuses for soldiers. We will not cost America one ounce of its moral authority," he said.

"How you treat people is very, very important. We're not gonna become racists. They (the enemy force) want you to hate every Iraqi out here... You treat those women and children the way you do your own. You make certain you don't do anything that would smear the Marine Corps. It is absolutely essential you know what I won't f--ing tolerate," he said, and related the details of a recent case in which a Marine administered an electric shock to a detainee he had in jail. He was swiftly court-martialed. "He thought it was funny. It is, if you like five years in Leavenworth (prison)," Mattis said. "You are free men. No one forced you into the Marine Corps. You are going to prove the enemy wrong out here," he said.

Mattis is as likely to mention a battle in ancient Rome as one in Vietnam when making a point to his troops. Every conversation with his Marines seems an opportunity for some history and criticism, usually so subtly the Marine doesn't realize he has been corrected. He feels like he is changing his path on his own. Mattis is thoughtful without being calculating, and includes his team - which includes me by sheer proximity from time to time - in on his leadership decisions.

While in Asad after a brief stop on the Syrian border, he learned of a coordinated and deadly mortar attack on his headquarters base at Blue Diamond. It seriously injured five. At least one - a well-loved sergeant - died from his wounds. Mattis sat on the information for the duration of a solemn helicopter ride. When we landed he gathered us together and broke the news. "Now we're going to go in there like nothing is wrong. Cool and calm. Cool and calm," he said, imbuing everyone in the circle with responsibility for maintaining morale.

There are plenty of Marines who have concerns about the original case for the war. They are certainly a minority, and one that no doubt singled me out to discuss their views because of my fairly unusual uniform on base (straw hat, long skirts, braids). But none who question the case for war doubt what will happen if they are pulled out before the job is done - this place will devolve into murderous anarchy, and quickly. There is a mental separation here. The debate about the war is one thing. The commitment to fighting it is quite another. They mourn every loss of a comrade, but they accept it as part of the job. There is an obscene bumper sticker Marines are fond of. It says, "U.S. Marine Corps: Because a Natural Death is for Pussies."

Late one night an officer was leaving the command operations center when he said pleasantly to a corporal standing guard, "How are you, Marine?" The corporal was completely alone in the pitch-black of one of Saddam's former palaces, and would be there for hours more before he was relieved. "Motivated!" he thundered back, cheerily, from the dark.

A GHOST IS BORN

Owen West

"He insisted on giving his life so that forty of his fellow Marines might live and triumph. He had freely chosen loyalty above life." – 1stLt Michael Stick, speaking of Corporal Larry Maxam, KIA RVN 1968

Every infantry unit has ghosts. They are conduits to the heartbreak of war, reminders of the brutal individual sacrifice often required so that others might live. The infantry is a guild. So what happens when there are no knights to emulate? Tears of anger dry, days pass, and the ghosts - and war itself - become mythical.

Before arriving in Fallujah this February, the 1st Marine Reconnaissance Battalion had produced no ghosts since the storied days of Vietnam, when recon Marines operating in small teams had clashed with entire North Vietnamese battalions. In 1974, the fallen were not mythical creatures but fathers and husbands and sons and friends. Alongside emulation came bugles and flags and sobs. Thirty years later, their achievements stood tall. But their collective sacrifice had dimmed.

On April 7, 2004 the ghosts returned. One gave his hands. One gave his legs. One gave his arm. And one gave his soul. Those men are no longer in-country, but Marine units are like giant families, and families do not dismiss tragedy. They embrace it. There's a sweet-and-sour mix of pride and despair that accompanies the memory of bravery under fire.

Captain Brent Morel had missed Iraqi Freedom I. Not that the men in his platoon really cared. Yes, most of them had seen combat, but they valued decisiveness as much as experience. And Morel had plenty of pluck. If inexperience made him a bit eager on the battlefield, that was just fine with them.

The recon platoon was traveling in the first five Humvees of a convoy, each man watching a sector of landscape. The terrain was perfect ambush territory - the road was elevated and exposed, it was paralleled by a series of chest-high berms, and there was even a canal that could act like a moat if the insurgents picked a fight. Some of the Marines hoped they would. A week earlier, Fallujah had erupted when four American contractors were murdered. The desire for contact was not driven by revenge, however. It was something innate that was swelling even as Fallujah deteriorated, a mix of adrenaline sprinkled with just enough dread to make it confusing. There was going to be a big fight. Might as well start today.

The lead vehicle was hit first. A rocket-propelled grenade sailed over a berm and slammed into the machine gun Corporal Eddie Wright had mounted on his door. "Grenade" is really the wrong term for this weapon - its warhead is the size of a football. When it exploded, all five men in the lead vehicle were wounded. Wright lost both hands. Shawn Talbert, standing behind the machine gun on the roof, was raked with metal below the knees. Something broke Eric Kocher's arm. The other two men took minor injuries – "minor" for Marines meaning bits of tumbling steel burrowing into the skin like hornets. Concussions, blown eardrums, and non-arterial blood flow. Minor.

The enemy - insurgents, mujahideen, Syrians, Fedayeen, who cares? - opened fire with machine guns and rifles from the safety of the berms, 100 to 150 meters away. In Marine infantry school, this is known as a close ambush. And the only way to escape a close ambush is to attack it. The last part always elicits a few chuckles. Who would be crazy enough to charge a machine gun? Captain Morel was in the second vehicle. "Stop and dismount," he said, already running toward the enemy position. Those other Marines in the bullet-swept column that could follow him did so, racing toward the berms before their brains caught up with their legs.

Sergeant Michael Mendoza was one of them. He hadn't seen combat in the first war either. Now bullets were sailing all around his head, cracking like whips as they snapped through the sound barrier. When he reached the first berm (alive!) he took cover, pumping some rifle grenades into the enemy position. That's when he noticed the guys were moving again. Hell, he thought, I'd better go too.

Morel had practically hurdled the first berm and was now scrambling across the second. Sergeants Dan Lalota and Willie Copeland wondered if he was ever going to stop. They were providing cover fire, then sprinting to catch up. The incoming fire was thick now. It was a big ambush. Maybe fifty people. All five Marines followed Morel into the canal and started to wade across. It was chest deep and had a sinkhole bottom. None were aware that a second element of the platoon was rolling up the right flank.

Seeing the first three vehicles in the kill zone, Gunnery Sergeant Dan Griego had turned the last two platoon Humvees and rumbled up a road to provide a flanking element. When they crested the hill, the Marines saw dozens of Iraqis scrambling around behind the ambushers. They opened fire, killing a few Iraqis and disabling two vehicles that looked to be shuttling soldiers into the ambush and taking bodies out. The Iraqis shifted their attention and fired on them with a machine gun, but the Marines kept pouring it on.

Across the canal, the band of attacking Marines paused behind the final berm. "Cover me. We're assaulting through," was all Morel said.

"You want to assault through?" asked Lalota.

"Yes."

"Roger that."

Brent Morel crested the hill and shuffled down into the open ground. He was struck by a bullet that penetrated his arm and disappeared under his armpit. The exit wound was found on his lower back. It was likely an armor piercing round.

Lance Corporal Maurice Scott was the first to reach Morel. He dragged him across the open ground into a small culvert, eighteen inches deep. Other Marines piled in to help, terribly exposed to fire, shocked that their leader had fallen. By some miracle, no Marines were shot as they gently stripped their captain's gear free and applied battle dressings. Maybe it was Griego's crew pounding the ambush position. Maybe one brave Marine - and another's hands, and another's legs, and thirty Iraqi lives - was all the war required that day.

A press release would be drafted reading, "Captain Scott Morel was killed while conducting security operations in the Al Anbar Province, Iraq." It would be sent after the personal notification of his wife by the casualty assistance team.

"I thought about Captain Morel a lot," says Michael Mendoza, who was sent spinning by a rocket-propelled grenade that exploded at his feet as he crested the final berm. "What we could have done differently. Could he still be alive if we said, 'Stop!'? But maybe others wouldn't be."

Owen West is a former Marine who trades for Goldman Sachs. His writings can be found at www.westwrite.com

THE LIST

"The best medal is a live man's smile."
– Lieutenant Colonel H. Lee Bell

This is an email from a Navy psychiatrist and former flight surgeon as she neared the end of her deployment.

Greetings to all from hot, hot, hot Iraq,

We are short indeed... although not quite as short as we had originally thought... our flight home has been posted and is showing up three days later than planned. The good news is that we leave in the middle of the night and arrive (all admin complete, including turning our weapons in to the armory!) around dinnertime at Pendleton on the same day we leave (due to the eleven hour time difference). The other good news is it appears we've got commercial contract air carriers taking us home... so we don't have to worry about sleeping on the cold steel deck of an Air Force C-17.

So... we turned over authority of the surgical company last week to our replacements, who had a serious trial by fire here in multiple ways, including multiple traumas, surgeries, increased risk to their personal safety, power outages, water outages, and camel spiders in the hospital... all in their first four days. But a few days ago, we heard the helicopters coming and knew they were dealing with multiple traumas, several of which were going to the O.R... and we sat in our barracks and waited for them to call if they needed us. They never did. Last week was the ceremony to mark the official end of our role here. Now we just wait.

As the days move very slowly by, just waiting, I decided

that one of the things I should work on for my own closure and therapeutic healing... is a list. The list would be a comparison: - "Things That Were Good" about Iraq and being deployed with the Marines as one of the providers in a surgical company, and "Things That Were Not Good." Of course, it's quite obvious that this list will be very lopsided. But I thought I would do it anyway, hoping that somehow the trauma, the fear, the grief, the laughter, the pride and the patriotism that have marked this long seven months for me will begin to make sense, through my writing.

Interestingly, it sort of turned into a poem. To be expected, I guess. Most of all it's just therapy, and by now I should be relatively good at that. Hard to do for yourself, though. So here goes... in reverse order of importance...

Things That Were *Good*:

- Sunset over the desert - almost always orange...
- Sunrise over the desert - almost always red...
- The childlike excitement of having fresh fruit at dinner after going weeks without it...
- Being allowed to be the kind of clinician I know I can be, and want to be, with no limits placed and no doubts expressed...
- But most of all, the United States Marines, our patients...
- Walking, every day, and having literally every single person who passes by say, "Hoorah, Ma'am..."
- Having them tell us, one after the other, through blinding pain or morphine-induced euphoria... "When can I get out of here? I just want to get back to my unit..."
- Meeting a young sergeant, who had lost an eye in an explosion... he asked his surgeon if he could open the other one... when he did, he sat up and looked at the young Marines from his fire team who were being treated for

superficial shrapnel wounds in the next room... he smiled, laid back down, and said, "I only have one good eye, Doc, but at least I can see that my Marines are OK!"...

- And of course, meeting the one who threw himself on a grenade to save the men at his side...who will likely be the first Medal of Honor recipient in over eleven years...

- My friends - some of them will be lifelong in a way that is indescribable...

- My patients - some of them had courage unlike anything I've ever experienced before...

- My comrades, Alpha Surgical Company - some of the things witnessed will traumatize them forever, but still they provided outstanding care to these Marines, day in and day out, sometimes for days at a time with no break, for seven endless months...

- And last, but not least... holding the hand of that dying Marine...

Things That Were *Not* Good:

- Terrifying camel spiders, poisonous scorpions, flapping bats in the darkness, howling, territorial wild dogs, flies that insisted on landing on our faces, giant, looming mosquitoes, and invisible sand flies that carry leischmaniasis...

- 132 degree temperatures...

- Wearing long sleeves, full pants and combat boots in 132 degrees...

- Random and totally predictable power outages that led to sweating throughout the night...

- Sweating in places I didn't know I could sweat... like wrists, and ears...

- The roar of helicopters overhead...

- The resounding thud of exploding artillery in the distance...

- The popping of gunfire...

- Not knowing if any of the above sounds is a good thing, or a bad thing...

- The siren, and the inevitable "big voice" yelling at us to take cover...

- Not knowing if that siren was on someone's DVD or if the "big voice" would soon follow...

- The cracking sound of giant artillery rounds splitting open against rock and dirt...

- The rumble of the ground...

- The shattering of the windows...

- Hiding under flak jackets and kevlar helmets, away from the broken windows, waiting to be told we can come to the hospital to treat the ones who were not so lucky...

- Watching the helicopter with the big red cross on its side landing at our pad...

- Worse - watching Marine helicopters filled with patients landing at our pad - because we usually did not realize they were coming...

- Ushering a sobbing Marine Colonel away from the trauma bay while several of his Marines bled and cried out in pain inside...

- Meeting that twenty-one-year-old Marine with three Purple Hearts, and listening to him weep because he felt ashamed of being afraid to go back...

- Telling a room full of stunned Marines in blood-soaked uniforms that their comrade, that they had tried to save, had just died of his wounds...

- Trying, as if in total futility, to do anything I could, to ease the trauma of group after group, that suffered loss after loss, grief after inconsolable grief...

- Washing blood off the boots of one of our young nurses while she told me about the one who bled out in the trauma bay, and then the one who she had to tell, when he pleaded for the truth, that his best friend didn't make it...

- Listening to another of our nurses tell of the Marine who came in talking, telling her his name - about how she pleaded with him not to give up, told him that she was there for him - about how she could see his eyes go dull when he couldn't fight any longer...

And last, but not least... holding the hand of that dying Marine...

THE HOG BOARD

Ed Aldridge

"All men profess honesty as long as they can. To believe all men honest would be folly. To believe none so is something worse." - John Quincy Adams

When I was at MCRD Parris Island in April of 1976 I experienced one of the most harrowing experiences of my life, but at the same time one of the funniest. We were in the sixth week of training and had just put up a hog board (a bulletin board with pictures of our girlfriends wearing bikinis or less) at the front of the squad bay, just outside of the Drill Instructors quarters.

Everyone had sent home for pictures, and that include the DI's. The only time we were allowed to view this was in the evening just before racking out. It was a sacred board, and the DI's had told us so. They told us if we looked at it any other time before the allowed time there would be dire consequences.

So one day the DI locked us all up at attention, on line, and he went into his quarters, which was a small room that had Venetian blinds around it, which were closed. We had been bunked in alphabetical order. My name started with the letter 'A' so I was the first in line. The guy next to me also started with an 'A' and he was second. This guy had the attention span of a two year old. His eyes and body were always wandering around.

I noticed through my peripheral vision that he had gotten fidgety, and was looking across my body at the Hog board (which was positioned about arms reach from me).

Not As Lean, Not As Mean, Still a Marine!

All of a sudden all hell broke loose. The DI came out of his quarters screaming. He threw his clipboard halfway down the squadbay and went straight for my eyeballing buddy.

The conversation went like this…

"What in the hell do you think you are doing, Alexander!?"

"Nothing Sir!"

"Don't lie, maggot. I know what you were doing. Would you like to tell the rest of the platoon, you shit for brains!"

"No Sir, the Private did nothing Sir!"

"Oh, so now I am a damn liar trying to make a victim out of you, am I?"

"No Sir!"

"Were you not eye f*****g my wife?"

"No Sir!"

"So, my wife isn't good enough for a maggot like you, huh?"

"No sir??? The Private doesn't know sir???"

"Son, you have just made my death list! Drop to the ground and give me pushups until I am exhausted!"

Then he came up to me, got within an inch of my face, and asked me if I had been eyeballing his wife. I answered "No sir!" He then asked if during free time I had noticed his wife, and I replied, "Yes sir!" Next he asked me if I wanted his wife. I replied, "Yes sir, she is the hog I desire most on our board, sir!"

He didn't laugh, but it took a lot of effort on his part. On graduation day he said it was the moment he knew I was going to make a fine Marine!

NOTHING BUT FAITH

"If, as a people, we don't have the stomach to endure the inevitable difficulties we've faced in Iraq, how will we have the will to endure the war on terror over the long haul?" - David Limbaugh

One of the Marines lost in the car bombing mentioned in the following letter was Captain Allan Rowe. We served together at 1st Force Recon Company, and I was shocked to learn of his death. Captain Rowe was a fine officer, an outstanding Marine, and a devoted husband and father - and for those reasons his name is included in the dedication of this book.

As you have heard, we lost seven Marines to a suicide car bomber the other day. We also lost three Iraqi Special Forces Soldiers. All were exceptionally brave men. The Marines are from a battalion that has fought as hard or harder than any other here in Iraq. These were the guys that were knee deep in the hardest fighting in Fallujah back in April, and who have been going hard ever since. Even more tragic is that they were close to getting out of here.

As heart-broken as the Marines of the battalion were, last night they really took it to the insurgents inside of Fallujah. Contrary to what might be in the media, the mission was not retribution for the suicide bombing. It was part of a regular operation that was slightly accelerated in light of what happened. We had been watching the city for quite a while and killed many, many terrorists last night. The battle lasted for hours, and many hours later we were still getting secondary explosions from the objectives that we destroyed. You must have faith that the Marines are giving much better that they are getting.

Such action does not lessen the pain for the Marines who lost their buddies, but it gives them a chance to fight and that is what they want. I saw the Sergeant Major for the battalion that lost the seven Marines the morning after the explosion. He told me, "There is still plenty of fight left in them" (i.e., the Marines). Sure enough, that night (last night), they delivered. Regardless of what the enemy throws at them, the Marines will always be laying in the tall grass looking to take the fight to them. There is a major effort to "keep the noise level down and stay out of the news" but it does not mean that the Marines are not out there every day performing. I cannot say it enough, they are amazing!

The Iraqi Special Forces soldiers were outraged by the attack and were also full of fight afterwards. They wanted to go into Fallujah that day and attack the mujahadeen. Their commander stood in front of them and told them to bide their time. It came soon enough. They participated in last night's action and did well. In fact, we just took on two hundred more recruits and continue to have high expectations for them. These guys are under constant threats. When they go home on leave, it is not uncommon for them to have to move their families around in order to avoid kidnappings or murders of not only themselves but their entire families, children and all. We just spoke to them today about having faith that we will win and to believe that things will get better. In fact, I am much less tolerant of Americans who are losing their stomach to see this through. These Iraqis have never known freedom and have no idea what life could be like if they see it through, yet they put their lives on the lines - based on nothing but faith.

THE MARINE LEGACY

George J. Flynn III

"The Spartans do not ask how many the enemy number, but where they are." - Ages of Sparta, circa 415 BC

I joined the Marine Corps because my father is a Marine. I just always wanted to be like him. One of my earliest memories of him is seeing him come downstairs, dressed for the Marine Corps Ball, with white gloves and blue trousers with the red stripe. He looked like Superman.

When 9/11 happened I was an ROTC scholarship student at Virginia Tech, so I already knew I was going into the Marine Corps. 9/11 simply made me realize the importance of what I was going to be doing.

My father was an artilleryman, but I wanted to have a different route at some point so that's why I went infantry. The infantry is what made the Marine Corps. Infantry is what stormed Mount Suribachi at Iwo Jima.

We deployed to Kuwait in January of 2003, two months after I joined my regiment, and went into southern Iraq during Operation Iraqi Freedom. I was a platoon commander. There were no combat veterans in my platoon. We all learned together, and got our baptism by fire. We returned home in June 2003, but headed for Afghanistan last November, returning home in May 2004.

My non-military friends ask why we bother in Iraq and Afghanistan. I think we are making a difference. There were some people over there that needed some help, and we gave it to them. There are people who have a chance at a better life now.

Not As Lean, Not As Mean, Still a Marine!

Preparing for combat, you always wonder what you're going to be like. At TBS (The Basic School at Quantico) they always told us that at some point the training just kicks in and takes over. You get this sense of calm as your training takes over.

Setting an example is the most difficult thing about leading men in combat, 24/7. In combat, you're the one they're looking at for leadership. You need to be one step ahead and always have them on your mind. Somebody is watching everything you're doing - all of your decisions, your emotions and your actions.

They say that the Marine officer/enlisted relationship is father and son, but being a platoon commander, the age difference is so small it's more like being an older brother to these guys. The officer/enlisted admiration goes both ways. There are a lot of bonds forged. I like the fact that I get to hang out with the Marines I go home and brag about every day. It's nice to know that twenty years from now, we will be able to say we were serving together and doing something good for the world.

I motivate my Marines by being out in the field with them. If they see you out there, doing everything they're doing, they're going to realize it's important because their platoon commander is doing it. I really want these guys to know I care about them. I hope my enthusiasm rubs off on them. I hope that they leave work with the enthusiasm that I come to work with. If they move on, I want them to go out into the world a better person than they were when they first decided to enlist.

I teach my Marines honor and to understand the legacy they've inherited. They need to understand how they are part of something bigger than they are. We're the best of the best. You can't get around it. Right now in high school kids are learning about the Spartans. I'd like to think that two thousand years from now guys in high school are going to be learning about the U.S. Marine Corps.

First Lieutenant George J. Flynn is the Executive Officer of Company G, 2nd Battalion, 8th Marine Regiment, 2nd Marine Division. This essay originally appeared in *Sea Power* during September 2004.

THE POP IN

"I have noticed that nothing I *never* said ever did me any harm." – Calvin Coolidge

Don't you hate it when someone just "pops in"? You know what I mean – a friend who drops by without calling first. I don't know why, but they *always* seem to come at the most inopportune time… if you know what I mean. This is the story of a pop-in, Marine Corps style.

In garrison one of the responsibilities of a Force Recon communications section is to manage the company's Information Systems Management Office, or ISMO. That is a fancy name for the section responsible for the maintenance and operation of the unit's computer equipment. It wasn't nearly as glamorous as jumping out of airplanes, but it was an essential job all the same.

The corporal who worked in my ISMO was a bit of a free spirit, but we cut him a bit of slack because he really knew his stuff. His office was around in the back of the compound, and since it was rare for anyone to go back there he sometimes tended to forget where he was. This was one of those times.

One fine day I was sitting at my desk working on something or other when one of my Marines came running in and said, "Hey Gunny, come check out the vehicle parked in the compound!" Even though no vehicles were allowed inside the fence line I thought it was a bit odd for him to be as agitated as he was, so I went out to take a look.

When I emerged from the door of the communications shop I saw an official Marine Corps sedan sitting in the middle of the compound. Just as I wondered who it could belong to, a gust of wind caught the small red flag attached to the front of the vehicle, and as it flapped in the breeze I saw that it contained four white stars. General C. C. Krulak, the Commandant of the Marine Corps, was in the area – but he wasn't in the car.

I then noticed an unfamiliar staff sergeant running around the area, looking in doors. He appeared a bit flustered. When asked to identify himself he said he was the Commandant's driver, and was in the process of trying to locate his boss. The General, it turned out, had a habit of disappearing when making unannounced visits, despite the driver's best efforts to keep track of him. All we could do was hope he didn't walk into the "wrong" door.

It just happened to be lunchtime, and my ISMO corporal was sitting with his back to the door, feet propped up on his desk, and the radio on so loud the walls would have been shaking if they hadn't been made of cinder blocks. The music was so loud, in fact, that the corporal didn't hear the door open. Suddenly the radio was switched off, and silence filled the air. The corporal blurted out, "Hey, what are you doing, asshole? Turn it back on!"

When there was no response my Marine looked up and saw the four gleaming stars on the General's collar, and nearly fell out of his chair. As he scrambled to his fleet his eyes flicked back and forth between the Commandant and a poster on the wall (which featured a photo of General Krulak) to confirm the identity of his visitor. He then assumed the position of attention and commenced sweating.

While this was going on the Commandant's aide, a female major, was wandering around the office looking at the posters on the bulkhead. Most were of the typical Marine Corps variety, but one decidedly was not. It featured a pretty, large-breasted girl with a bare midriff holding an ice cold can of Coors beer. The caption was something of a play on words, and said, "Come to the mountains." Mountains indeed! When the major got to that one she stopped, and made a comment to the Commandant which the corporal couldn't hear.

The Commandant's eyes then came to rest on the "suggestive" poster, and as he turned back to the corporal he said, "Marine, do you think my aide appreciates coming in here and seeing that kind of thing?"

The corporal looked over at the major, who had exceedingly short hair for a woman and an exceptionally athletic build, shrugged his shoulders, and said, "Well sir... to be honest, I'm not really sure..."

WE WERE MARINES
We Are Marines

James Brady

"Whatever else we are or may become for the rest of our lives, if you have once been a Marine, you are always a Marine." – James Brady

On the field at Agincourt, before the battle, Henry V addressed the troops in the most famous of Shakespearean battle speeches. "We few, we happy few, we band of brothers…"

Whatever we are or may become for the rest of our lives, if you have once been a Marine, you are always a Marine. A couple of years ago, on the fortieth anniversary of the start of the Korean War, I published a memoir called *The Coldest War*. It was about being a young Marine officer in a rifle company up in the mountains of North Korea in the winter and about the men with whom I was privileged to serve. As soon as the book appeared, Marines began coming out of the woodwork and down the long forgotten years. Men I thought long dead, men I didn't know, men I love, and men I didn't even like.

Like many of us, I'm not much for reunions - even with other old Marines. I've got a 1st Marine Division sticker on the rear window of the car and that's about it - and even with that people inquire, after a careless glance, if I belong to the National Rifle Association. So much for rear window stickers.

But there is something beyond reunions or books or

stickers that pulls us back ineluctably into our Marine past. And it hasn't got all that much to do with being gung-ho. It is simply that we all, once upon a time, for a matter of months or for a career of thirty years, served together in what is arguably the finest fighting organization the world has ever seen.

We were Marines. We are Marines.

In the summer of 1991, somewhat belatedly one might admit, they held a little parade in New York for Korean War vets. A modest affair, compared to the gaudy Persian Gulf extravaganza staged a few weeks earlier. But embarrassed by others into making at least a token appearance, at the appointed hour, I went downtown in a business suit and milled about a bit in the pleasant confusion and hubbub before finding the Marine detachment where I fell in, just another middle-aged man shuffling along in the morning sun toward Broadway.

Then an odd thing happened. We were marching (strolling, really, not nearly in step) behind a bank, looking around like tourists, when I realized that quite a few people had turned out - some of them waving little flags. It wasn't really much of a parade, but it was nice to see the folks there in the sun along the sidewalks and to hear them calling out as our detachment of several hundred neared.

"It's the Marines... look, the Marines... hey, it's the Marines."

Somewhere near me I heard a voice, unknown to me but familiar in its growl, suggesting rather loudly, "Let's dress it up now. Let's at least *try* to get in step!"

An old gunny, surely, and we dressed up the ragged line and fell into something approximating a march instead of a stroll - and from the people along the way, there rose up a little cheer and, quite unaccountably and surprising myself, I found that I was crying.

I don't know why. I didn't expect it to happen.

I hadn't lined up with other Marines for nearly four decades, hadn't marched, hadn't thought that much about it - and now the years and the miles were falling away and in some small and very personal way, I was again a Marine.

But then, I guess, I always had been.

James Brady was well-known author and journalist. This essay originally appeared as the Foreword to *Anybody Here a Marine?* by Dennis Carpenter.

LIKE NO OTHER

"We need never be ashamed of our tears." – Charles Dickens

When God created the first United States Marine, it was into the sixth day of overtime. Finally an angel appeared and said, "You're having a lot of trouble with this one, Lord. What's wrong with the standard model?"

The Lord replied, "Have you seen the specs on this order? It has to be able to think independently, yet be able to take orders. Have the qualities of both a military mind, and a compassionate heart. Be a leader of junior Marines, and learn from seniors. Run on black coffee. Handle critical ops without a Military Procedure Manual. Be able to manage a difficult subordinate, an irate supervisor and a demanding OIC. Have the patience of a saint and six pairs of hands, not to mention the strength of three its size."

The angel shook her head slowly and said, "Six pairs of hands - no way!"

The Lord answered, "Don't worry, we'll make other Marines to help. Besides, it's not the hands which are causing the problem. It's the heart. It must swell with pride when other Marines do well, sustain the incredible hardship of combat, beat on soundly when it's too tired to do so, and be strong enough to continue to carry on when he's given all he had."

"Lord," said the angel, touching the Lord's sleeve gently, "Come to bed!"

"I can't," said the Lord. "I'm so close to creating something unique. Already I have one who can complete a twenty-mile forced march with full pack, handle a 9mm and an M16 with astounding accuracy, conduct land navigation in the dark, and operate field communications."

The angel circled the model of the Marine very slowly. "It's too serious," she sighed.

"But tough," said the Lord excitedly. "You cannot imagine what this Marine can do or endure!"

"Can it feel?" asked the angel.

"Can it feel!" replied the Lord. "It loves Corps and country like no other!"

Finally the angel bent over and ran her finger across the Marine's cheek. "There's a leak," she pronounced. "I told you you're trying to put too much into this model."

"That's not a leak," said the Lord. "That's a tear."

"What's it for?" asked the angel.

"It's for joy, sadness, disappointment, frustration, pain, loneliness and pride."

"You're a genius!" exclaimed the angel.

The Lord looked at her somberly and replied, "I didn't put it there."

THE GRUNT

"For it's Tommy this, and Tommy that, and 'Chuck him out, the brute!' But it's 'Saviour of his country' when the guns begin to shoot; And it's Tommy this, and Tommy that, and anything you please; And Tommy ain't a bloomin' fool - you bet that Tommy sees!" - Rudyard Kipling

The average age of a grunt is nineteen years. He is a short haired, tight-muscled kid who, under normal circumstances, is considered by society as half man, half boy. Not old enough to drink, but old enough to die for his country. He never really cared much for work and he would rather wax his own car than wash his father's - but he has never collected unemployment either.

He's a recent High School graduate. He was probably an average student, pursued some form of sport activities, drives a ten-year-old jalopy, and has a steady girlfriend who either broke up with him when he left, or swears to be waiting when he returns from half a world away. He listens to rock and roll, or jazz, or rap - and 155mm howitzers. He is ten or fifteen pounds lighter now than when he was at home because he is working or fighting from before dawn to well after dusk.

He has trouble spelling, thus letter writing is a pain for him, but he can field strip a rifle in thirty seconds and reassemble it in less. He can recite to you the nomenclature of a machine gun or grenade launcher and use either one effectively if he must. He digs fighting holes and latrines and can apply first aid like a professional. He can march until he is told to stop, or stop until he is told to march. He obeys

286

orders instantly and without hesitation, but is not without spirit or individual dignity.

He is self-sufficient. He has two sets of fatigues - he washes one and wears the other. He keeps his canteens full, and his feet dry. He sometimes forgets to brush his teeth, but never to clean his rifle. He can cook his own meals, mend his own clothes, and fix his own hurts. If you're thirsty, he'll share his water with you. If you are hungry, his food. He'll even split his ammunition with you in the midst of battle when you run low. He has learned to use his hands like weapons, and his weapons like they were his hands. He can save your life - or take it, because that is his job.

He will often do twice the work of a civilian, draw half the pay, and still find ironic humor in it all. He has seen more suffering and death than he should have in his short lifetime. He has stood atop mountains of dead bodies, and helped to create them. He has wept in public and in private for friends who have fallen in combat, and is unashamed. Just as did his Father, Grandfather, and Great-grandfather, he is paying the price for our freedom. Beardless or not, he is not a boy. He is the American Fighting Man that has kept this country free for over two hundred years. He has asked nothing in return, except our friendship and understanding. Remember him, always, for he has earned our respect and admiration with his blood.

He is the Grunt!

THE ARMOR OF INTEGRITY

General Charles C. Krulak

"If I had to rank the Leadership Traits, I'd have to place 'integrity' at the top." – Major H.G. "Dunk" Duncan

The Leadership Principles are a cornerstone of our Marine Corps' ethos, but if we don't take the time to really understand each of them they are nothing more than a list of fourteen words. Take integrity, for example. Simply put, it tells us that Marines do not lie, cheat or steal – or tolerate those who do.

We study and we discuss ethical principles because it serves to strengthen and validate our own inner value system... it gives direction to what I call our moral compass. It is the understanding of ethics that becomes the foundation upon which we can deliberately commit to inviolate principles. It becomes the basis of what we are - of what we include in our character. Based on it, we commit to doing what is right. We expect such commitment from our leaders. But most importantly, we must demand it of ourselves.

Sound morals and ethical behavior cannot be established or created in a day, a semester, or a year. They must be institutionalized within our character over time - they must become a way of life. They go beyond our individual services and beyond our ranks or positions. They cut to the heart and to the soul of who we are and what we are and what we must be - men and women of character. They arm us for the challenges to come, and they impart to us a sense of wholeness. They unite us in the calling we now know as the profession of arms.

Of all the moral and ethical guideposts that we have been brought up to recognize, the one that, for me, stands above the rest - the one that I have kept in the forefront of my mind - is integrity. It is my ethical and personal touchstone.

Integrity, as we know it today, stands for soundness of moral principle and character - uprightness - honesty. Yet there is more. Integrity is also an ideal - a goal to strive for - and for a man or woman to "walk in their integrity" is to require constant discipline and usage. The word integrity itself is a martial word that comes to us from an ancient Roman army tradition.

During the time of the twelve Caesars, the Roman army would conduct morning inspections. As the inspecting centurion would come in front of each legionnaire, the soldier would strike with his right fist the armor breastplate that covered his heart. The armor had to be strongest there in order to protect the heart from sword thrusts and from arrow strikes. As the soldier struck his armor, he would shout "integritas," (in-teg-ri-tas) which in Latin means material wholeness, completeness, and entirety. The inspecting centurion would listen closely for this affirmation, and also for the ring that well kept armor would give off. Satisfied that the armor was sound and that the soldier beneath it was protected, he would then move on to the next man.

At about the same time, the praetorians or imperial bodyguard were ascending into power and influence. Drawn from the best "politically correct" soldiers of the legions, they received the finest equipment and armor. They no longer had to shout "integritas" to signify that their armor was sound. Instead, as they struck their breastplate, they would shout "Hail Caesar!" to signify that their heart belonged to the imperial personage - not to their unit - not to an institution - not to a code of ideals. They armored themselves to serve the cause of a single man.

A century passed and the rift between the legion and the imperial bodyguard and its excesses grew larger. To signify the difference between the two organizations, the legionnaire, upon striking his armor would no longer shout "integritas," but instead would shout "integer" (in-te-ger).

Integer means undiminished - complete - perfect. It not only indicated that the armor was sound, it also indicated that the soldier wearing the armor was sound of character. He was complete in his integrity. His heart was in the right place. His standards and morals were high. He was not associated with the immoral conduct that was rapidly becoming the signature of the praetorian guards.

The armor of integrity continued to serve the legion well. For over four centuries they held the line against the marauding Goths and Vandals, but by 383 AD the social decline that infected the republic and the praetorian guard had its effects upon the legion.

As a 4th century Roman general wrote, "When, because of negligence and laziness, parade ground drills were abandoned, the customary armor began to feel heavy since the soldiers rarely, if ever, wore it. Therefore, they first asked the Emperor to set aside the breastplates and mail, and then the helmets. So our soldiers fought the Goths without any protection for the heart and head and were often beaten by archers. Although there were many disasters, which lead to the loss of great cities, no one tried to restore the armor to the infantry. They took their armor off, and when the armor came off - so too came their integrity." It was only a matter of a few years until the legion rotted from within and was unable to hold the frontiers - and the barbarians were at the gates.

Not As Lean, Not As Mean, Still a Marine!

Integrity - it is a combination of the words, "integritas" and "integer." It refers to the putting on of armor, of building a completeness, a wholeness. A wholeness in character. How appropriate that the word integrity is a derivative of two words describing the character of a member of the profession of arms.

The military has a tradition of producing great leaders that possess the highest ethical standards and integrity. It produces men and women of character - character that allows them to deal ethically with the challenges of today and to make conscious decisions about how they will approach tomorrow. However, this is not done instantly. It requires that integrity becomes a way of life. It must be woven into the very fabric of our soul. Just as was true in the days of Imperial Rome, you either walk in your integrity daily, or you take off the armor of the "integer" and leave your heart and soul exposed and open to attack.

My challenge to you is simple, but often very difficult. Wear your armor of integrity. Take full measure of its weight. Find comfort in its protection. Do not become lax. And always, always, remember that no one can take your integrity from you. You and *only* you can give it away!

General Charles Krulak is a former Commandant of the United States Marine Corps

KEEPERS OF THE FLAME

"It is essential to understand that battles are won primarily in the hearts of men." – Field Marshal Bernard Law Montgomery

Colonel James M. Lowe, Commanding Officer of Marine Corps Base Quantico, made the following remarks to the TBS lieutenants of Charlie Company at a unit Mess Night.

From that elegant introduction, you may or not have picked up on the fact that I have had five tours in Marine divisions, serving in all four divisions and 3rd MarDiv twice. I have made eight Marine Expeditionary Unit deployments, served with the Special Operations Command, and have been to every level of PME possible in order to hone my warfighting skills. Utilizing your great deductive abilities, intellect and experience as lieutenants, you should have questioned the Corps' collective judgment when they decided to make me a base commander! I sure as hell did, and I still do! Look up "base" in the dictionary. According to Mr. Webster it's "the lowest part or bottom; having or showing little or no honor, courage or decency; mean; ignoble; contemptible; menial or degrading; inferior in quality; of comparative low worth." So, after twenty-eight years of focusing on locating, closing with and destroying the enemy, I've got that going for me! That's okay! Go ahead and laugh! There is at least one future Base Commander sitting among you right now!

Seriously, I am honored to return to the Basic School as your guest at this, one of our most time honored traditions. I have been asked to speak on my insights and experiences as a leader of Marines. Basically, I was told to talk about what I have learned over the last twenty-eight years of leading Marines. So let's talk about something I like - Marines! Up front, let me tell you how much I admire you. Why is that? Unlike the vast majority of your fellow citizens, you stepped forward and committed yourself to a greater cause without concern for your personal safety or comfort. And you did it knowing that you would gain nothing in return, except the honor and cherished privilege of earning the title of "Marine officer."

Individually, you are as different as apples and oranges, but you are linked for eternity by the title "Marine," and the fact that you are part of the finest fighting force that has ever existed in history.

If you haven't picked up on it... I like being a Marine, and I like being around Marines. Like most of you are probably thinking, I came into the Corps to do four years and four years only. But a strange thing happened. I was having so much fun that I simply forgot to get out. Hell, at this point, I am thinking seriously about making the Corps a career! So, what is that I like about Marines?

I like the fact that you always know where you stand with a Marine! With Marines, there is no middle ground or gray area. There are only missions, objectives and facts.

I like the fact that if you are a self-declared enemy of America, that running into a Marine outfit in combat is your worst nightmare - and your health record is about to get a lot thicker or be closed out entirely!

I like the fact that Marines are steadfast and consistent in everything they do, regardless if you agree with them or not.

I like it that Marines say the term "politically correct" with nothing but pure disdain.

I like that Marines stand tall and rigid in their actions,

thoughts and deeds when others bend with the direction of the wind and are as confused as a dog looking at a ceiling fan!

I like the fact that each and every Marine considers the honor and legacy of the Corps as his personal and sacred trust to protect and defend.

I like the fact that most civilians don't have a clue what makes us tick! And, that's *not* a bad thing. Because if they did, it would scare the hell out of them!

I like the fact that others say they want to be like us, but don't have what it takes in the "pain-gain-pride" department to make it happen.

I like the fact that the Marines came into being in a bar, Tun Tavern, and that Marines still gather in pubs, bars and slop chutes to share sea stories and hot scoop.

I like the fact that Marines do not consider it a coincidence that there are twenty-four hours in a day and twenty-four beers in a case - because Marines know there is a reason for everything that happens!

I like our motto, Semper Fidelis, and the fact that we don't shed it when the going gets tough, the battlefield gets deadly or when we hang up our uniform for the last time.

I like the fact that Marines take care of each other... in combat and in time of peace.

I like the fact that Marines consider the term "Marines take care of their own" as meaning we will give up our very life for our fellow Marines, if necessary.

I like the fact that Marines know the difference between "chicken salad" and "chicken shit," and aren't afraid to call either what it is!

I like the fact that Marines have never failed the people of America, and that we don't use the words "can't," "retreat," or "lose."

Not As Lean, Not As Mean, Still a Marine!

I like the fact that the people of America hold Marines in the highest esteem, and that they know that they can count of us to locate, close with and destroy those who would harm them!

I like Marines… and being around Marines.

I like the fact that a couple of years ago an elected member of congress felt compelled to publicly accuse the Marine Corps of being "radical and extreme."

I like the fact that our Commandant informed that member of congress that he was absolutely correct, and that he passed on his thanks for the compliment.

I like the fact that Marine leaders - of every rank - know that issuing every man and woman a black beret - or polka-dotted boxer shorts for that matter - does absolutely nothing to promote morale, fighting spirit or combat effectiveness.

I like the fact that Marines are Marines first… regardless of age, race, creed, color, sex, national origin or how long they served or what goals they achieve in life!

Let me give you one example. A young man enlisted in the Navy in WWI. When the war was over, he shipped over and joined the Army. He next enlisted in the Marine Corps and served from 1920-1922. There was no Air Force back then, so I guess he felt he had put all the checks in the block! When he served out his time in the Corps, he went after an education, receiving various degrees in engineering, history and political science from UCLA and Montana State University. He entered politics and served for eleven years in the House of Representatives. Next he tackled the Senate where he served for twenty-four years, as both the Democratic Whip and later as the Senate Majority Leader. He was then appointed as the Ambassador to Japan where he served for eleven years. This gentleman went from "snuffy" to national and international prominence… and when he passed away in 2001, he was rightly buried in Arlington. If you want to visit his grave, don't look for him near the Kennedy eternal flame where so many of our political leaders are laid to rest. Look for a small, common marker shared by the majority of our heroes.... look for the marker that says "Michael J. Mansfield... PFC... U. S. Marine Corps. You see, Senator Mike Mansfield, like each of us gathered here tonight, was more proud of being a Marine than of anything else in his incredible life of national service.

There is one thing I have learned for sure over the last twenty-eight years... the years fly by, names change, the weapons and the gear change, political leaders and agendas change, national priorities and budgets change, the threats to our nation change... but through it all, there is one abiding constant - the basic issue, do-or-die Marine.

He or she will do damn near anything asked of them, under terrible conditions, with better results and fewer complaints than any civilized human being should have reason to expect. And we... we who have the privilege to serve them and lead them, make our plans and execute crucial missions based primarily on one fact of life... that the basic Marine will not fail his country, his Corps and his fellow Marines, and that they will overcome any threat - if allowed to do so.

Think about that, and remember that for 228 years it has worked and it has kept the wolf away from America's door.

I like Marines, because being a Marine is serious business. We're not a social club or a fraternal organization and we don't pretend to be one. We're a brotherhood of "warriors" - nothing more, nothing less, pure and simple.

We are in the ass-kicking business, and unfortunately, these days business is good. But don't worry about that. What you need to remember is that the mere association of the word "Marine" with a crisis is an automatic source of confidence to America, and encouragement to all nations who stand with us.

As Marines, our message to our foes has always been essentially the same. "We own this side of the street! Threaten my country or our allies and we will come over to *your* side of the street, burn your hut down, and whisper in your ear, "Can you hear me now!?"... and then secure their heartbeat.

Now I must tell you that I had an opportunity to review your MOS assignments. I remember that time in my life well as a real group tightener! Regardless of what MOS you now have, if you don't already know it, being a leader of Marines is about as much fun as you can legally have with your clothes on!

And that's true regardless if you are a grunt, datadink, sparkchaser, stewburner, wiredog, buttplate, remington raider, rotorhead, legal beagle, fast stick, cannon cocker, track head, skivvie stacker, dual fool or a boxkicker. And if you don't believe it, you will! Trust me!

Why is that? Because each us fought to gain the coveted title of Marine. It wasn't given to us - we earned it. And on the day we finally became Marines, an eternal flame of devotion and fierce pride was ignited in our souls.

Let's not fool ourselves. You know it and I know it. You have some challenging times and emotional events ahead of you. I am not talking about tomorrow morning's headache, either. I am talking about the fact that the world is a dangerous place and as leaders of Marines, you will be walking point on world events.

Make sure you keep that flame that I mentioned earlier burning brightly. It will keep you warm when times are hard. It will provide light in the darkest of nights. Use it and draw strength from it, as generations of leathernecks have done since our beginning.

Before transferring to Quantico, I completed a twenty-four-month tour with the 31st MEU aboard *USS Essex*. Some of the Marines here tonight were with me, like Beak Vest, Rudy Whalen and Flounder Foley. *Essex* is a great ship, and one of six to bear that name in defense of our nation. In 1813, the first *Essex* was commanded by a tough skipper named Captain David Porter. By all accounts, Captain Porter was the type of man you did not want to see at captain's mast. He was tough, but he was a true warrior. On one particular mission, *Essex* was ordered to sail alone to the Pacific and attack Great Britain's Pacific whaling fleet. Obviously, Captain Porter knew the fleet was well-guarded by British men-of-war and he knew his job would be a tough one and that he would be severely out-gunned in his task. Prior to sailing, Captain Porter addressed the assembled crew of sailors and Marines on the deck and explained the task at hand. He asked for volunteers only, and told his men to take "seven steps forward" if they would willingly go in harm's way with him. He then turned his back and waited. After a few moments, he turned to face his crew and noticed no holes in the ranks. The ranks looked just as they had, and not a single Marine or sailor stood to the front of the formation. It is reported that he went on a tirade and screamed, "What is this? Not a *single* volunteer among you?" With this, an aide leaned over and whispered in Porter's ear, "Sir, the whole line has stepped forward seven paces."

I think of this story often. And when I do, I think of Marines like you. On behalf of the generations of Marine lieutenants who have gone before you, thank you for taking the "seven steps forward," thank you for your love of country. Thank you for your life-long commitment as a

Not As Lean, Not As Mean, Still a Marine!

United States Marine.

For those of you who are wondering, "Am I up to it?" forget it. You will be magnificent, just as Marine officers always have been. I realize that many of your young Marines are going to be "been there, done that" warriors and that they will wear the decorations to prove it. But you need to know that they respect you, and admire you. You need to know that they want and need your leadership. All you have to do is never fail them in this regard and everything will turn out great. Hold up your end of the bargain and they will not fail.

I am pretty sure I can speak for the entire group of distinguished guest here tonight when I say, "We admire you and would trade places with you in a minute to do it all over again." Sooooo... if you're interesting in giving up a platoon in order to be a base commander, see me at the bar!

One last thing. When you check into your first unit and start the fantastic voyage that only Marines will ever know, kick some serious ass, because it is a full time job and there is a lot of that activity that must occur for America and her allies to survive.

"Long live the United States... and success to the Marines!

FLYING GRUNTS

The first time Chesty Puller was shown a flame thrower his only question was "Where does the bayonet go?"

All Marines are riflemen first...

A couple of years ago a Marine Harrier squadron was invited by the Air Force to participate in one of the "Red Flag" exercises they periodically conduct at Nellis Air Force Base in Nevada.

In keeping with the Corps' expeditionary nature, the Marines had their birds prepped and ready to go with the same equipment they used in the field, while the Air Force birds (on the opposite side of the flight line) pulled out all manner of rear echelon type APUs (Auxiliary Power Units) and other such equipment to start their aircraft. As a result, it looked to onlookers like the Marine pilots simply walked up to their aircraft, kicked the tires, turned the key, and lit the fires. This seemed to offend the Air Force folks, and they began to cut loose with the usual, "You jarheads are nothing more than grunts that know how to fly..." comments.

Anyway, the squadron commander and his First Sergeant decided to make the most of it. There's a "pitot tube" that sticks out of the forward end of an AV-8 Harrier which happens to be the size of the barrel ring of a bayonet. One of the crew chiefs came up with the idea of welding a "bayonet lug" on those screw type hose clamps, and these were affixed to said pitot tube in the wee hours of the morning.

By the dawn's early light the Air Force types watched as the Marine pilots marched, in a column of twos, to their posts in front of their planes. The squadron commander gave the command, "Fix… *Bayonets!*" and each pilot proceeded to attach a bayonet to these "bayonet lugs."

Then they got in their Harriers and lifted off into the wild blue yonder, with bayonets still fixed.

Chaaaaaaaaarge!

A MARINE'S STORY

Captain John Miller: "Mike, Are you all right?"
Sergeant Horvath (after getting shot for the third time):
"I just got the wind knocked out of me. I'm fine!"
– From the movie *Saving Private Ryan*

The bullet in his back hadn't damaged his spirit. Corporal Lonnie Young knelt next to a wounded Marine. In boot camp, recruits learn that every Marine is a rifleman, and this is reinforced annually when each Marine must re-qualify on the rifle range.

Corporal Young put that training to good use when the base he was working at in An-Najaf, Iraq came under attack by approximately eight hundred anti-coalition militiamen on April 4, 2004. That day Young fought alongside seven Blackwater Security personnel to secure the base and defeat the enemy.

Here's his account of the day's events. The day was Sunday, April 4th. Corporal Lonnie Young had been in Iraq since January, three long, hot months in the war-torn country and a far cry from his hometown of Dry Ridge, Kentucky - small-town America with a population of two thousand.

Being called to the frontlines as a Defense Messaging System administrator, he quickly found himself providing convoy security and personal security for visiting general officers, but on this day he was setting up communication throughout the different camps.

Young and his co-workers, approximately seven civilian contractors and coalition fighters, pulled into the gates of Camp Golf in An Najaf to establish a communication link at the coalition base.

Not As Lean, Not As Mean, Still a Marine!

"While entering the front gate, I noticed a small group of protesters out in the streets," Young recalled. "As we proceeded onto the base there were numerous coalition soldiers in 'riot gear' near the front gate. Our rendezvous point was behind the first building in a large parking lot."

After a short briefing, the convoy moved to the rear of the base to continue their mission. Young and his team remained with the five-ton truck, and went to work installing a Motorola base-station radio in the Spanish Forces headquarters building.

"We entered the building and had a quick discussion with the Spanish commander. After the short introduction, we went to the roof and began installing the radio antenna," Young said.

While on the roof, Young stopped for a brief moment to clear his head and admire the view of the cityscape. He recalls not seeing many people in the streets. Everything seemed tranquil and peaceful, a scarce sight in Iraq. Little did he know this was the calm before the storm.

"We went back downstairs to the radio room to continue the installs, and after about twenty minutes finished up everything. I then grabbed all of our gear and took it back outside to the five-ton truck. Since we were about twenty minutes from chow time, I removed my cammie blouse and caught a quick ten-minute nap in the back of the truck. Andy, a civilian contractor, came outside, woke me up, and exclaimed that we were not getting a good signal on the radio and needed to fix it. I told him I would be right in to help, got dressed, grabbed my weapon, and was about to get out of the truck when I heard the unmistakable sound of an AK-47 rifle firing a few rounds out in the street."

The shots Young heard fired were just the beginning of what would turn out to be a brutal four-hour firefight between eight commandos from Blackwater Security Consulting, a handful of U.S. and coalition force troops, and approximately eight hundred anti-coalition militia members.

Upon hearing the shots, Young threw on his gear, grabbed his M-249 Squad Automatic Weapon, and assumed a clear vantage point atop the roof alongside his comrades. He peered through his rear site aperture at the armed mob below, awaiting further orders to engage.

"After what seemed like an eternity, but which was maybe just a few seconds, I could see people getting out of the truck and start running. One of the Iraqis quickly dropped down into a prone position and fired several round at us. I started yelling that I had one in my sights, and asked if I could engage. 'With your permission sir, I have acquired a target,' I yelled over and over until finally the Blackwater Security guys gave the call of commence firing," Young explained.

"I leveled the sights on my target and squeezed the trigger. I could see that the man had on an all white robe and was carrying an AK-47 rifle in his right hand. He seemed to be running as hard as he could when I fired off a short burst of 5.56 mm rounds. Through my sights I could see the man fall onto the pavement. I stopped for a second, raised my head from my weapon, and watched the man lay in the street motionless. I had a weird feeling come over me. I had many emotions kick in at once. I felt a sense of purpose, happiness, and sorrow, which all hit me at once."

The battle raged on with rounds whizzing closely overhead. Young unrelentingly fired belt after belt of ammunition and suppressing fire, deterring the rebel fighters.

"I was getting ready to make an ammo run when out of the corner of my eye, I saw Captain Eddy get hit and fall to the cement rooftop," he explained. "He made a short scream and then yelled for a medic. I leaned my weapon up against the wall and dove to his side. I started to remove Captain Eddy's gear carefully, one piece at a time. At that moment, I could hear bullets ricocheting off through the air and smacking a tin air duct. I removed Captain Eddy's Interceptor vest and continued to cut off his brown T-shirt. I could see a small hole in his left arm that was gushing blood. I looked around him and found another hole close to the center of his back. Quickly grabbing my medical kit from my load bearing vest, I dumped it out onto the ground and started to search through its contents." Young then grabbed a couple of gauze patches and applied pressure to the blood spurting wounds.

"We came up with a plan. He said that he could run, so I put his right arm around my neck and called for covering fire. I heard everybody firing their weapons rapidly as we made our run for the door. The sounds were ear-piercing and very intense. I continued on, and carried the Captain down the stairs and into the tactical medical room they had set up on the first floor."

"I then saw a beautiful sight. There were two tanks rolling out into the drive that leads to the front gate. I could hear their machine guns lighting up and their tracks slapping the pavement as they moved. You could sometimes see sparks come off of the tanks as bullets ricocheted against their armored hulls. It was a great sense of relief to see them out there. It gave me motivation to continue on without noticing any of the fatigue or pain that was throbbing through my knees from diving around and trying to dodge bullets."

Young loaded up a few magazines and returned back to his rooftop position. Suddenly, out of the corner of his eye, he saw something red flash out in front of him... SMACK! Again, the unforgettable sound of bullets ripping through human flesh rang in the young corporal's ears.

"It sounded just like a bullet smacking a target at the rifle range - a really sharp crack. I had heard that same crack when Captain Eddy was hit. I looked down and to my left, and saw a horrific sight. I saw blood gushing and squirting out of the side of a guy's face."

That guy was a linguist for Blackwater Security. To this day, Young has yet to figure out his name. It was the first time he had ever seen the man, but he still considered him to be a brother. He set down his weapon and leaped to the injured man's side.

"I could see a quarter-sized hole in his jaw. By this time, the guy had lost about a pint of blood. I tried to press on the wound and stop the bleeding that way, but the blood was squirting out between my fingers. I had thought to myself that his carotid artery had to be cut. Using my index finger, I reached inside the hole and began to feel around. It took a few seconds to find it, but I finally felt something like a large vein. I wrapped my finger around it and pinched as hard as I could."

With bullets raining down on them, Young grabbed the guy by the back of his Interceptor vest and began to drag him. As he was dragging him, the Marine heard an ear-piercing smack, much like the all too familiar smack that he had earlier when the guys beside him had been hit. He then found himself hurtling through the air and collapsing to the concrete rooftop.

"I had a burning sensation like I had never felt before on the backside of my left shoulder. My left eye was throbbing as I tried to rub out what I thought was dirt. I could no longer see out of my left eye. I picked myself up and looked around for who had been hit. I knew that I'd heard the unmistakable smack, but no one appeared to be shot. I went back to the guy that I was previously dragging and moved him behind a concrete air duct in the center of the front wall. There, the Blackwater medic came sliding in by the guy's other side. I reached back inside the hole in his neck and pinched once again."

With every ounce of energy left in the weary Marine's body he hauled the badly injured man down off the rooftop and down to the floor below where medics were still administering first aid to the wounded captain. As the battle raged outside, the Marine grabbed his SAW and some more ammunition and ran back to his rooftop perch.

"I gazed over the streets with straining eyes, only to see dozens of dead Iraqis lying all over the ground," Young recollects. "It was an unbelievable sight. Even though there were so many dead, the Iraqis were still running towards the front gate. I opened fire once again. Emptying magazine after magazine, I watched the people dressed in white and black robes drop to the ground as my sights passed by them. All I could think about at that time was that I had to either kill, or be killed. It felt as if we were losing ground. In many senses we were, but that feeling just made me fight harder."

Suddenly Young felt someone tugging on his back. He turned and looked over his right shoulder to see one of his officers yelling at him, ordering him off of the roof. It was then the Marine realized he was standing in a pool of his own blood. The last smack he had heard was in fact his own flesh being torn.

"I was a little bit confused about what was going on," Young said. He asked me where I was hit. I told him that I wasn't sure, but I thought that it was my back. I was sweating heavily and it was getting in my eyes, so I took off my Kevlar helmet and wiped the right side of my face. I could feel the sweat dripping off my hand, so I flung my hand really quickly, as to fling all the water off. My hand was painted bright red from fresh blood."

Feelings of dread overtook Young as he frantically felt around his face for a bullet hole. Someone with Ka-Bar in hand cut his green T-shirt to expose the bloodied wound. One entrance hole was found, right in line with his heart - and there were no exit holes.

"I said to the captain that I was good to go and started to put my Interceptor vest back on. I felt that I was able to get back in the fight, but the captain thought differently. After a short argument, the captain convinced me to get down off the roof. A small bit of time passed, and the room started spinning. My eyelids felt like they had bricks tied to them, and I was hot all over. I heard the 'doc' say that they had to get me out of there. They started to pick me up and I gained enough sense to walk on my own. We ran outside and I saw three Blackwater helicopters sitting there. I ran to the farthest helicopter and got inside the front passenger seat. I felt very nervous as we took off. I didn't have any body armor at all, nor did I have a weapon. I looked all around the base and saw that everybody was firing their weapons... I felt almost helpless sitting there."

Young explained that the helicopter ride to the hospital in Baghdad seemed like an eternity. Upon arrival, he went straight into surgery. After a successful operation, the round was removed from his back, and a piece of shrapnel was removed from his left eye, but no major damage was done. The doctor even let Young keep the troublesome hunk of metal as a war trophy.

In the words of Major Douglas Fordham, the only other Marine attached to the DMS team of technicians, Young was critical to the success of the militia deterrence. "I can tell you this... before this attack ever broke out, in the two days of operations that preceded it, I was very confident placing the security of my team and indeed my own life in the hands of this corporal. I had no doubts in him. He exuded a level of confidence and professionalism found in few seniors and even fewer peers. As I look back on all of this, I believe I have Corporal Young to thank that I am still alive. Period."

Young has seen the horrors of war. He's experienced hell firsthand, and learned the hard way that truth is far stranger than the fiction of movies. What could possibly make a man sacrifice his own well-being for the safety of two complete strangers? The answer is simple... he is a Marine.

The title Marine - earned, never given - has inspired ordinary men to do extraordinary things for over two hundred years. Corporal Lonnie Young isn't the first, and won't be the last, Marine to ignore his own injuries to protect others.

A MESSAGE
For Corporal Ramirez

James Webb

"The fight in Afghanistan is often overlooked. We must not forget those who still serve there on a lonely and dangerous mission." – James Webb

The four-engine C-130 Hercules descends toward total darkness above Tarin Kowt in the plains of central Afghanistan, seventy miles north of the ancient capital of Kandahar. Its wheels finally bite into an unmarked dirt airstrip. The aircraft brakes hard, then taxis along the strip. Billows of dust engulf us. The rear door yawns open, and we trundle down the tailgate onto an eerie, empty landscape lit only by the brightness of the moon. As I step onto the runway, my boots sink into six inches of powder so fine and dry that it might be talc.

In the moonscape I can see the silhouettes of Marines moving through a small city of tents, concertina wire and military vehicles. I have arrived at Camp Ripley, the desolate forward operating base of the 22nd Marine Expeditionary Unit (MEU). From here Alabaman Colonel Kenneth McKenzie Jr., the 22nd MEU's commander, has been directing two thousand Marines, and recently Army infantry troops as well, in combat operations against Taliban and other forces across an area half the size of North Carolina.

I have come to Afghanistan to observe the 22nd MEU and other Marine Corps units fighting in this often-neglected theater. My son Jim, with me as my photographer, is also carrying a message for Marine Corporal Jose Ramirez, whom we are determined to locate during our visit.

Two days earlier we had left Ramstein Air Base in Germany, a busy hub linking medevacs and cargo to Iraq and Afghanistan. During the seven-hour flight we sat on canvas jump seats and napped on the metal floor of an Air Force C-17 loaded with fresh cargo, and finally landed at the main American base at Bagram.

Built by the Soviets during their ill-fated occupation of the country, Bagram is a lesson in history and of the contrasts in living styles that attend all wars. Its perimeter is littered with old Soviet weaponry and crisscrossed with still-active minefields.

We slept in an odorous, dusty room that was once part of a Soviet-built hospital. All around us, the American military - plus soldiers from at least a dozen other nations and hundreds of civilian workers - live in a world almost surreal in its contradictions.

Bagram, home to more than six thousand soldiers, offers up the heat and isolation of a war zone and at the same time emits an unreality that might be found in an episode of M*A*S*H. The base has never been attacked other than by occasional rocket fire from distant mountains, but every person in military uniform carries a loaded weapon, even when walking to the base exchange or the day spa or pizza parlor. At the transient quarters, a visiting Army general even straps a shoulder-holstered pistol over his undershirt as he travels from his bedroom to the latrine one floor below.

And yet, throughout the day, hundreds of soldiers in official Army gym clothes jog on Bagram's roads and sidewalks, weaponless and worry-free. Just outside the Internet café, I watch an aerobics class where dozens of solemn-faced soldiers kick up their knees in unison, step-dancing to the rhythm of Britney Spears.

Not As Lean, Not As Mean, Still a Marine!

Unarmed, full-bellied civilians with thick Southern accents dish out food in the chow halls, run the laundry and operate supply trucks, compliments of the ever-present Halliburton Corporation, which even announces when you sign onto the Internet that it has provided the connection.

The Marines' Camp Ripley offers neither the distractions nor the contradictions of Bagram. It is a place of wind and dust, sitting on an arid, empty plateau. The seriousness of the Marines' mission permeates the air. At night the camp is eerily quiet and the darkness is nearly complete, interrupted only by green chem sticks marking pathways through the concertina wire and an occasional blue-lensed flashlight.

Struggling in the thick dust, we carry our gear from the airstrip to the small group of tents that mark Colonel McKenzie's command post. Iron-gray Sergeant Major George Mason sits at a small table in the darkness, smoking a cigar as he converses in a near-whisper with another Marine. Rising to greet us, the New Jersey-born Mason hands us thin mats and gestures toward two nearby one-man pup tents, where we will stow our gear and sleep on the ground. There is not one cot in the hundreds of tents that dot Camp Ripley's moonscape. Colonel McKenzie and Sergeant Major Mason are testimony that the Marine Corps leads by example, sleeping on the dust-filled deck inside their own pup tents no differently from the rest of their Marines.

The command operations center is a low-lit tent jammed with sophisticated computers. I learn that a recently arrived Army unit is in contact with guerrillas in the mountains to the east, not far from where the 22nd MEU's Marines recently killed more than one hundred enemy, including at least one Chechen. This largely unreported operation, the most extensive in Afghanistan in more than two years, has been overshadowed by events in Iraq and represents the farthest inland penetration by ship-borne amphibious forces in the history of the Marine Corps.

The next morning we board a helicopter and fly north over vast reaches of desert, banking through sharp mountain passes. Gunships ride our flanks. A second helicopter follows in our trace. Bare scrapes of road mark the desert floor and the edges of many mountains.

Every now and then we see a lone vehicle, a herd of goats, even wild camels. Occasionally there are squares of mud walls, denoting an Afghan housing compound. Finally we fly past a half-dozen Marines manning a hilltop outpost, and on the other side we descend toward a streambed at the edge of a village. Green smoke from a grenade curls into the air, marking the landing zone. And in minutes, we are at the command post of "One-Six" - the 1st Battalion, 6th Marine Regiment.

1/6 is now in its seventy-fourth consecutive day of offensive combat operations. Led by Pakistani-born Lieutenant Colonel Asad Khan, whose call sign, appropriately, is "Genghis," and a particularly daring sergeant major, Kentuckian Thomas Hall, the three two-hundred-man rifle companies have covered enormous distances along the rough roads and narrow mountain passes. Early on, the Taliban attempted a series of three-point, V-shaped ambushes and learned a costly lesson. Rather than going on the defensive once ambushed, the Marines attacked in classic fashion, stunning the ambushers and chasing them down one by one.

A five-vehicle convoy picks us up, along with several bags of precious mail brought in by the helicopters. It is brutally hot in the Humvees as we drive along craggy mountain roads. Dust pours into the open windows, mixing with the odor of the fuel cans behind us. On the roofs of the

Not As Lean, Not As Mean, Still a Marine!

Humvees gunners stand watch, dark goggles on their eyes, their boots fixed into canvas straps that descend into the center of the cab.

The square mud housing compounds seem to blend into the desert as we pass. Young children stare curiously, a few daring to wave. A vehicle breaks down, and we leave it behind with another one for security. It is a risky but daily occurrence, with the Marines stretched out so far and wide.

Charlie Company, along with several dozen Afghan soldiers, is set up at the edge of a swiftly flowing river, its vehicles marking the edges of the patrol base. On the far side of the river a group of villagers has gathered to watch, and a smaller group of nomads has set up its own tents. We have reached the very tip of the spear whose hilt began in Bagram, and these Marines have an edge to them. They are well-disciplined but cocky, the series of recent firefights having cost them few casualties. At the same time they are weary, knowing they are toward the end of their deployment and soon will be heading home.

That afternoon we wade the chest-deep river, moving quickly through a large portion of the village on the other side as the Marines cordon and search different compounds, looking for Taliban and stashed weapons. It is intricate, exhausting work that will carry over into the next day and the next in other remote villages. Dogs are barking and snarling. Bearded men are protesting. Women with long memories of abuse during the Soviet occupation are hiding with their female children. A few gritty female Marines are attached to the company in order to search the women without insulting local traditions. Afghan interpreters conduct in-depth interrogations under the direction of Marine counterintelligence. Four-man fire teams work with quick precision, tempers occasionally flaring from the tension and

314

the heat, searching room after room, compound after compound, then marking large X's on the mud doorways with their bayonets. Opium and marijuana are omnipresent, drawing frequent jeers from Marines who must deal with stoned-out Afghans, but who are not allowed to even drink a beer inside this country for fear of offending Muslim sensibilities.

Then it is over, and we wade back across the river. At night I lay amid the smooth round stones of the riverbank. My clothes are still wet from the patrol. A soft, cooling wind rises off the river, and I pull my flak jacket up to my chin as if it were a blanket. The sky is brittle clear and the stars shine with amazing clarity. As I lay on my back, I see a satellite slowly crossing the sky. I wonder if it is watching us.

Kilo Company of the 3rd Battalion, 6th Marine Regiment is far to the north of Camp Ripley, strung out along a series of remote platoon outposts that look directly at the Pakistani border. We find Kilo's third platoon at a Special Forces camp high above a gorgeous river, looking down at a valley so green that it could be in Vietnam. In this odd war that combines so many aspects of national security, it is no small irony that vast fields of opium sprawl in plain view just on the other side of the river.

The Marines' work up here is different - defensive rather than offensive, with Kilo's platoons under the operational control of the Army's Special Forces. For eight days at a time, combined squads of Marines and Afghans man dangerous outposts on top of nearby mountains that are reachable only by helicopter. Daily squad-sized security patrols trace the hills overlooking the main compound. In the cave-pocked valleys along the border, small Special Operations teams are frequently inserted by helicopter, conducting long-range patrols in search of al-Qaeda and other terrorists' base camps.

To reach this distant outpost, we hitch a ride in an Army CH-47 Chinook helicopter whose missions for the day include delivering resupply loads. As we fly, Apache helicopters constantly cover our flanks. The many-houred journey from Bagram is routine for these highly skilled pilots, who on the trip must negotiate a foglike sandstorm through hazardous mountain passes and drop off large loads by hovering at the edge of sharp terrain that leaves no room for error.

And here, in the shadow of the Pakistani border at the far edge of Afghanistan, we finally link up with Corporal Ramirez. Dripping sweat, he breaks from a working party when our helicopter arrives, greeting Jim and me with a handshake and a quick embrace before getting back to work. My son later joins his squad on a combat patrol up into the steep mountains. Then, as night falls, we talk for more than an hour of home and of Afghanistan. The seductive quiet of the mountains, where al-Qaeda's forces watch, listen and hide, can be deceptive. Shortly before our arrival, a three-man patrol repeated an earlier route and was quickly wiped out as it stepped down a ridgeline into a ravine. The platoon is still haunted by the bravery of the patrol's radio operator, a nineteen-year-old Tennessean who fought the attackers to his death, giving up his radio only when they cracked his forearm on a rock to pry it out of his hand.

The message for Corporal Ramirez, carried so many thousands of miles by my son, is a letter from my daughter, Sarah. I have no need to read it to know the gist of what she said. This is the second time that Corporal Ramirez has deployed to Afghanistan in little more than a year. I have seen her struggle with the pain of these separations - forgoing normal college rituals, forcing herself to learn more about this proud oddity called the Marine Corps and this remote country that has the potential to so drastically alter her life. I have listened on the phone as her calmness descended into sudden tears when asking about news of casualties. Two days before my trip, I watched her celebrate her twenty-first birthday, an evening of forced gaiety with one glaring, remembered absence.

And yet, saying good-bye to Jose the next morning as a Black Hawk helicopter swoops in to take us back to Bagram, I know something else - that he and I, and so many others, cannot allow ourselves to feel unique in these emotions. Indeed, they are being repeated a hundred thousand times over, every day, among those who have been sent into harm's way. My only wish is that the rest of America might somehow comprehend their depth and their intensity.

Senator James Webb, author of six novels, served with the Marines in Vietnam and was awarded the Navy Cross, Silver Star, Bronze Star and Purple Heart. He was also Secretary of the Navy under President Reagan.

MAN OF GOD
Man of War

"Liberty is not a *gift* of God, but a hard-won achievement with the *help* of God."

It was Christmas of 1999 in Richmond, Virginia. Sitting with quiet humility on a wooden pew in Watts Chapel at Union Theological Seminary and Presbyterian School of Christian Education is a man of peace, a student of the Scriptures. Next to his heart he holds a Bible, worn from hours of study. Mid-term finals are finally done, and with a whispered prayer he says, "Lord, if I can make it through one more semester, I'll have it made." For years now this student has struggled through daily classes, fought to maintain his grades, and cleaved to the dream of ministering peace to others. In many respects he is not at all unlike the other seminary students, struggling with class work, meeting in study groups, worrying about his performance on the next test, and looking forward to graduation.

A closer look at the aspiring minister, however, reflects many differences between the man and his fellow students. The wrinkles in his face reflect the character of a man who has been to hell and back. The hair is grayer, the posture a little more stooped, the demeanor more that of a kindly old grandfather than a giddy, young college student. But one look in his eyes reveals the soul of the man, a man who deeply loves God, cares about others, and desires with all that is within him to serve others. Thus, one can finally conclude, this man really *isn't* any different than the idealistic young people with whom he attends class. Slowly

318

one's eyes are drawn from the Scriptures over his heart, to the small pin on his lapel. The blue, six-sided cloth pin bears the likeness of several small stars... and then recognition dawns. This man of God wears our Nation's highest award for military valor... the Medal of Honor.

Carl Leonard Sitter was born in Syracuse, Missouri in 1922. In his early years the family moved to Pueblo, Colorado to follow work. Carl's father was a steelworker, and found steady employment in Pueblo's steel mill. Carl grew up in the city that would one day be named the "Home of Heroes" by the United States Congress, never suspecting that one day he would be part of the reason for that title. He was typical as a lad, an only child who learned the value of hard work and a good education. In his youth he delivered newspapers for the *Pueblo Star Journal* (now the *Pueblo Chieftain*). In his high school years he studied hard, graduating from Pueblo's Central High School in 1940. (Four years earlier Bill Crawford, who would receive the Medal of Honor during World War II, had graduated from the same school.)

As a teen, Carl Sitter was tough... not mean... just a kid who developed a character as strong and hard as the steel his father smelted every day. By his own admission, he didn't think much about God, certainly not becoming a minister. In fact, it was the Marine Corps that challenged and beckoned the new graduate like a seductress. "It was," he said, "the first of my *three* careers." It was that career that took him to the "brink of hell" and taught him the importance of God. Carl's grandfather was a Presbyterian minister, and Carl had grown up in church... only to drift away for a time.

As a young officer and leader of Marines in combat, the lessons of those early days in church and the words of his grandfather began to take on a new importance. In the

Pacific, Lieutenant Sitter found himself leading other young men into battle, their lives under his command. "That's when I started getting close to God," he said in an interview for his hometown newspaper. It was also when he learned the importance of protecting the heart, for it was the pistol covering his heart that saved his life at Guam. His faith... and his .45... enabled him to return home to build a life with his wife in Pueblo.

In the summer of 1944 the sound of gunfire filled the air as hidden Japanese soldiers continued to rain death on the Marines who struggled to reclaim the small island of Guam in the Pacific Ocean. From the first American landings in July through the fall leading up to Thanksgiving, some of the Marine Corps rifle companies suffered fifty to seventy-five percent casualty rates. Carl pushed his young Marines forward, encouraging them to meet the enemy and defeat them. He shouted encouragement, pushed them from position to position, ducking only when needing immediate cover from some new threat. A new burst of enemy gunfire drove him to the ground. Pinned down for the moment, he would not allow his Marines to stay pinned down for any length of time. That would be fatal for all of them. Shouting orders, he rose from his position to attack the enemy. As quickly as he had risen, he was driven back to the ground by a horrible blow to the chest. In that milli-second between the moment when the fatal bullet arrives and the conscious mind records its last impulse, he knew he had been shot in the heart. There was a moment when all was numb... then the young officer realized that he was still breathing... still conscious of the gunfire around him. Instinctively he reached his hand to his chest, felt the ragged edges of his uniform and the warm flow of blood. And cold, hard, shattered steel. Too much steel for a single bullet.

Not As Lean, Not As Mean, Still a Marine!

Slowly Lieutenant Sitter's mind began to clear, and he came to an amazing realization. The torn, cold steel he felt was the shattered remnants of the .45-caliber pistol holstered below his left shoulder. It had taken the direct impact of the enemy round, and saved his life. Surging to his feet with a yell, he began the attack anew. This time the enemy rounds hit the soft flesh of his shoulder. Though painful, the wounds were not fatal. World War II Marine Corps Lieutenant Carl L. Sitter would live to receive his Purple Heart Medal, as well as the Silver Star that would also be awarded for his heroic leadership that day. He would also live to face even greater tests of his courage and leadership in years... and wars... to come.

Six years later Captain Carl Sitter returned to hell, only this time "hell froze over." On the frigid road to the Chosin Reservoir in North Korea, Captain Sitter faced the greatest challenges of his life. During his most trying hours, Carl Sitter remembered the importance of his personal faith. He also remembered the importance of protecting the heart. Throughout his entire tour of duty in Korea, Captain Carl Sitter always wore a .45 caliber pistol holstered over his left shoulder. It was no "John Wayne" gesture, but was the result of the lesson learned earlier at Guam when such a pistol had saved his life.

The battle at the Chosin Reservoir of North Korea in the days following Thanksgiving Day, 1950 was one of the most bitter and difficult trials in American history. Captain Sitter and his fellow Marines faced the coldest winter in a century, surrounded by a well supplied Chinese Communist force that outnumbered them more than ten to one. Through it all, Captain Sitter held his force of young Marines together and taught them to fight, and survive, with pride. During two of their darkest days a young Marine observed the hopelessness of the company's situation and asked, "What are we going to do?"

"What are you gonna do?" Captain Sitter growled. "You're gonna fight, damn it! You've gotta fight, or we aren't getting out of here. It's just that simple."

Stephen Olmstead, who would eventually rise to the rank of Lieutenant General, was a young private under Captain Sitter's command. "Carl Sitter was just one hell of an inspiration to us at a time when we were really in big trouble," he said during an interview. "His skills, his leadership and his inspiration are the reasons that a lot of us are still alive today."

Two days of intense fighting on East Hill outside of Hagru-ri are cited in the citation for Carl Sitter's Medal of Honor. Those two days reflected only a portion of the week of hell Captain Sitter and his company survived. And when the job was done Captain Sitter, wounded repeatedly, led his battered company back out of the Chosin Reservoir. In all, he would wear four Purple Hearts, as well as that ever-present pistol to protect his *own* heart.

CORPS VALUES

Zell Miller

"My experience in the United States Marine Corps steered me onto the path of success. The Marine Corps instilled in me honor, courage and commitment - core values that have sustained me through thick and thin."
- Senator Zell Miller

Zell Miller credits the Marine Corps for turning his life around as a young man. He had dropped out of Emory University and landed in the drunk tank for a night in 1953 when he decided to sign up for a three-year enlistment in the Marines. Miller went through boot camp at Parris Island, S.C., followed by time at the Naval Training Station in Great Lakes, IL and the 2nd Marine Division at Camp Lejeune, NC. By the end of the three years, he had earned the rank of sergeant and was an Expert Rifleman. Miller went on to become a history professor, mayor of his hometown of Young Harris, Georgia, a state senator, lieutenant governor for sixteen years, governor for eight years and finally, a U.S. senator.

Drunk, dirty, disheveled and dejected, I sat cross-legged on the floor of the Gilmer County Jail in the Appalachian town of Ellijay, Georgia. It was a hot Saturday night in August of 1953. Drunk out of my skull from rot-gut moonshine liquor, I had side-swiped a car and run headlong into a ditch. Within minutes I was handcuffed, thrown into the back of a sheriff's car and carted off to where I belonged. Behind bars with me were four others, all of us in the same dark cell. Three old, grizzled mountaineers in bib overalls and a "dandy" in seersucker pants and what had once been a white starched shirt. And me. All were older, and all were just as drunk as I was.

I was twenty-one years old. One thing was clear in my woozy head - I was in a bad, bad situation, and it was no one's fault but my own. Certainly not my mama's. Birdie Bryan Miller had raised me and my sister alone, a "single mother" long before that term became well known. My father had died when I was seventeen days old. My mama didn't just do the best she could - she did the best that *anyone* could. She raised us in a loving home, took us to church twice each Sunday, taught us about values, and read to us. *The Little Engine That Could* was my favorite story.

We grew up in a house built from rocks that my mother had hauled out of a nearby creek. My six-year-old sister watched me on a blanket under a tree near the creek while my mother stooped and lifted and waded in that cold mountain water day after day as she stacked hundreds of beautiful, smooth rocks on the creek bank. Today that rock house is the Miller home place and, in certain places, her handprints in the concrete are still visible. Her handprints were on me as well. And that night I sat in jail with my head in my hands wondering how anyone could have sunk so low. How could anyone have done their mother so wrong?

The life into which I was born in the mountain environment of all-white Towns County, Georgia, in 1932 was as different as night is from day from the metropolitan, multicultural Atlanta, Georgia, I now live in. Poverty was as general then as it is stratified along class lines now. There were no race or religion problems, because we were all of the same color and of similar Protestant persuasions. There were some family feuds and political rifts between Democrats and Republicans, but nothing even closely approximating the divisions and conflicts of modern, urban society.

However narrow or insular the outlook of the average citizen of my native area might have been, character - as personified by honesty and respect for parents, elders, peers and self - was taught by word and example and emulated by deed. Discipline was expected and, if necessary, enforced by hickory sticks and woodshed visits. Children had chores, which they were expected to perform as faithfully and thoroughly as their school homework, and the youngster who "got a whippin'" at school could expect to get another when he or she got home. Teachers were regarded as sacrosanct as parents were.

Life was a serious business, and it was treated as such. Children were trained from the earliest to speak only when spoken to and to respond to their elders with the appropriate "Yes, sir" or "No, ma'am." Whining and "talking back" or "sassin'," were certain to bring swift retribution.

My mother was a talented artist who was regarded by some as an independent and free spirit and different in her ideas and approach to life's trials and tribulations. But she worked twice as hard as any man I ever knew to educate her two children. My maiden aunt, Verdie Miller, was a teacher of awesome presence, a demanding taskmaster, and a loving confidant. I also had an English teacher, Edna Herren, who was a major influence on me as a student.

But with all that I had going for me, I did not have a male role model in my life. And when I left my cocoon of insulated, mountain, female-dominated life, I found myself overly challenged and shockingly frustrated. The worldly, metropolitan atmosphere of Emory University in Atlanta was very different from the safe and sedate atmosphere of Young Harris College.

Not As Lean, Not As Mean, Still a Marine!

I felt overwhelmed by the sophistication of my fellow students, and for the first time - but not the last - had someone laugh at the twang of my "hillbilly" accent. The classes were harder, the students more articulate, and I became lonely, miserable and depressed. A feeling of inferiority permeated my whole being. Unlike the "Little Engine," I quit, dropped out, and returned to my mountain home to the great disappointment of my mother, my aunt, and the arched brows of the town and college gentry, who had wondered if the orphaned boy would be able to make it in the real world. I began to drink, run wild, and finally wound up in that drunk tank in Ellijay.

And so when my buddy Max Nicholson finally came and bailed me out Sunday afternoon I went home, cleaned up, and with my tail between my legs, sneaked onto the back pew of Sharp Memorial Methodist Church. As Pastor Tom Smith spoke that Sunday evening service and the choir sang those old familiar hymns I knew by heart, I sat alone, surrounded by my shame. I realized I needed more than the tender mercies of my little local church, more even than a strong mother and loving friends had been able to provide. I was heading in the wrong direction, and I knew it. My thoughts drifted back to a sign I had seen in Atlanta. "The Marine Corps Builds Men," it proclaimed. Then and there I decided either to cure or kill myself by signing up for a three-year enlistment in that elite outfit.

The kill almost came before the cure, but it was the turning point of my life. Everything that has happened to me since has been at least an indirect product of that decision and, in the twelve weeks of hell and transformation that were Marine Corps boot camp, I learned the values of achieving a successful life that have guided and sustained me on the course which, although sometimes checkered and detoured, I have followed ever since. That weak, mixed-up lad on the back pew never came back home – instead, a strong disciplined man in olive drab did. And when that guy quit at Emory, it was the last time he quit at *anything.*

The best analogy I have heard describing what it is like to go through Marine Corps boot camp is that it is the closest thing to a birth experience grown men will ever go through. The main difference is the gestation period is compressed into three instead of nine months. Even the geography of Parris Island, South Carolina - site of Marine Corps boot camp - can be seen by a raw recruit as the equivalent of the female birthing anatomy. It is configured like a giant womb into which the only entry and exit is a two-mile long causeway ending in a two-lane bridge over Archer's Creek, a tidal arm of Broad River. The base, which is surrounded by alligator infested swamps, is the uterus, and the recruits, who are introduced into it in platoon-sized increments of approximately seventy-four, are the fertilized eggs. There are sixty-five or so who manage to take root and survive the rigorous and demanding training of the following twelve weeks, and who subsequently emerge from the same channel as newborn Marines who will never again look upon life and its challenges as they did some ninety days earlier.

In the course of one season of the calendar, boot camp turns sometimes aimless youths into proud and self-disciplined Marines who have well-honed senses of self-esteem and dedication to themselves, their mission and their country. The differences of economic classes and prejudices of race and religion, which they brought with them, have been transformed into respect for others and an ability to follow orders to achieve mutual goals.

Humorist Art Buchwald, one of the most famous alumni of the Marines, characterized his Corps training and discipline as "the right service in the right place at the right time." He called the experience "a very painful one, which is exactly how the Marines intended it to be," explaining that the purpose of boot camp is "to break you down, and then rebuild you into the person... who will never question an order, who will always worry about his buddy and who, someday, will walk as tall as John Wayne."

Not everyone can join the Marines and, quite frankly, the Marine Corps is not for everyone. But the basic lessons Marines teach their recruits are important ones. I believe that more of our citizens must learn these lessons if a democratic society in our republican form of government is to survive and thrive. I not only believe that with all my heart, but I also know it to be true from the lessons of my own life. I am as certain as the words on this page that I would not be in the position to do the things I have done in my life had I not sought to "make a man of myself" by joining the Marine Corps as a troubled and insecure lad.

Like Art Buchwald, I remember my trips onto and out of Parris Island as if they were yesterday. I recall with clarity the thoughts I had about what I learned and what I must do to make those values a positive force in my life thereafter, regardless of what course it might take. I made a list of those values on a piece of paper and have kept it in my pocket, and over the years, I have added to it. Also, over the years, the more I have thought about them, the more convinced I have become that these values constitute a formula for the survival of a society in which individuals can achieve for themselves and, at the same time, contribute to the advancement of mankind as a whole.

I believe these are values that should be common to all people regardless of the color of their skin, the tenets of their denomination, or the places of their residence. I submit it is the only basis upon which diversity can coexist with commonality, and by which all people can pursue individual goals for themselves while contributing to the general well-being and advancement of society as a whole.

Those who think otherwise need to go through twelve weeks of boot camp and see how they feel about it afterwards.

The preceding is adapted from the prologue to Senator Miller's 1996 book, *Corps Values: Everything You Need to Know I Learned in the Marines.*

THE PANIC BUTTON

"The only thing we have to fear is fear itself."
– President Franklin D. Roosevelt

When I first assumed command of the Marine Detachment in Brazzaville, the State Department's Regional Security Officer there was a fellow by the name of Jim Schnaible. It was my first post and I wanted to hit the ground running, so once I had gotten settled in one of my first official duties was to go around with Jim to the homes and compounds belonging to the Embassy and assist him in conducting a security survey. That consisted of evaluating such things as compound walls, lighting, guard posts and alarm systems - and we had had an extensive checklist to make sure we didn't miss anything.

The last residence to be checked was the Marine House where my detachment resided, and the last item on the checklist was the alarm system "panic button." I had seen these in the other residences, but wasn't yet familiar enough with the Marines' quarters to know where it was located. While Jim waited, I called the Marine on duty at Post One to find out where it was, and the moment I hung up the phone the RSO appeared in front of me with pen and clipboard in hand and an expectant look on his face.

"Well?" he asked.

"There isn't one," I replied.

"What do you mean?"

"There is no panic button in the Marine House."

After letting that sink in for a few moments Jim just shrugged his shoulders and wrote in the space allotted, "N/A - Marines don't panic!"

PERSONA NON GRATA

"When you teach a Marine a rule, make him repeat it back to you. Make him explain it. You can never be sure *what* he heard." – Major H. G. "Dunk" Duncan

One of the jokes the other services like to tell at our expense is that 'MARINE' means "Muscles Are Required, Intelligence Not Essential." What those detractors often fail to realize is Marines are trained to obey rules and regulations, and what could appear "stupid" to an outside observer might simply be a Marine following the rules - as he understands them to be.

Marines who serve at our Embassies abroad are known as Marine Security Guards, or MSGs, and those who go on the program must go through a rigorous screening process - and with good reason. At most posts around the world, a single Marine is often responsible for the security of the Embassy or Consulate at any given time, and above-average intelligence is required in order to make critical decisions in the face of a variety of unexpected emergencies. Attacks have been launched, bombs have been detonated, and fires have broken out in the blink of an eye - and in each case the State Department employees in the building look to the Marine manning Post One for the appropriate response.

Because of the exceptionally high caliber of Marines being sent out to MSG posts, I sometimes forget that while they are certainly squared-away and competent watch standers, these guys are also young and still a bit naive in some matters. I would always be amazed when a young hard-charger who was capable of programming a computer with his eyes closed would turn around and say or do something absolutely outrageous.

A good example occurred while I was commanding the MSG Detachment in Canberra, Australia. Unlike many of the third-world or "hardship" posts we had to serve at, Canberra is a modern and cosmopolitan city - and we often took advantage of that by dining in the many fine eating establishments located in the vicinity of the Marine House. In fact, we dined out so often that in a matter of months my Marines had eaten in each of the restaurants several times. So it came as quite a surprise to me when I discovered one of my guys had never eaten in the Chinese restaurant located right next door to our favorite watering hole. I knew for a fact that he liked a variety of food, so I asked why he hadn't gone there. His response was, "I thought you knew, Gunny. We're not *allowed* to eat in there."

I was dumbfounded by that, and ready to march down to the restaurant and "read the riot act" to the restaurant owner. But before doing so, I wanted more information.

"Who *told* you that you can't eat there?"

"Well, nobody. But there's a sign on the door."

"A sign? What does it say?"

"No MSG!"

For those unfamiliar with it, MSG (Monosodium Glutamate) is a preservative sometimes used in Chinese food which has been shown to be unhealthy.

NO MAS, SIR!

Stan Smith

"I'd give a million dollars to be a Marine." - Former heavyweight boxing champion Riddick Bowe

You are not a Marine until graduation day. Period. Just showing up at Receiving and becoming part of a 'forming gang' doesn't mean a thing. Take Dan Rather of CBS News for example-- he never made it through boot camp, but does nothing to dispel the notion he is a Marine. That makes him just another POSER!

Riddick Bowe has traded haymakers with some of the toughest men in the boxing ring. Anyone who can go toe to toe with Evander Holyfield three times, and twice survive the brawling antics of Andrew Golota, can deal with anything. Well, *almost* anything.

Apparently, the Marine Corps has a training program that can knock out even a former heavyweight champion of the world. On February 21, 1997 Bowe said "no mas" after eleven days of boot camp at Parris Island.

It seems, according to a *Washington Post* article, that Bowe may have wanted out as early as day one of his odyssey into the Marine Corps Reserve. That same article also said Bowe had visited Parris Island before he decided to become a Leatherneck. So what happened?

You'd think Bowe wouldn't need a visit to a Marine Corps training base to figure that discipline and the Devil Dogs is like a Mike Tyson left hook and the resulting thud of his opponent hitting the canvas.

Well, what I know about Marine boot camp is restricted to

what I've seen on TV with *Gomer Pyle* and movies like *Full Metal Jacket*. For something closer to the truth I went to the source, at least as close as I can find it on Fort Lee - our local Marine Corps Detachment.

One of Fort Lee's Marines, who wanted to remain anonymous, thought Bowe's going to boot camp was nothing but hype from the start. "I thought it was a publicity stunt. I was told he was going in because his trainers couldn't get him in shape."

That's a thought. Bowe, looking toward a possible war with Evander or Mike, opted for the military's premier training camp. Thirteen weeks and about $15,000 of taxpayers' money later, and he's a lean, mean, twenty-nine-year-old multimillionaire on an amphibious assault ship cruising the Mediterranean for six months.

Another Marine, Gunnery Sergeant Wiley Tiller, a food service instructor and former recruiter, said Bowe's trek through Parris Island was going to test his mental toughness more than his muscles.

"It would have been a big culture shock as soon as he got off the bus... as an athlete, he was probably used to a coach yelling at him, but after a while you can kinda tell him to get off your back. He had it that way. But here (the Marines) you don't have it that way. He would've been totally stripped of anything he ever was, and then he would have been brought back up. That was probably messing with his manhood. I know he could've done the physical training - everybody knows how tough training is for boxers - but being told what to do, when to do it, how to do it, that's not easy for a twenty-nine-year-old to handle."

There would have been no entourages, no private showers or rooms, special food or any allowances because of the fact that he was Riddick Bowe. The Gunny said he respected

Bowe as a boxer, but suggested that if he couldn't handle boot camp, maybe he lacks the mental toughness to resurrect his career.

My anonymous Marine said Bowe can't claim the title of being a Marine, not even for eleven days. "When you graduate, that's when you are a Marine. When you walk in, you are nothing."

After Bowe's two lackluster performances against Golota and his increasing problems at making weight, "The Few" may be his chances left at another heavyweight title… "The Proud," his refusal to quit the ring in the face of declining skills… and "The Marines," still a dream unfulfilled.

HOME FOR CHRISTMAS

John McCain

"God favors the bold and the strong of heart."
– General A.A. Vandegrift, USMC before D-Day at Guadalcanal

Although I am not in favor of all of his political philosophies, I have a tremendous amount of respect for the way Senator John McCain conducted himself while a prisoner of the North Vietnamese. And naturally, I don't think it was a coincidence the man who encouraged him in those dark days was a Marine.

Nothing crushes your spirit more effectively than solitary confinement. Having no one else to rely on, to share confidences with, to seek counsel from, you begin to doubt your judgment and your courage. The loneliness robs you of everything - everything but time. When you are in solitary confinement you have nothing to think about other than time and just making it through another day. So needless to say, keeping track of the date is not difficult for a man held at length in solitary confinement.

In the five and a half years I was a prisoner of war in Vietnam, Christmas was always the most difficult time of year for me. I distinctly remember Christmas Eve 1969. I had been a POW for more than two years already, most of which was spent alone in my cell. Like many other cells in the Hanoi Hilton, mine was a small, empty room, roughly seven feet by ten feet with a concrete slab on the floor, which served as my bed. The walls were eighteen inched thick, and the windows of each cell were boarded up so that the POWs could not communicate with each other. I remember there being a single, naked lightbulb dangling on a cord in the center of the ceiling, and a small loudspeaker in the corner on which the Vietnamese would play various propaganda pieces.

It was about eight o'clock on Christmas Eve 1969. I was in pretty bad shape, having received some severe beatings from the North Vietnamese. On top of that, I had still not recovered from the injuries I received when I was shot down two years earlier. I was cold. I was injured. And as I lay there in my cell listening to Hanoi Hanna report on "the latest heroic victory over the American imperialists," I had some real serious doubts about my chances for survival.

Then the prison guards began to play a series of Christmas songs over the camp's public address system, the last of which was Dinah Shore singing *I'll Be Home for Christmas.* As I lay there listening to that particular song, my spirits dropped to the lowest possible point. I was not sure if I would survive another night, let alone ever return home for another Christmas with my family.

It was then that I heard the tapping on my wall.

Despite the strict rule against it, the POWs communicated to each other by rapping on the walls of our cells. The secretive tap code was a simple system. We divided the alphabet into five columns of five letters each. The letter K was dropped. A, F, L, Q and V were the key letters. Simply tap once for the five letters in the A column, twice for F, three times for L, and so on. After indicating the column, pause for a beat, then tap one to five times to indicate the right letter. For example, the letter C is sent as: *tap... tap tap tap.*

We became so proficient at the tap code that in time the whole prison system became a complex information network. With each new addition to our population, word quickly passed from cell to cell about every POW's circumstances and information from home. The tap code was my sanity's saving grace. That daily personal contact through the drumming on my wall made my isolation more bearable. It affirmed my humanity and kept me alive.

The cell on one side of me was empty, but in the other adjacent room was a guy named Ernie Brace. Ernie was a decorated former Marine who had flown more than one hundred combat mission in the Korean War. He had volunteered as a civilian pilot to fly missions to secretly supply CIA-supported military units in the Laotian jungle. During one such operation in 1965 he was captured and handed over to the North Vietnamese. He was brutally tortured and kept in solitary confinement for three years at a remote outpost near Dien Bien Phu before he was even brought to the Hanoi Hilton in 1968.

As soon as I heard the tapping on Christmas Eve, I knew it was Ernie. I got up and pressed my ear against the cold stone wall of my cell. At first it was difficult to make out the faint tapping of my neighbor. But it soon became very clear.

"We'll all be home for Christmas," Ernie tapped. "God bless America."

With that I began to cry.

When you are imprisoned, the enemy can take almost everything from you but they cannot take your spirit. Those unspoken words coming from Ernie - who, due to his work with the CIA, had the least chance of getting out of the camp alive - were a poignant affirmation that as Americans, we possessed a divine spark that our enemies could not extinguish - hope.

"We'll all be home for Christmas. God bless America."

That simple message, in my darkest hour, strengthened my will to live. Ernie helped me realize that we would get home when we got home. Until then, we had to manage our hardships as best we could. Without his strength, I doubt I would have survived solitary confinement with my mind and self-respect intact.

It was long ago and far away. But around the holidays, when I hear "I'll Be Home for Christmas," I am always reminded of that time, that place, and the words of my friend Ernie Brace. He kept me going and lifted my spirits when they were in their greatest need of lifting. When I hear that song I think about Ernie. I think about my friends that never made it home for another Christmas. And I think of what a blessing it is to be an American.

TAPS

Ed Johnson

"Go to sleep, peaceful sleep, may the soldier or sailor, God keep. On the land, or in the deep, safe in sleep."
– Second verse of "Taps"

I just wanted to get the day over with and go down to Smokey's for a few cold ones. Sneaking a look at my watch, I saw the time - 1655. Five minutes to go. My full dress uniform was hot in the August sun. Oklahoma summertime was as bad as ever - the heat and humidity at the same level - too damned high.

I saw the car pull into the drive, a '69 or '70 model DeVille - it looked factory-new. It pulled into the parking slot at a snail's pace.

An old woman got out so damned slow I thought she was paralyzed. She had a cane and a sheaf of flowers, about four or five bunches as best I could tell. I couldn't help myself. The thought came unwanted, and left a slightly bitter taste. "Sh*t! She's going to spend an hour, my damned hip hurts like hell, and I'm ready to get the hell out of here right, by-God, now!"

But my duty was to assist anyone coming into the cemetery. Kevin would lock the "in" gate, and if I could hurry the old biddy along, we might make the last half of happy hour.

I broke Post Attention. The hip made gritty noises when I took the first step, and the pain went up a notch. I must have made a real military sight - a middle-aged man with a small pot-gut and half a limp, in Marine Full Dress Uniform, which had lost its razor creases about thirty minutes after I began my watch.

I stopped in front of her, halfway up the walk. She looked up at me with an old woman's squint. "Ma'am, can I assist you in any way?"

She took long enough to answer. "Yes, son. Can you carry these flowers? I seem to be moving a tad slow these days."

"My pleasure, ma'am." Well, it wasn't *too* much of a lie.

She looked again. "Marine, where were you stationed?"

"Vietnam, ma'am. Ground-pounder. '69 to '71."

She looked at me closer. "Wounded in action, I see. Well, done, Marine. I'll be as quick as I can."

I lied a little bigger. "No hurry, Ma'am."

She smiled, and winked at me. "Son, I'm eighty-five years old, and I can tell a lie from a long way off. Let's get this done. Might be the last time I can come. My name's Joanne Wieserman, and I've a few Marines I'd like to see one more time."

"Yes, ma'am. At your service."

She headed for the World War I section, stopping at a stone. She picked one of the bunches out of my arm and laid it on top of the stone. She murmured something I couldn't quite make out. The name on the marble was Donald S. Davidson, USMC, France 1918.

She turned away and made a straight line for the World War II section, stopping at one stone. I saw a tear slowly tracking its way down her cheek. She put a bunch on a stone. The name was Stephen X. Davidson, USMC, 1943. She went up the row a ways and laid another bunch on a stone, Stanley J. Wieserman USMC, 1944.

She paused for a second, "Two more, son, and we'll be done."

I almost didn't say anything, but, "Yes, ma'am. Take your

time."

She looked confused. "Where's the Vietnam section, son? I seem to have lost my way."

I pointed with my chin. "That way, ma'am."

"Oh!" she chuckled quietly. "Son, me and old age ain't too friendly."

She headed down the walk I'd pointed at. She stopped at a couple of stones before she found the ones she wanted. She placed a bunch on Larry Wieserman USMC, 1968, and the last on Darrel Wieserman USMC, 1970. She stood there and murmured a few words I still couldn't make out. "Okay son, I'm finished. Get me back to my car and you can go home."

"Yes, ma'am. If I may ask, were those your kinfolk?"

She paused. "Yes, Donald Davidson was my father. Stephan was my uncle. Stanley was my husband. Larry and Darrel were our sons. All killed in action, all Marines." She stopped. Whether she had finished, or couldn't finish, I don't know. And never have. She made her way to her car, slowly and painfully.

I waited for a polite distance to come between us and double-timed it over to Kevin who was waiting by the car. "Get to the out-gate quick, Kev. I have something I've got to do."

Kev started to say something but saw the look I gave him. He broke the rules to get us there down the service road, but we beat her - she hadn't made it around the rotunda yet.

"Kev, stand to attention next to the gate post. Follow my lead." I humped it across the drive to the other post.

When the Cadillac came puttering around from the hedges and began the short straight traverse to the gate, I called out in my best gunny's voice, "A-Ten *Hut!* Present *Haaaarms!*"

I have to hand it to Kev, he never blinked an eye. Full dress attention and a salute that would have made his DI proud. She drove through that gate with two old worn-out Marines giving her a send off she deserved, for service rendered to her country, and for knowing Duty, Honor and Sacrifice.

I am not sure, but I think I saw a salute returned from that Cadillac.

Instead of "The End".... just think of "Taps."

THE HONOR OF OUR CORPS

Robert A. Hall

"We fought for each other, and to uphold the honor of the Corps." – Captain Angus Deming, USMC

When the beer, it flows like water,
And the talk, it turns to war,
Then we speak of absent comrades,
And the Honor of our Corps.

Of the fights in distant places,
And the friends who are no more,
Dying faithful to the nation,
And the Honor of our Corps.

Though our bones are growing brittle,
And our eyes are growing poor,
Still our hearts are young and valiant,
For the Honor of our Corps.

Should the Eagle, Globe and Anchor,
Call us to the field once more,
We would muster at the summons,
For the Honor of our Corps.

When the years have told our story,
And we close the final door,
We will pass to you for keeping,
Bright the Honor of our Corps.

Will you take the awesome burden?
Will you face the fire of war?
Will you proudly bear the title,
For the Honor of our Corps?

ABOUT THE AUTHOR

Andy Bufalo retired from the Marine Corps as a Master Sergeant in January of 2000 after more than twenty-five years service. A communicator by trade, he spent most of his career in Reconnaissance and Force Reconnaissance units but also spent time with Amtracs, Combat Engineers, a reserve infantry battalion, and commanded MSG Detachments in the Congo and Australia.

He shares the view of Major Gene Duncan, who once wrote "I'd rather be a Marine private than a civilian executive." Since he is neither, he has taken to writing about the Corps he loves. He currently resides in Tampa, Florida.

Semper Fi!

CPSIA information can be obtained at www.ICGtesting.com
Printed in the USA
BVOW08s2351180713

326196BV00010B/419/P

9 780974 579337